BEWARE
FALSE TIGERS

BEWARE
FALSE TIGERS

Strategies and Antidotes
for an Age of Stress

FRANK FORENCICH

Foreword by Alessandro Pelizzon

EXUBERANT
ANIMAL

Published by Exuberant Animal, Bend, Oregon
www.exuberantanimal.com

Edited and designed by Girl Friday Productions
www.girlfridayproductions.com

Cover design: Kathleen Lynch
Project management: Alexander Rigby
Image credits: cover © Jinoytommanjaly via Wikimedia Commons

ISBN (paperback): 978-0-9851263-2-2
ISBN (e-book): 978-0-9851263-3-9

There is no education like adversity.

—Benjamin Disraeli (1804–81)

CONTENTS

Foreword ix

Introduction: A Walk in the Bush 1

Chapter 1: Planet of Stress .7

Chapter 2: The Fundamentals of Adaptation 19

Chapter 3: Surrounded by Tigers. 58

Chapter 4: Humans Under Pressure 138

Chapter 5: Strategies and Antidotes 164

Chapter 6: Teaching, Leadership, and Activism 294

Chapter 7: Practice is Perfect 305

Gratitudes 309

Notes 311

FOREWORD

I first discovered Frank Forencich's beautiful oeuvre well over a decade ago. At the time, I was just starting my journey in documenting the emergence of what I have come to call an *ecological jurisprudence*, and Frank's *Exuberant Animal* helped me to frame and situate my own position, not only in relation to an observation of the world mediated by an intellectual lens, but also in relation to my own embodied self. I was thrilled to meet Frank around a virtual fire ten years later, when he invited me to be part of his *Sapience Project* to discuss the meaning and implications of my research—mapping and investigating the Ecuadorian Constitution of 2008 recognizing Nature, or "Pacha Mama," as having "the right to integral respect for its existence and for the maintenance and regeneration of its life cycles, structure, functions, and evolutionary processes." In just a few sentences, Ecuador fully enshrined the birth of the Rights of Nature movement within modern jurisprudence, an example soon to be followed by India, Colombia, France, and New Zealand, to name just a few. This was the focus of the conversation Frank and I had around his virtual campfire, a conversation inscribed in a chorus of compelling voices of many wise fellow searchers, all dedicated to interrogating and reflecting upon our collective human trajectory in relation to the world that surrounds us. And thus, when Frank asked me to write the foreword for his latest book, I was profoundly honored. There is nothing such as an intellectual challenge to fire up an academic's imagination, and soon I found myself seeking the deeper connections between Frank's analysis of stress and the legal journey toward an ecological jurisprudence I have been so focused on. The answers I found were far more than what I expected.

That we are facing an era of climate emergency is now virtually uncontroversial. Five IPCC reports (the most rigorously peer reviewed documents in the history of scientific research) and countless academic publications confirm the fact that we, humans, are now a force capable of shaping the future of the planet for millennia to come. Mathematical cosmologist Brian Swimme and scholar of religions Mary Evelyn Tucker note that "we have crossed over into an Earth whose very atmosphere and biosphere are being shaped by human decisions . . . We live on a . . . planet now, where not biology but symbolic consciousness is the determining factor for evolution. Cultural selection has overwhelmed natural selection. That is, the survival of species and entire ecosystems now depends primarily on human activities. We are faced with a challenge no previous human has ever contemplated: How are we to make decisions that will benefit an entire planet for the next several millennia?"

So far, it looks like a fully successful answer to that question still escapes us as a species and an international community. In an era of climate uncertainty and upheaval, stress is thus inevitable, both at the individual and at the collective level. The first connection between Frank's analysis of stress and my investigation of an ecological jurisprudence had emerged. Moreover, stress, as Frank notes in multiple sections of his book, is as much a response to a *perceived* or *imagined* threat as to a real one. And, while the fact of profound and potentially catastrophic environmental changes is undeniable, the construction of our current predicament as an "environmental apocalypse" is a construct of our collective imagination, a modern permutation of what John Michael Greer called the "apocalypse meme." And to tell such an apocalyptic story, after all, is to imagine the possibility of those very behaviors that the story originally warns against: to imagine the world on the brink of sudden collapse may indeed act as a *nocebo*, justifying greed because of fear, hoarding "stuff" at the expense of others because of imagined near-future scarcity, and hyperindividualism because of a modern version of Hobbes's *bellum omnium contra omnes*, the "war of all against all." Against the effects of this apocalyptic storytelling, the construction of Nature as a legal subject with rights, interests, and standing, therefore, acts as a powerful tool to reframe our collective position in relation to the cosmos, to suggest a far greater degree of interconnectedness with the whole of Nature mediated by law, and, in so doing, to address our current degree of stress caused by our current environmental narrative. Stress, as Frank very clearly suggests, is a problem to be dealt with by reframing our *Weltanschauung*, our worldview, rather than merely by deploying a series of individual stress-relieving techniques.

Where does stress come from, though? That is the first question that Frank's book endeavors to answer. While stress, like pain, forms part of the normal biological makeup of all humans (in fact, of all life-forms), the degree and intensity of chronic stress experienced in modern settings do not. Frank applies the "evolutionary discordance hypothesis" to this predicament, and very convincingly shows that the contemporary epidemic of chronic stress is a result of mismatch, of living outside the ecological range within which humans have evolved over hundreds of millennia.

We all live well outside our evolutionary ecological range, and this has a profound impact on both our daily lives and our collective choices. The term *ecological range* is here to be preferred to the concept of planetary "boundaries" or "limits" introduced by Johan Rockström and Will Steffen, since the latter term conveys a restrictive, inherently stifling undertone, whereas the former suggests that "natural" is that which most aligns with evolutionary trends. Frank's application of the evolutionary lens to the stress question, and his unveiling of the connection between history and biology, is inscribed within a well-established anthropological tradition, one initiated by cultural materialist scholars such as Marvin Harris and continued, more recently, by authors such as Colin Tudge and Jared Diamond. This long view of human evolution bridges the divide between "nature" and "culture," shedding the traditional dualism of much Western anthropology and modern philosophy, fully embracing what French anthropologist Philippe Descola articulates as the invitation to a novel nature-culture monism.

Extending well beyond the traditional medical field within which stress is commonly located as a "well-being" issue, Frank thus offers a deconstructive approach to the very *idea* of stress, and provides an almost Foucauldian analysis of stress as a very specific discourse, one that has been over-medicalized and has been exclusively located within the biological boundaries of the individual. In fact, as Frank shows, the main contemporary narratives around stress as an individual problem actually help to constitute and reaffirm the "individual" itself as a reified and atomistic entity. In this sense, Frank's analysis shows, the contemporary discourse of stress is profoundly linked to liberal individualism and the humanist project. Words such as stress "*management,*" like all other similar modernisms, "see an external world that needs to be controlled" and lead, in Frank's own words, to an "otherizing of the cosmos, and externalization of the world—another expression of alienated consciousness." Rather than being a merely individual "well-being" issue, stress lies at the center of the social discourse, and can highlight the many shortcomings of a modern worldview focused

on endless economic growth achieved by exploiting a world
of otherwise meaningless resources. How different this worldview is from that of so many cultures, in particular (although
not exclusively) those indigenous cultures that still "assume a
continuity between their bodies, [their] habitat, [their] tribe,
and [the] cosmos" (the "long body" of the Iroquois tradition)!

The many ailments of modern society, in light of this view,
can thus be clearly identified because of the stress they cause
on us all at a very biological level. In this light, ethical judgment and biological awareness become deeply intertwined.
Separation anxiety, cognitive overload, cultural dysfunction, compulsive hoarding, the ever-present "darkness deficit," lack of physical and social "vagility," the neck-breaking
pace of change (also described as the "great acceleration"),
the obsessive narcissism of a culture immersed in constant
self-awareness because of ever-present mirrors and cameras
(the "selfie-culture"): these are just some items on the long
list of cultural traits profoundly mismatched with our human
evolutionary range. It is no wonder that individuals feel utterly
and overwhelmingly powerless in the face of a world they seem
unable to understand, or at least deeply relate to, at a genetic
level. The result, Frank notes, is that, "lost in our species-level
narcissism, we no longer converse with the habitat that keeps
us alive."

What can be done to address the issues that stress reveals,
and, in so doing, heal not only oneself but also the world as
a whole? After all, as Chief Seattle said, "What we do to the
Earth, we do to ourselves," but the inverse is also true: what we
do to ourselves, we do to the Earth. And thus, Frank's suggestions in addressing the epidemic of chronic stress we all face
are not so much posthumanist as they are "preter-humanist":
they attempt to move beyond the current discourse of what it
means to be "human" without sacrificing (in fact, by embracing

in full) our very own "humanity." Stress, just like pain, is not
to be rejected. After all, an individual who does not experience
pain is bound to have a very short life span, and what medical
researchers call "congenital insensitivity to pain," always leads
to inadvertent, and often self-inflicted, gruesome injuries. The
same is true of stress, and thus, Frank reminds us, we should
stop being "stress illiterates, dangers to ourselves and to others," and instead learn to read—and, most important, carefully
listen to—the stress messages our bodies send us. Once we do,
the options open to us are both many and easily within reach:
embrace a slower pace in doing things, including writing and
thinking, extending the lessons of the Slow Food movement
to all facets of our lives; stop trying to "exercise" and rather
think of it as movement, seeing and seeking opportunities for
it everywhere around us; reject the pressure to seek status and
fame, and do not internalize the perceived "rank" society may
attempt to impose upon us; get rid of the "narrative noise" in
which we constantly drown, choose carefully the stories we
wish to consume, reject the manufactured "plastic narratives"
that manipulate our attention every moment of our life; sleep
deeply, walk simply, and seek both darkness and silence; put
down our phones, put down our cameras, and don't "record"
our experiences merely to publicize them: just live.

As the natural evolution of Frank's previous book, *The
Sapience Curriculum*, this book reminds us that "sapience
takes time," but it is that very sapience that makes us both
more fulfilled and more in tune with the world around us.
Stress, after all, is not "just a human problem, it's a biological
problem that extends beyond our own species, to forests, coral
reefs, wetlands, and beyond." Stress, therefore, is a profoundly
ecological problem. But while our own individual experience
of, and our collective narratives about, stress are shaped by
"powerful forces that operate beyond our individual bodies
and lives," it is by focusing on our lived experience that we

can become more effective ecological actors. As anthropologist Wade Davis points out, we culturally co-create a socio-ecological world, and both the experience and the discourse of stress represent a powerful node in which to determine and define the world we wish to co-create. It is this insight that finally showed me why Frank had asked me to write this foreword, even though I could not initially see all the connections. Stress becomes one of the most important tools by which an ecological jurisprudence can emerge: far from being merely a quest to "save the world" (a failing idea in and of itself), the journey toward an ecological jurisprudence that the Rights of Nature movement initiated more than a decade ago is a journey of self-discovery, one in which a full understanding of stress as both an experience and a discursive creation plays a central role.

Know thyself, γνῶθι σεαυτόν, was one of the maxims inscribed on the Temple of Apollo at Delphi, and it has always been the ultimate goal for all practices of self-mastery. Clearly the result of deep, accumulated wisdom, which makes Frank an undeniable elder who has clearly deeply lived—and continues to live—this book is an unforgettable guide on the journey of knowing oneself, and, in healing our fragmented, tortured, stressed selves, toward healing the world around us.

Dr. Alessandro Pelizzon
Faculty of Business, Law and Arts
Southern Cross University, Australia

INTRODUCTION

A WALK IN THE BUSH

Imagine this . . .

It's one hundred thousand years ago, anywhere in eastern or southern Africa, long before agriculture, written language, numbers, hierarchy, nation states, and gee-whiz technology. It's just you, your tribe, and the glorious habitat that surrounds you.

You've been out hunting with your people for a couple of days and all is well. The travel is mostly easy, with stands of trees and bushes here and there, tall grass in between. You'd like to see more of where you're going, but it's early summer and the foliage is thick in places. You've seen a few lions along the way, as well as leopard and hyena, but your group has an intimidating presence and you feel safe.

You've already bagged one animal, and at the moment, things are looking promising. But over the course of the afternoon, your group thins out across a broad expanse of semi-wooded grassland, and suddenly, you realize you're alone. Your friends have gotten too far ahead, and now it's just you and the bush.

Cautious and vigilant, you slow your pace, scanning left and right with powerful focus. Doubt creeps in and you start to worry. A minute ago, you were the hunter, but now you're beginning to feel like the hunted. Your body goes on full alert. Walking even more softly, you're extra careful with your posture and your foot placements. Easy does it, listen carefully.

Suddenly, there's movement in the tall grass, just a stone's throw away. You freeze and your mind sharpens to a single point. Your pulse races and the question courses through your mind-body: Is this a real, hungry predator on the hunt? Or is it a false alarm, a false carnivore? A baboon, perhaps, or an impala or zebra? Is this my overactive imagination or an authentic threat to my life?

How you respond will have big consequences for your day, your health and longevity, and even the nature of your descendants, if you're lucky enough to have any.

HERE AND NOW

Back in the modern world, this nerve-racking encounter is emblematic of the problems that all of us face throughout life. Like hunters in wild habitat, we encounter ambiguous stimuli, often with incomplete or conflicting information. If we judge poorly, we'll either waste a lot of time and energy dealing with minor, inconsequential threats or fall victim to the sharp teeth and claws of the genuine beast.

And if the hunter-gatherers of our deep past had it hard, ours is a far more difficult challenge. Every day brings a new round of ambiguity and novelty, strange combinations of sensation and evidence, genuine threats and trivial annoyances, all overlapping and in flux. And for most of us, "the bush" isn't a real geographic habitat that we can touch and feel—it's a digital-social-cultural space, a shifting, fluid, abstract land-scape with its own unique set of demands.

Real tigers? False tigers? It's getting more and more diffi-cult to sort them all out. An email appears on-screen with a link from an unfamiliar source; it looks dangerous, possibly a tiger. Should you click on it? A friend or partner seems sud-denly disconnected, distant and vaguely hostile. Should you be concerned? Take action or let it pass as someone having a bad day? You wake up one morning and notice a minor but persistent discomfort in the back of your throat. Is this a false tiger—a minor cold or flu? Or is it a real coronavirus tiger that will send you into quarantine or even bring you down?

The challenge is everywhere now. A neighbor or coworker tells us about a strange but plausible conspiracy theory that might be life changing. A politician makes an outrageous claim about a satanic pedophile cult; a post on a dating site looks promising, but with a strange twist. A news report tells us that there's something in the water, a book claims that artifi-cial intelligence will soon make humans irrelevant, a YouTube video tells us that an asteroid will soon strike the Earth. It's no wonder we're on edge. It's no wonder we're experiencing so much anxiety, depression, anger, and confusion.

If we could just sort out the tigers in our world and our lives, everything would be so much easier. We'd be more relaxed, more effective, and more creative. We'd be healthier, happier, and maybe even a little wiser. We'd have more time for our families and friends, and best of all, we'd be better positioned to create a functional, sustainable, ecologically viable future.

HOW THIS BOOK WILL HELP YOU—AND US

This book will help you zero in on precise, proportional, and appropriate responses to the stressors you face. In short, it'll help you sort out the tigers in your life. With some insight and practice, you'll learn how to respond to the right stressors at the right time, with the right intensity and for the right duration. You'll stop wasting so much time and psychic energy on trivial threats and focus instead on the things that really matter. In the process, you'll find yourself feeling more effective, more connected, and more at ease with the challenges in your life.

If all goes well, this book will help you reframe your experience, broaden your perspective, and give you more options. It'll help you make your stress more tolerable, more productive, and more meaningful. You might even come to the conclusion that stress is an ally that can work in your favor. Along the way, you'll come to see that stress is not an experience to be abolished but an essential path toward living a more enjoyable and effective life.

The ideas in this book will challenge you, and you may well find yourself intimidated by the scope and magnitude of the stresses that we face. But you'll also come to realize that you're not alone, that the stress, anxiety, and depression you're feeling aren't unique to you. Even better, this book will remind you of your innate animal strength, capability, and resilience. You are not a weak and hapless victim, suffering under the crushing weight of an impossible predicament—you're a powerful human animal with immense biological ancestry at your back. You have deep vitality and resilience in every cell in your body.

And while this book is for you, it's also for us. As it stands, our planetary predicament is an all-hands-on-deck emergency, one that requires creative action and engagement by everyone. To succeed, we need people who are functional, courageous, and free from imaginary fear. Green technological wizardry may well be useful and necessary in the creation of a functional future, but it will never be sufficient.

Our ultimate success will depend on our emotional and psychological skills, especially our relationship to challenge and ambiguity. When people live in fear of imaginary tigers, it doesn't just compromise their own performance and happiness, it makes life more difficult for all of us. When entire populations are gripped by anxiety and angst, even the simplest challenges become overwhelming. But if we get stress right, we've got a chance to create something that works.

Our grand tour of stress will come in four parts. We'll start our journey by taking a look at the fundamentals of the stress response, the autonomic nervous system, neuroplasticity, and some basic strategies for success. Then we'll look at the systemic, historical, and cultural forces that impact our personal lives—the big tigers of the modern human predicament. In turn, we'll look at the ways we're responding to the challenges we face as "humans under pressure." As you'll see, there's a lot that can go sideways when we're under stress, a thousand dysfunctions that can wreak havoc on our personal, social, and ecological lives. And finally, we'll consider some strategies and antidotes, a selection of remedies and solutions that we can use to make our stress work for us.

As you engage, take some time to let the material sink in and to reflect on your personal experience. As you'll discover, some of these ideas are disruptive, controversial, or contrary to popular, established culture. You may well disagree with some of what you find here, but it's the experience that counts. Sit with the ideas and talk with your friends. Let these ideas do their work as they stimulate fresh connections and insights. There's no telling exactly where the process will lead, but one thing is certain: you'll wind up with more options and a greater sense of possibility. Your experience with stress will never be the same.

CHAPTER 1

PLANET OF STRESS

Living here in the modern world, you're no doubt familiar with stress and all the frustrations that go with it. You're comfortable with the word itself, and you might even suppose that it's a regular feature of human life. Isn't it normal for people to feel chronically pressured, anxious, harried, and overloaded? Isn't this the human condition?

Actually, it's not.

Historically, humans have always experienced adversity. But as for all animals living in wild habitat, most of that adversity was occasional and episodic. There were hard times and even life-threatening emergencies, but those challenges usually passed and gave way to a more comfortable, familiar pace of life.

In fact, the word *stress* didn't really enter into popular use until the early twentieth century, beginning with the work of Harvard physiologist Walter Cannon and his description of the "fight-flight" response. Years later, the pioneering endocrinologist Hans Selye, sometimes called "the grandfather of stress," observed that patients with various chronic illnesses appeared to display a common set of symptoms. He also noticed that laboratory animals exposed to cold, drugs, or surgical injury exhibited a typical pattern of responses, a "general adaptation syndrome."[1] Later in the century, books such as *Why Zebras Don't Get Ulcers* by Robert Sapolsky and *Full Catastrophe Living* by Jon Kabat-Zinn brought stress into popular conversation and awareness.

And today, everyone's talking about it. Google's Ngram Viewer, an online tool that tracks the frequency of words that appear in print, shows that the word *stress* barely made an appearance in the nineteenth century, and then rose gradually throughout the twentieth. And now it's everywhere. Even before the social justice protests and COVID-19 pandemic of 2020, almost everyone was claiming to be "under stress" in one way or another, and even children were claiming that their schoolwork was "stressing them out."

We all feel it now: this maddening sense of urgency, the impending loss of control, the pervasive cognitive overload, the squeeze of temporal poverty and economic uncertainty. Stress has become a ubiquitous, chronic, and even debilitating feature of the modern world. We often joke about it and sometimes even brag about it, but this is serious, even lethal, business on a vast scale. Not only does stress wreck our bodies, it also has extremely negative consequences for cognition and imagination and, in turn, our ability to create a viable future for humanity and the biosphere.

THE STRESS EPIDEMIC

In 1996, the World Health Organization declared stress a "worldwide epidemic," and if it was bad then, it's a thousand times worse now. Global pandemics, widespread economic insecurity, social injustice and racism, political polarization, overwork, lifestyle disease, food and water insecurity, political corruption, misinformation, health care disparities, and, looming above it all, the impending collapse of the biosphere. It's no wonder that the World Health Organization numbers look as bad as they do:[2]

+ Close to 1 billion people have a mental disorder.
+ Depression is a leading cause of illness and disability; globally, an estimated 264 million people are affected by depression.
+ A person dies every forty seconds from suicide.
+ Every year, 3 million people die due to the harmful use of alcohol.

In other words, people are suffering on an unprecedented scale. Stress has become a defining experience of our age, and yet, we mostly ignore it and sometimes even glorify it, declaring it a badge of honor for entrepreneurs and other go-getters who are willing to push the limits.

The problem goes deep, something that psychologist Carl Jung would have recognized immediately. Stress is surging through the collective unconscious of humanity, where it exerts a profound influence on our personal experience and our behavior. Our bodies feel the rampant destruction of habitat around the world, the social turmoil, inequality, racism, and injustice. We feel it in the anxiety that courses through our tissue and our lives, but we're mistaken about its source. Trained by culture to view ourselves as individuals, we blame ourselves for our feelings and our experience. We believe that our stress is our fault alone, a personal failing, a shameful inability to deal with challenge. But in fact, stress is a shared human predicament that extends to all people across the planet. Stress isn't just *your* problem or *my* problem, it's *our* problem. But it's even worse than all that. Stress isn't just a human problem; it even afflicts nonhuman animals. For example, a 2021 study published in the journal *Scientific Reports* found that animals living in fragmented forests have higher levels of stress hormones than those in larger forest patches. A team of scientists collected fur samples from rodents and marsupials in the Atlantic Forest of Paraguay: "We suspected that organisms in deforested areas would show higher levels of stress than animals in more pristine forests, and we found evidence that that's true," reported one of the study's coauthors.[3]

Likewise, biologists in the Pacific Northwest have reported increased levels of stress hormones in the orcas (killer whales) of Puget Sound. Unable to find adequate food because of extensive dam building and destruction of salmon habitat, these creatures are suffering. In fact, it's safe to assume there are similar stress effects in other mammals in disturbed habitats around the world. In other words, stress is more than a human problem; it's a biological problem that extends beyond our own species to forests, coral reefs, wetlands, and beyond. All of us—humans and nonhuman animals alike—are feeling the effects.

Far from being a mere lifestyle and health annoyance, stress is one of the most pressing problems on our planet. It's a foundational issue that compromises our cognition and our ability to deal with reality:

- **Stress contracts our imagination, our intelligence, and, most of all, our sapience.** When people are under pressure, they're less likely to take chances on new ideas that might prove vital in creating a functional, livable future. Stress exacerbates our fear and anxiety, leading to denial, social polarization, and an overreliance on status quo ideas, organizations, and processes.

• **Stress encourages short-term thinking.** Everything that's not considered absolutely urgent is moved to the back burner, and thus, all our slow-motion crises—climate, biodiversity, habitat destruction, and all the rest—get pigeonholed into the catchall category of "let's worry about it later."

• **Stress impairs our judgment.** When people are under the influence of the stress hormone cortisol, they tend to make horrible decisions. We lapse into dysfunctional behavior and fail to meet our responsibilities. We ignore evidence, act rashly, focus on trivial matters, and fight one another, all of which compromise our ability to deal with a complex and demanding world.

In short, stress makes everything worse, both individually and collectively. Not only does it ruin our personal health, it also degrades the very abilities we so desperately need at this moment in history. To put it another way, we might well rank cortisol as one of the most problematic substances on the planet—along with plastic, endocrine disruptors, excess antibiotics, and carbon. In other words, stress isn't just a health problem—it's an ecological problem, a social problem, a national security problem, a problem of national culture and character, and a problem for the totality of life on Earth. And we ignore it at our peril.

THE STANDARD NARRATIVE

Of course, most of us have heard about stress, and we think we know what it's all about. We've heard the conventional narrative in popular books, magazines, websites, and in casual conversations with friends and coworkers. That is, stress is an individual problem with individual solutions. It's an isolated, personal experience that has nothing to do with history, society, culture, or context. If you're feeling overwhelmed, harried, or exhausted, it's up to you to make an adjustment. And of course, we've all heard the typical lifestyle prescription for stress relief: get plenty of exercise, take the right supplements, talk to your friends, write in your journal, practice mindfulness, listen to soothing music, and, of course, take some deep breaths.

WRONG PIGEONHOLE

The standard narrative does give us some useful ideas to play with, but sadly, it doesn't go far enough. What we see at the supermarket checkout stand is a simplistic story that fails to reflect the complexity, meaning, potential, and benefits of stress. Most important, the narrative fails because it puts stress in the wrong category. Most of us have been conditioned to believe that stress belongs in the health-medicine-lifestyle pigeonhole, closely related to themes of fitness, wellness, and well-being. It's a personal issue. If you're feeling stressed, there's something wrong with you, your body, your life, or your attitude.

If this perspective sounds familiar, that's because this individualistic orientation is baked into modern culture at large. In the world of medicine, disease is something that takes place inside our skins; the body is examined and treated as an isolated, stand-alone organism—a medical object. In the world of psychology, mental health is often treated as something that takes place inside the skulls of isolated human beings: depression, anxiety, and mood disorders are individual problems with individual solutions. Even the word *health* is generally taken to mean *personal health*, in spite of the fact that modern science now shows that many of our physical ailments are highly contagious and shared across populations. For a hypersocial species such as ourselves, health is always interconnected, and in fact, the very idea of a *healthy individual* is something of a misnomer. There can be no health in isolation.

To be sure, some physicians and health providers do advise their patients to "get more sleep," "try some meditation," or "manage your stress." And for the affluent and the "worried well," there are plenty of exotic options, including spas, retreats, and workshops. Some corporate programs attempt to address the issue in-house, but most rely on the standard narrative and the belief that, ultimately, it's up to the individual to adapt.

In short, the standard stress narrative fails to account for the fact that hypersocial human animals are radically connected to one another and that we share in the creation of our experience and the world. To be sure, individuals do experience stress, but it's also true that stress is contagious across families, workplaces, society, and culture. The new sciences of interpersonal neurobiology and social neuroscience vividly demonstrate that thinking, feeling, emotion, and stress are widely shared, distributed across tribes and, now, populations. In other words, human psychology is radically interdependent. So is stress.[4]

WRONG OBJECTIVE

The standard narrative also gets it wrong by suggesting that stress is nothing more than a problem to be solved. It's described as an abnormal deviation from our regular lives, something to be eliminated. In other words, if you're feeling distress, anxiety, depression, or fragmented attention, there's something wrong with your life that needs to be fixed, adjusted, medicated, or resolved. You, my friend, are broken. But if you follow the recommendations of the standard narrative, you might be able to get back to equanimity. And if not, well, there's something *really* wrong with you.

But all of this ignores history and context. Today, we live in a historically abnormal world, one that's marked by extraordinarily high levels of ecological stress, social stress, and economic stress, all of which is chronic. Of course we feel anxious and depressed. This is the normal reaction of animals that are forced to live in an abnormal, alien environment. In other words, we're behaving and responding in a way that's consistent with our ancestry and our circumstances.

But the standard narrative tells us that stress is something unpleasant that we need to somehow "get over." If we practice the right techniques and use the right products, we can get past it and back to our normal, peaceful lives. On the face of it, this might sound right, but on deeper reflection, we begin to realize that there are actually some stresses that we really don't want to "get over."

Suppose that the people in your life or your community are suffering from illness or injustice. Do you really want to get over this stress and move on to a state of peace and equanimity? Suppose that the precious natural habitat of your region is bulldozed for yet another shopping mall or chemical plant, while biodiversity is crashing around the world. Do you really want to get over this? Suppose that rich and powerful corporations are using their power to suck the life out of your community and hoard their wealth, leaving your people stranded. Do you really want to get over this fact and just let it go?

In fact, maybe this desire to "get over" our stress is really part of our problem. Maybe what we really need is to feel the stress more acutely and fight back with highly focused action. Maybe some kinds of stress actually shouldn't go away; maybe we should even be *more* stressed about the conditions we're living in.

WRONG TIGERS

The problem with the standard narrative is that it deals mostly with the small tigers in our lives—our overloaded schedules, our workplace confusion, and the typical culprits of modern living. Stress is cast as an annoying but mostly benign inconvenience. It's unpleasant, but thankfully, there's a set of easy "tips" to help us feel better. But this approach ignores the blunt-force reality that stress can crush our lives and our spirits and obliterate our ability to function in the world. The focus on easy lifestyle tips obscures the fact that stress goes all the way to the heart of the human experience. It also obscures the fact that if we really want to feel better, we might need to make substantive, even wholesale revisions to our relationship to life and the world at large, none of which is easy in the slightest. Stress is deeply serious business and ought to be treated as such.

As it stands, the standard narrative has little or nothing to tell us about the truly epic forms of stress that shatter our lives and cause us so much suffering. It tells us little about the life-crushing traumas of death, divorce, grinding poverty, and social injustice and, above all, the precarious state of the biosphere and the looming threat of ecological collapse.

There are a host of challenges facing humanity at this moment, but without question, one of the most pressing is our inability to distinguish between outright lies, illusory dangers (false tigers), and catastrophic threats to the future (real tigers). For the massively stressed modern human, living under the constant influence of hyperactive, shock-value media, all threats are presented as equal in their urgency and consequence. We act as if there's no substantive difference between the demise of the last Blockbuster video outlet and the extinction of animals, birds, and insects. We make poor assessments of authentic dangers and overrespond to trivial, even illusory threats. We are stress illiterates, dangers to ourselves and to others.

To put it another way, the standard narrative has virtually nothing to say about the really big tigers of our day. It'll tell you how to keep stress from compromising your youthful appearance, but it won't tell you how to stop fossil fuel destruction of the atmosphere. It'll tell you how to live a long life, but it won't tell you how to preserve a functional biosphere. It'll tell you how to feel less harried at work, but it won't tell you how to make your life meaningful in the face of radical social inequality.

WRONG ORIENTATION

Ultimately, the standard narrative fails because it frames stress as an external problem. Stress is something that comes from outside our bodies, as an alien visitor from beyond. We complain about being "under" stress, as if it's an external force bearing down on our heads and shoulders, forcing us into ill health and unhappiness. This externalized orientation is captured in the popular phrase *stress management*. That is, stress is something "out there," and if we could just contain it or manipulate it in the right way, all would be well.

This view of stress reminds us of similar modernisms such as *time management, risk management, crisis management, human resource management,* and *ecosystem management,* all of which imply an external world that needs to be controlled. So too for our popular practice of declaring war on anything we don't like: the war on cancer; the war on poverty; the war on terrorism, climate change, COVID-19; and, inevitably, the war on stress. But these dualistic approaches amount to an otherizing of the cosmos, the externalization of the world— yet another expression of alienated consciousness. The locus of our difficulties and our stress lies outside of us. When in doubt, manage something.

To be sure, it's obviously the case that external, objective tigers can and do "attack" us from time to time. And yes, there are external agents, forces, and processes that sometimes need to be controlled and managed. But as you'll see, most of our stressful experiences are matters of perception, interpretation, meaning, and, above all, relationship. In other words, our stress may well be "out there," but it's also "in here."

A NEW NARRATIVE

The time has come to give stress the respect that it deserves, but sadly, we just don't have much of a curriculum for dealing with stress on any scale, either individually, culturally, or systemically. The standard narrative is typically offered as a supplemental program, an add-on or enrichment to our regular curriculums. We wait until people are massively overloaded, teetering on burnout and lifestyle disease, then step in with stress-management workshops to help people regain their equanimity. But this is often a downstream act of desperation, an emergency measure that's too little, too late.

Given our lack of substantive stress education, it's no wonder that so many of us get things so wildly wrong. Our behaviors are often out of sync and out of proportion. We respond to stressors with the wrong intensity, at the wrong time, and for the wrong duration. We overreact to minor insults and underreact to genuinely threatening challenges. To put it in physiological terms, we're autonomic slop artists—we freak out about false tigers while we ignore the real ones.

Our problem is compounded by the fact that our brains—primed by evolution for survival in natural, outdoor habitats—are not particularly good at distinguishing real tigers from false ones in a hypercomplex modern world. Uneducated in the arts of threat assessment and proportional response, we overreact to trivial matters, personal dramas, local narratives, and petty politics. At the same time, we radically underreact to the really big tigers that threaten to bring down our planetary life-support systems: ecological overshoot, the climate crisis, destruction of habitat and biodiversity, social injustice, and other systemic failures that literally threaten our ability to have a functional future on this planet.

In short, our failure to recognize the difference between real and false tigers is having radical, cascading consequences, not just for us as individuals but for all of us, humans and nonhumans alike. All of which calls for a new approach. We need a curriculum that's more expansive, richer, and more nuanced. We need something that speaks not just to the plight of the individual but also to the systemic, interconnected nature of our predicament, especially the big historical, social, and ecological tigers of our age. This new narrative will serve as a remedy, not by promising to banish stress from our lives but by giving it meaning and making it relevant to the challenges of our day. The goal is not to make our stress disappear, but to listen and learn what it's teaching us.

CHAPTER 2

THE FUNDAMENTALS OF ADAPTATION

The key to success in any discipline is to build on foundational ideas and practices, and in this sense, stress is no different. We start at the beginning with the fundamentals of the autonomic nervous system, especially the far-reaching implications of neuroplasticity and what they mean in practice. In turn, this puts us in a good position to exercise some foundational strategies for success: knowledge, flexibility, specificity, and continuous adaptation. These qualities will take us a long way on our journey to skill, equanimity, and intelligent action in the face of ambiguity.

USE AND ABUSE OF THE AUTONOMIC NERVOUS SYSTEM

> Any man could, if he were so inclined, be the sculptor of his own brain.
> —Santiago Ramón y Cajal, Nobel Prize in Physiology or Medicine, 1906

To make stress work for us—to make our stress functional— it's essential to begin at the beginning, with the anatomical fundamentals of the human body, especially the autonomic nervous system and its two branches, one devoted to physical action (the fight-flight response) and the other to tissue repair and healing, a state that's often described as "rest-and-digest" or "feed-and-breed" (so-called because, when we're nice and relaxed, we want to feast and have sex).

Most of us have seen anatomy charts in high school and have heard the conventional explanations about the two branches, each with its particular mind-body effect, and maybe we've even heard something about how the autonomic nervous system affects our behavior, but that's it. For most of us, it's all just a bunch of wiring running down the center of the body, branching out to some squishy organs. It's vaguely interesting, but so what?

The problem is that we're failing to see the potential and the downstream consequences, not just for our individual lives but also for society and culture as a whole. The autonomic nervous system is far more powerful and influential than most people realize. It impacts every single cell in the body and, in turn, all our behaviors and, in turn again, all our relationships with the world at large. A human life spent fighting and fleeing is a whole lot different from one spent resting and digesting or feeding and breeding.

In every moment of every day, we live our lives at a cross-roads: Take one autonomic path and you may end up being miserable and ineffective. Take the other and you may end up performing at a high level. In fact, the wiring that lives in your body isn't really anything like the wiring that lives in your house or your car. Those wires are static; they perform their function with great reliability, but that's all they do. They never learn, adapt, or change. In contrast, the autonomic nervous system, like so many other systems in the body, is plastic and therefore trainable. In other words, the wiring is alive and learns based on how it's used. If we expose the system to the right kind of training and experience, we can enjoy some incredible benefits. Not only will our bodies work better, our entire lives will become more functional and meaningful.

MEET YOUR AUTONOMIC NERVOUS SYSTEM

Strictly speaking, the autonomic nervous system is not the only structure that participates in the human stress response. Other players include the hypothalamic-pituitary-adrenal axis, the vagus nerve, the limbic system, the amygdala, and even the prefrontal cortex. In short, the system is a kluge, a haphazard collection of parts, assembled by evolution over the course of millions of years, that nevertheless functions with incredible sophistication and efficiency.[5]

Also, to be completely accurate, the stress hormone cortisol is just one of many such hormones in a class called glucocorticoids. All of these informational substances and subsystems are tightly interlinked, and each has a role to play in regulating the body and behavior. To be perfectly precise, we'd have to address each one of these elements in turn and describe their particular actions, but such an effort would span thousands of pages and tax our attention to the limit. For now, we'll use the term *autonomic nervous system* as a label for the entire stress-response system in the body.[6]

At the same time, it's essential that we expand our view to get the complete picture of the autonomic nervous system. If we look strictly at anatomical charts, we might get the impression that the system is self-contained within the boundary of the skin and that it operates autonomously. But this would be a mistake. In fact, the autonomic nervous system is massively connected to the outside world and, in particular, to our social world. In a functional sense, the autonomic nervous system is actually bigger than the body itself.

This may sound odd or even metaphysical, but it makes perfect sense in light of human evolution. In a Paleolithic setting, people were massively dependent on other human beings for survival. Ancient Africa was a dangerous, predator-rich environment (lions and tigers and bears, oh my!), and tribal membership was essential for survival.[7] There were simply no viable alternatives to social living. The consequence is that people lived every moment on the cusp of acceptance and rejection, inclusion and exclusion. For all our Paleolithic ancestors, the predicament was stark: tribe or die.

In this kind of circumstance, it makes sense to suppose that evolution would favor the development of extreme social sensitivity. Autonomic nervous systems would be highly attuned to signals of danger or safety that are communicated through other people's posture, facial expressions, and tone of voice. In effect, other people functioned as sensory organs that helped us navigate the world, and they still do.

This extended social nervous system is now widely recognized by the neuroscience community in the field of interpersonal neurobiology. As neuroscientist Louis Cozolino puts it in *The Neuroscience of Human Relationships*, "the brain is a social organ" and "there are no single human brains." Likewise, Robert Sapolsky tells us that "no brain is an island."[8] Or as

Steven Sloman and Philip Fernbach put it in *The Knowledge Illusion,* "we never think alone."

In addition, the mechanism has been pretty well worked out. In *The Neurobiology of "We,"* psychiatrist Daniel J. Siegel describes a "resonance circuit" that operates between individual human bodies.[9] In a drastically simplified form, it goes like this:

As we observe the movements, postures, eye gaze, and microexpressions of other people's bodies and faces, we become sensitive to the pace of their conversation and their tone of voice, intonation, stress, and rhythm, the so-called *prosody* of communication. This information is processed by mirror neurons in the cortex of the brain, then relayed downward into the limbic, emotional brain centers. From there, this emotional content flows deep into the observer's body (the enteric nervous system) where it's experienced as gut feeling and a sense of what others are experiencing.

In effect, this circuitry allows us to run nonverbal simulations of what other people are feeling and experiencing. When the system works properly, we actually feel what others are feeling. But when this resonance circuit atrophies through disuse or is sabotaged by electronic devices, trouble is sure to follow. All of which has huge implications for our efforts to understand and work with stress. In short, our experience of stress and safety is bound to be highly social and contagious. In other words, there can be no "stress management" in isolation. All of our efforts will both touch and be touched by others. It's always interdependent.

THE POWER OF PLASTICITY

The details of the autonomic nervous system are fascinating in their own right, but our first priority is to understand the principle of plasticity, the physiological basis of the "use it or lose it" principle. The details are complex, but the essence is quite simple: the more we use a particular pathway, system, or component of the body, the stronger and faster it's likely to become.

The prime example is the plasticity of the nervous system, officially described as *neuroplasticity*. With use, nerve-cell fibers become more efficient and areas of the brain's cortex expand or contract, depending on our experience. But by far the most interesting example of neuroplastic change is the "long-term potentiation" (LTP) of synapses, the microscopic junctions between nerve cells.[10]

In technical terms, LTP is defined as "long-lasting enhancement of synaptic strength." In short, the more you use a synapse, the more efficient it becomes. And when we consider the fact that there are trillions of synapses in the human nervous system, this process can add up to profound, life-altering, and even culture-altering consequences.

Given our modern understanding of physiology, it's safe to assume that most structures of the body have at least some degree of plasticity. In general, the more we use a particular system, the more robust it's likely to become. So too for the autonomic nervous system—the more we fire the fight-flight system or the rest-and-digest system, the stronger and faster it becomes. We've all heard about the "use it or lose it" principle, but we can also phrase it this way: "Using it makes it stronger and faster." Or as Hippocrates put it: "That which is used develops. That which is not used wastes away."

Experience is everything in this process. If you happen to live in a genuinely dangerous environment, repeated activation of your fight-flight system will make you better equipped for survival. Your fight-flight reactions are probably appropriate and will become increasingly functional over time. You'll probably pay a price in weakened tissues and organs and in longevity, but if you can stay alive in the short term, it's a price worth paying. But what if you live in a modern, ambiguous environment where the dangers and threats are abstract or sub-ject to interpretation? What if some of the tigers we encounter are actually false?

This is where things get interesting. If you continually "teach" your autonomic nervous system by stimulating it with false tigers and imaginary threats, you'll train yourself for inappropriate reactions to the world. Your fight-flight system will become stronger and faster, but it might not do you much good in the face of the ambiguous and complex challenges of the modern world. On the contrary, it may well lead to inappropriate behavior and long-term health problems.

We can also look at this in terms of resilience. In good times, the body holds an ample supply of psychophysical energy and capability in reserve. Think of this as a "resilience reservoir," the sum total of our metabolic and psychospiritual resources. Every time we fire a fight-flight response, we deplete the reservoir; every time we rest-and-digest, we replenish it. The implications are obvious: if we continually deplete the resilience reservoir by living in a state of fight-flight, we aren't going to have much to draw on when the real tigers come around.

Like individuals, societies, organizations, and families also have their own resilience reservoirs—reserves of equanimity and flexibility that live in the collective unconscious of the group. When the reservoirs are full, the group can weather and adapt to all manner of challenges, but when these psychosocial reserves are depleted through continual pressure, hostility, and polarization—as they are today—the group becomes increasingly strained, brittle, and wary. And it's all contagious. Every time we run ourselves into fight-flight exhaustion, we also diminish the reserves of whatever group we belong to. But every time we replenish our personal resilience, we contribute to the adaptability of the whole.[11]

Just as the human body and the brain are substantially plastic, it makes sense to assume that the imagination is as well. This is where things get really interesting, because imagination no doubt follows the same principles of plasticity that we see in tissues throughout the body. That is, it's specific and use dependent. Use your imagination in a particular way and it'll become stronger and faster in precisely that way. Stop using a part of it and that part will atrophy in short order.[12]

Likewise, our imagination is also vulnerable to the same kind of habit formation that we see in muscle memory, nervous systems, and behavior. In short, it's all watershed. A drop of water falls in one place and starts a trickle, an early watercourse. Subsequent drops are increasingly likely to follow that same course, eroding a rivulet, a rut, and eventually a valley, a gorge, and even a canyon. What starts as simple pondering eventually builds into a powerful force and inclination, for better or for worse.

All of which contains an important lesson for resilience. Use the imagination in the right way and you'll become strong and stress resistant. Use it in the wrong way and you'll become vulnerable, automated, weak, and confused. Imagine yourself as a powerful animal, massively connected to your biological ancestry, and you'll be quick to rebound from adversity and trauma. Imagine yourself as a victim of circumstance and you'll become progressively weaker as the years go by.

PLASTIC VERSUS PLASTICITY

This would be a good time to pause and make sure of our definitions, especially the words *plastic* and *plasticity*. There's ample room for confusion here, so let's get it right at the outset. The word *plastic* might refer to the synthetic substance that's produced in factories to create the thousands of modern products that we both love and loathe. This kind of material is incredibly useful, but it's also an environmental menace. Or the word *plastic* might refer to the malleability or flexibility of almost anything—a material, a process, a tissue, an organism, or a culture.

To say that something is *plastic* might mean that it's fake, synthetic, artificial, or cheap. If we talk about plastic relationships, plastic narratives, or plastic experiences, we're saying that they're overproduced, sterile, and lacking in authenticity. They feel as if they came from a factory, wrapped in even more plastic. In other words, they don't feel genuinely human or alive.

Or we can use the word *plastic* to refer to a living system that's moldable and trainable, as in the *neuroplasticity* of the human brain. In general, the plasticity of plants, animals, nervous systems, and the imagination is a good thing because it facilitates adaptation and saves effort. But it can also be a bad thing when it generates deeply rutted habits that are inappropriate to circumstances. In any case, let's be precise: stop dumping plastic into the ocean and avoid the single-use packages, but celebrate the plasticity of your brain and body.

THE IDEAL: BE AN AUTONOMIC ATHLETE

Ultimately, everything we do with our bodies and lives depends on context. If you happen to live in an overtly dangerous environment, it makes sense to train yourself for faster and stronger fight-flight responses. But most of us live in an ambiguous world, one that's filled with tigers of all varieties, some real but many false. In this kind of world, it just doesn't pay to overtrain for always-on fight-flight reactivity. You might remain physically safe, but you'll generate wildly disproportionate responses to minor challenges and, in the process, alienate people and drive yourself even deeper into stress.

A better approach is to become an autonomic athlete, relaxed and poised but ready for action when the time is right. In other words, our default state should be rest-and-digest/feed-and-breed, but the fight-flight system should be ready to go, fast and strong as needed. To put it yet another way, rest-and-digest should be our baseline state, while fight-flight should be reserved for real tigers and genuine emergencies.

But of course, we sometimes fail. Stress hormones are powerful and seductive, and the modern world is crawling with tigers of all kinds. It's easy to misjudge. It's easy to fall into the habit of overreaction, firing the fight-flight system impulsively or perversely, just for the sake of stimulation. But every time we do it, we increase the likelihood that we'll do it again, and before we know it, we're camped out in fight-flight. False tigers appear and we jump into action and then overreaction.

The life lesson here is to use the fight-flight system with discretion. Use it as needed, not by habit. Pay attention to the early warnings, inclinations, and whispers of reactivity. *Am I overreacting to a false tiger? Maybe I can just let this go.* Relax, take a breath, and save your fight-flight mobilization for when you really need it. And remember, we usually have a choice about which branch to fire. Not always, but often. The ancient, primal body is driving the action on most things and will make its own judgment calls as it sees fit; if danger is immediate, the fight-flight system is probably going to kick in whether you want it to or not. But in many circumstances, we do have a choice. When faced with an ambiguous challenge or minor threat, we can fire the fight-flight response or we can let it go. We don't have complete top-down control, but we do have *some* control.

Remember, the art we're seeking is a proportional stress response. The challenge is not to eliminate our stress, but to rewire our behavior for precision. That is, we need to get stressed about the right things in the right proportion, at the right time, in the right intensity, for the right duration, and with the right meaning. Don't let the false tigers train your autonomic nervous system into overreactivity. Save your power for the real dangers.

KNOW THE CURVE

On the face of it, the stress response sounds like a simple, binary teeter-totter: you're either in fight-flight or in rest-and-digest. But in the living animal, the body's response to stress actually follows a classic inverse U-shaped curve of rising benefit, a tipping point, and diminishing returns. If we're going to be good autonomic athletes, it's essential to understand how the curve works and what it means in daily life.

On the left side of the curve, rising levels of stress hormones mean good things for the body, the brain, and cognition. Metabolic fuels are released into the bloodstream to feed our attentive brains. At the same time, our brains secrete neurotrophic chemicals that stimulate the growth of new nerve cells, dendrites, and synapses. In this sweet spot, memory is sharp, and attention is focused. This condition is sometimes described as *eustress*.[13]

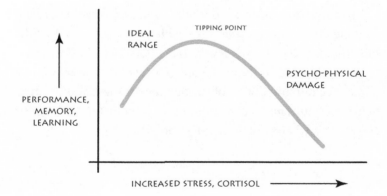

As stress increases, benefits also increase, but beyond the tipping point, the effect reverses itself and stress becomes destructive. Our cognitive, psychological, and spiritual resources begin to drain away, and our bodies are slower to recuperate from exertion, injury, and illness. In turn, this makes us increasingly vulnerable to other stressors, even those we would normally weather without a second thought. Aches and pains seem worse than usual, and we begin to worry about the trajectory of our health.

Over time, chronic activation of the stress response inhibits the growth and connectivity of precious neurons and can even damage brain centers that are involved in learning, memory, and impulse control. Key neurotransmitters such as dopamine become depleted, which leads to a loss of pleasure. If stress continues, our mood becomes increasingly serious, then grim. Our sense of humor declines, and then disappears entirely. We stop laughing. We stop loving life.

At this point, we enter the dark world of disease, dysfunction, and depression. Stress hormones may become neurotoxic, endangering neurons and even killing them outright. Chronic exposure erodes the structure and function of the hippocampus, a crucial brain center involved in explicit, short-term memory and learning.

In turn, this can lead to a host of neurological disorders, ranging from minor attention problems all the way to full-blown dementia. At this level, stress hormones become psychotoxic, leading to impulse-control problems and substance abuse. We fall into a state of learned helplessness and begin to generalize our lack of control to other circumstances, even to those cases when control is in fact possible.

HEED THE WARNING SIGNS

The inverse U-shaped curve provides some powerful life lessons. In the first place, it teaches us that stress has real value. In moderation, it's essential for learning, performance, and a good life. So, instead of trying to make our lives stress free, the superior strategy is to seek an optimal level of stress: the right kind of stress, in the right intensity, for the right duration. In other words, look for precision, not eradication. Whenever possible, fine-tune your adversities.

Second, the curve reminds us to honor the point of diminishing returns. As stress increases and you approach the tipping point, be alert for these warning signs:

- Anhedonia (loss of pleasure)
- Neophobia (avoidance of new things)
- Perseveration (mindless repetition of established habit patterns)
- Increased reliance on familiar experiences and ideas
- Reduced ambiguity tolerance, increased extremism, and black-and-white thinking
- Social withdrawal and isolation
- Cognitive distortions, especially overgeneralizing and small-picture, short-term thinking
- Physical lethargy, poor sleep quality, and decreased resilience
- Irritability and "making mountains out of molehills"
- Catastrophizing (going straight to the worst-case scenario)
- Decreased sense of humor and play
- Poor concentration and attention span

- Impulsive behaviors and reduced self-control
- Decision resistance, procrastination, and impatience

All of which makes us wonder about where we stand, not just as individuals but also as a culture at large. Are we coasting along on the left side of the curve, in the sweet spot of eustress; are we teetering on the tipping point of reversal; or are we headed toward the pain, dysfunction, and disease of the right side? Judging from the mental health challenges and dysfunctional behavior we see in today's world, it's safe to say that we're in real danger. Many of us—even most of us—are literally marinating in cortisol, dancing on the tipping point of the inverse U, perilously close to the edge of disaster. And thus, the challenge of our age: dampen the stress, reduce the fear, ease the pressure, and keep our lives working on the left side of the curve.

BEWARE THE FIGHT-FLIGHT HAIR TRIGGER

On the surface, it might seem easy enough to shift our lives in the right direction. All we need to do is turn down our fight-flight reactivity while we turn up the feed-and-breed, rest-and-digest system. We imagine the autonomic nervous system as a binary teeter-totter: when one side goes down, the other side goes up. When the fight-flight response turns on, the feed-and-breed system turns off and vice versa.

All of which is easy to understand, but there's a catch: the fight-flight system is hypersensitive, armed with a hair trigger. That is, it's really easy to turn on and difficult to turn off. This might seem oddly asymmetrical and unbalanced, but given our history, it makes perfect sense. Life on the open grasslands of East Africa may well have been nurturing and even easy at times, but it was also incredibly dangerous. Hungry predators were everywhere, as well as other large, dangerous creatures like rhino and hippo.

In this kind of world, it paid to have a hyperactive fight-flight response. If that rustle in the bushes turns out to be an authentic threat, you're ready to fight or flee. If it turns out to be a mouse, no harm is done, other than a slight cost to your tissue, organs, and longevity. The consequence is that the average human is slightly paranoid and overreactive, a tendency that becomes even more pronounced when we're stressed.

All of which defines our challenge: it's easy to turn on fight-flight, but feed-and-breed will take some time and even some "work." But this is not work in the familiar, conventional sense. Rather, it's a kind of anti-work or reverse work. It's a letting go of effort and ambition, a cultivation of contentment and ease. There's no urgency and no pressure for productivity. Life is perfectly good as is, no improvements required. Just settle in.

The good news is that the rest-and-digest recipe is conceptually simple. All it takes is a perceived sense of safety plus time. That's all there really is to it. No exotic techniques required. If we can create these conditions for ourselves and for one another, the body will respond and sink into a state of repair and rejuvenation. So, reverse your effort and let go of your attachment. Let go of your desire to control, to manipulate, and to achieve. Just breathe.

KNOW THE BEAST

> There are enough real enemies and threats in the world without having to invent imaginary ones.
> —Christina Engela, *Dead Man's Hammer*

As aspiring autonomic athletes, our goal is to make our stress responses appropriate to circumstances. The objective is simple: fire the autonomic nervous system in a way that fits the actual conditions we face. Just as you wouldn't want to be firing your feed-and-breed circuits at the top of a black-diamond ski run, you wouldn't want to be hypervigilant and primed for combat when you're lying on a massage table. Most of us would be quick to see these responses as inappropriate and dysfunctional.

And so, we ask a set of simple, powerful questions in our encounters: *In the context of my life, what kind of tiger am I facing? Is it real or false? Is it truly threatening, or is it simply a minor irritant? Is it a sensory illusion or the product of my imagination? Is this tiger a result of an outdated fear that's no longer relevant, or is this something that truly demands my attention?*

Of course, few of us take the time to actually ask these questions. More likely, we stumble through life and let the ancient, unconscious body call the shots along the way. But the body is fallible and error is always possible, especially in a world filled with novelty and random, confusing stimuli. Primed by evolution to respond to local, physical dangers, the body has no idea what to do with most of the modern world—a world filled with a vast array of artificial sights, sounds, and sensations that sometimes mimic real challenges. So, if we leave it up to the body, we're going to get it wrong some of the time, or even most of the time.

MEET FAUX TIGRIS

All of us have struggled with this predicament. When we reflect on our personal history, we're likely to realize that we often overreact to perceived dangers and even create adversities entirely from scratch. As Mark Twain famously quipped:

"I have known many sorrows in my life, most of which never happened." Or to put it in our terms, he might have said, "I have known many tigers in my life, most of which were false." The real tiger species is known as *Panthera tigris*, and so, in keeping with scientific convention, the false tiger must be *Faux tigris*. This curious species appears large, ferocious, and frightening, no matter its actual size. It monopolizes our attention and triggers an autonomic, fight-flight response. And sometimes, it even grows larger over time, becoming increasingly menacing the longer we think about it.

While the real *Panthera tigris* is endangered because of habitat destruction and poaching, *Faux tigris* thrives in the modern world and can be experienced in almost any setting. And while real tigers usually go away after a while, *Faux tigris* can linger in the human imagination for weeks, months, and years and can even be passed from one generation to the next. To put it another way, real tigers are usually acute stressors, but *Faux tigris* can be stubbornly chronic.

But where does *Faux tigris* come from? Unlike most of the other creatures that inhabit our world, this one is mostly a product of the human imagination. In a sense, this is to be expected. After all, we are largely ignorant and irrational animals ourselves. Modern life takes us by surprise and, suddenly, we're here, trying to make a go of it in an immense, dynamic world that we can barely understand. Of course, we're going to overreact at times. We project our fears onto the world and imagine dangerous animals where none exist. Knowing this about ourselves, it's safe to assume that many, if not most, of the tigers we meet are false. To put it another way, if you meet a tiger in your life, there's a good chance that it's a *Faux tigris*. It's probably not as dangerous as you're making it out to be. In fact, it may not be a tiger at all.

WHAT IS STRESS TELLING YOU?

So, how do we assess the tigers in our world? How do we distinguish between genuine dangers and things that only feel dangerous? One obvious solution is to follow the science. If we track actual events and collect the data, we can make reliable judgment calls about risk and danger. For example, most of us are inclined to believe that flying in an aircraft is more dangerous than driving in a car, but research shows otherwise. When we collect actual data, flying is revealed as a false tiger, while driving—especially at night—is a very real one.

But science can only take us so far. Most of our personal challenges haven't been tracked or studied in detail, and most of our predicaments are messy, complex, and personal. On many days, our experience is vague; we feel anxious or distressed, but we can't say exactly why. Desperate for an explanation, we pick whatever's handy and label it (or, him or her) as the perpetrator. If we happen to be right, things may go well. But more likely, our impulsive accusations only spread the stress toxin through the system.

Back in prehistory, making this call wasn't much of a problem because the voice of stress was almost always clear. If you were feeling anxious, it's probably because there was a direct and immediate threat to your survival. You're under stress because a rhino just gored your best friend and is rampaging through camp. Maybe there's a wildfire coming your way, a neighboring tribe is attacking your camp, the weather is freezing cold, or you've sprained your ankle on a river crossing. In cases like these, it's easy to understand what your body is telling you—no interpretation is necessary.

But for most of us in the modern world, the voice of stress is often garbled and even incomprehensible. We know that something is wrong, but we can't say exactly what it is. Possibilities abound: The feeling of stress might be trying to tell you about a direct threat to your body, or it might be warning you about an erosion of personal power and control. Maybe you're experiencing a narrowing of options. Maybe you're suffering from cognitive overload or temporal poverty. If the mind-body senses that it's at the limit of what it can absorb and deliver, stress will start yelling its head off.

Or maybe your stress is telling you that your status in the tribe is under threat and you're facing the possibility of rejection. Maybe your stress is telling you that your identity and sense of meaning are under attack. Or more generally, maybe your stress is telling you that you're in an adversarial relationship with the world at large. You've otherized the world and set yourself in opposition to people and events.

Finally, the voice of stress might be telling you that you're doing genuinely creative work in the world and that you're meeting the inevitable resistance that comes with new endeavors. In this case, you're simply experiencing what any creative person would experience; the stress comes with the territory. In other words, you're on the right track.

Even more perplexing, it might well be all of the above; sometimes multiple stressors are in motion simultaneously, and even more confusing, things can change by the minute. Today's stressor might be tomorrow's punch line; what bugs us this morning might well prove to be irrelevant by dinner. It can be hard, even maddening, to sort it all out.

And sometimes, stress just seems to come from nowhere. There's a vague sense of unease, a feeling that's somehow just "in the air," drifting and surging through the collective unconscious. It takes up residence in our bodies and our spirits, for no apparent reason. We feel anxious, nervous, or agitated, but our condition is inexplicable. We grope for reasons, but none of it really makes sense.

QUESTION DEEPLY

The conventional scientific definition that's commonly used in the behavioral sciences tells us that stress is "a perceived threat to the organism." It doesn't matter whether you're a laboratory rat, a baboon in the wild, or a human trying to make it through another challenging day, it's always the same: if you perceive a threat to your body or your life, you're going to feel stress. And naturally, the operative word here is *perceived*. If you think, feel, or imagine that something's a threat, that's what really matters.

But that's just the beginning. If we really want to get to the root of what's bugging us, we need to ask some pointed questions about our experience. What exactly is bugging us? What exactly is provoking our autonomic nervous system? Who or what are these tigers that come into our lives? If we can bring the tiger into focus, we can craft an appropriate response.

All of which calls for an exercise. Take a moment, slow down, and reflect on what you're thinking and feeling. Pause for a time, then try to answer these questions:

> *What's the source of my stress?*
> *Can I put my finger on it?*
> *Is it inside or outside? Or both?*
> *Is this an objectively real tiger, or is it subjective and open to interpretation?*
> *Is this tiger going to kill me if I let down my guard?*
> *Does this tiger threaten me with a physical death, a social death, a financial death, or a creative death?*
> *Is this tiger a real or perceived threat to my body or my livelihood? To my family, friends, or colleagues?*
> *Is this tiger a threat to my identity or to the cultural story that sustains me?*
> *Does it feel like a threat to my values? My sense of security, predictability, and control?*

What are the consequences if I ignore this tiger?
Is it worth my time and trouble?

Take all the time you need, and even better, make some notes that you can refer back to later. Likewise, talk to the people in your circle:

I feel stressed; it feels like a tiger is prowling the perimeter of camp. Have you seen it?
Do you feel it too, or is it just my imagination?
Do you think it's dangerous?
Have you ever seen this kind of creature before?
Do you think it'll go away on its own, or should I do something?

By the time you've reflected on these questions, you might well conclude that your tiger is false and not worth your time. Or you might come to realize that, yes, this tiger is real and demands your attention. In either case, you're better positioned to move forward.

SUFFER WELL

But sometimes our anxiety is just fundamentally inexplicable, and that's OK too. Maybe our stress is the result of large-scale historical or cultural forces that are flowing through our communities or our lives. Maybe it's the subtle contagion that comes in waves off the people around us, finally taking up residence in our bodies. It's mystifying and unsettling, but maybe it's OK that we leave it at that.

After all, acceptance is far better than our typical response to inexplicable stress: our impulsive, often random, targeting, projection, blaming, and conspiracy mongering. Uncomfortable with our condition, we grasp at an explanation and lash out at whatever's handy: the dog, the people around us, the government, the ideology of the people in power. But in our rush for security and certainty, we often make things worse.

So, maybe it's better to suffer our inexplicable stress—as some have put it, to "suffer well."[14] Maybe it's better to just sit with the enigmatic anxiety and the mystery. We don't have to explain every sensation and emotion in our bodies and our lives. We don't even have to understand why we feel the way we do. There are tigers out there in the dark, just as there have always been. And sometimes, we've just got to live with them. There's nothing to be gained by obsessing over their shadows. Just breathe.

BE FLEXIBLE

> It takes two to Tao.
> —Ana Claudia Antunes

When going in search of remedies and antidotes for stress, a good place to begin is with Robert Sapolsky and his book *Why Zebras Don't Get Ulcers.* Sapolsky is well known for his groundbreaking work in the neurobiology of stress and was one of the first to suggest that stress hormones might be toxic to neurons. In a 2005 *Scientific American* article, he summed up the findings, all of which are backed up by research on human and nonhuman animals:

> Individuals are more likely to activate a stress response and are more at risk for a stress sensitive disease if they . . .
>
> • feel as if they have minimal control

- feel as if they have no predictive information
- have few outlets for their frustration (aka hobbies)
- interpret the stressor as evidence of worsening circumstances
- lack social support

This list makes for a great starting point and suggests a strategy, or set of strategies, for working with the tigers in our lives. In short, we look for anything that would increase our sense of control, give us better predictions, especially evidence of better things to come, and give us some outlets for our frustration and a sense of social support. If we could do all these things together, our lives would be a whole lot easier. This would be the holy grail of stress reduction.

But there's also a paradox here. Our list emphasizes the importance of exercising control over our circumstances— what we might call the "yang arts." But there's also a body of teaching and research that emphasizes the importance of learning how to relinquish, accept, and adapt—what we might call the "yin arts." What makes this interesting is that both approaches can work and, as it turns out, being ambidextrous might well be the best approach.

YANG: TAKE CONTROL

The yang arts begin with the recognition that all animals need a sense of power, control, and predictability to thrive. When nonhuman animals are placed in laboratory conditions that decrease their sense of control, they show biological markers of stress, but when control is restored, they do better. In short, a rodent that can turn off an electric shock does better than a rodent that can't, even when the level of electrical stress is precisely the same. Even fake buttons and levers that offer the appearance of control can reduce the stress effect. Predictability helps too: a rat that gets a warning light before an electric shock does better than one that gets no such warning.

In this sense, the solution to stress lies in focusing our attention on executing the work at hand. When our lives are in chaos, we need to accomplish vital tasks that will help us get a grip on our situation. In these circumstances, it makes little sense to imagine you're lying on a beach in the South Pacific, breathing in the fresh air and contemplating the gentle waves as they caress the shore. No, you've got to redouble your efforts and get the work done.

There's no real mystery here. The yang arts are all about task management and the fundamentals of modern living: planning your days and your weeks, using a calendar, budgeting your time, making to-do lists, and keeping your schedule in order. Do the planning, get the work done, gain a sense of control, and your stress will diminish. To put it simply, work works.

Likewise, having the right tools gives us a sense of leverage. Good tools—whether physical or digital—help us get our work done and, in turn, give us a feeling of mastery. Education also increases our sense of power and control, especially when it's relevant to the actual circumstances on the ground. Knowledge gives us options and makes the world seem less arbitrary and more predictable. Even physical strength training can give us a feeling of mastery and resilience. When we work our bodies against gravity and build our physical competence against resistance, the rest of the world begins to feel more manageable by comparison.

All of which sounds promising, but we need to remember that, historically speaking, the yang arts are actually rather new to the human repertoire. Hunter-gatherers may have exercised some small measure of control over their circumstances, but there just weren't many options available. You might sharpen your skills and your arrows, work some animal hides into clothing, and build a better hut, but that was about it. No one even considered manipulating the world; we were participants, not masters.

It wasn't until the dawn of agriculture and civilization that people really went all in on manipulation and, later, domination. In fact, we can describe the entire arc of Western culture over the past several thousand years as the progressive intensification of yang strategies. And now, for people living in the Western tradition, the yang approach has become nearly universal and normalized.

This control-maximizing strategy sometimes works in our favor, but it appears to be running its course, beyond the tipping point into the realm of diminishing returns. We've perfected an incredible range of yang arts, but in the process, we've become one-trick ponies. As individuals and a culture, we've become fixated on control, but all our work doesn't seem to be working. We have more control over the world than ever before, but our stress only seems to escalate.

YIN: LET IT BE

Power and control are practical and even valuable antidotes to stress, but they can only take us so far. After all, there are only so many elements and forces in the world that the human animal can control. Even with the most advanced tools and technologies, there are practical, aesthetic, and even spiritual limits to what we can and should do.

And as individuals, our attempts at control often fail in the face of real-life challenges. We might be able to control our immediate physical environment, but when it comes to the hypercomplex, nonlinear realities of people, social relationships, culture, and modern large-scale systems, even our best efforts are likely to be inadequate. If we persist in our efforts to control the uncontrollable, we'll not only stress ourselves unnecessarily, we'll also wreak havoc on the people and systems around us.

This is precisely why we need the yin arts of letting go and letting things be. This approach, sometimes described as "reversed effort," is a deliberate letting go of whatever it is that's bugging us. We protect ourselves as need be, but mostly we observe and relax. This approach is particularly useful in dealing with the irritating and annoying false tigers that are so widespread in the modern world. Spam calls, tailgaters, noisemakers; if it's a false tiger, let it go. Save your energy for the real predators.

In contrast to the yang arts, the yin arts are humble in nature. We bow before the big forces of nature. We bow before the hypercomplex, nonlinear realities of bodies, ecosystems, social systems, and the biosphere herself. We relinquish attachment to any particular outcome. We accept our powerlessness in the face of ambiguity and uncertainty. We acknowledge our ignorance. There is maturity here, and sapience.

On the face of it, this "let it be" approach may well seem easy enough, but raised in a thoroughly yang culture as we are, it may feel alien, even absurd. Raised from birth to "just do it," the whole idea of leaving things alone might seem weak, impractical, and maybe even stupid. But exercising the yin arts doesn't mean simply giving up in the face of adversity or living on our knees. It means picking our battles; taking on some tigers and letting others go their own way. It means being powerful at the right time and place. It means being fluid and adaptable. And there's surprising power here. When we relinquish the desire for control, the autonomic nervous system relaxes and shifts away from fight-flight urgency. In the process, we regain our equanimity and our poise.

BE AMBIDEXTROUS

And so, the obvious question: When to yin and when to yang? When to control and when to relinquish? Naturally, this reminds us of the Serenity Prayer, written by the American theologian Reinhold Niebuhr:

> God, grant me the serenity to accept the
> things I cannot change,
> courage to change the things I can,
> and wisdom to know the difference.

It's well said, but, then again, not really that much help. After all, who really knows the difference? It's always a judgment call, and all of us, even the most sober, intelligent, and level headed among us, have gotten it backward on occasion. We've fought long and hard against things we cannot change, and we've practiced serenity in accepting things that really should be changed.

And who's to say which is which? Are we to exercise serenity in accepting megafauna threats like climate change and the biodiversity crisis, things so enormous that personal efforts seem insignificant? Or should we fight on principle, even against overwhelming odds, because to do otherwise would be unacceptable? Maybe it's not enough to simply change the things we can. Maybe we should fight long and hard, even when the challenges seem insurmountable.

In any case, the answer cannot be found in any book but only in our lived experience. However, one thing is certain: every human animal, every aspiring artist, and every activist must be capable of both temperaments. One-trick ponies are destined to fail in a hypercomplex, dynamic world. If all you've got are the yang arts of power and control, you'll inevitably destroy your world and create more stress for everyone. If all you've got are the yin arts of acceptance and yielding, you'll get run over, abused, and violated. You'll be stressed, ineffective, and of no use to anyone.

The solution: know them both, practice them both. If yin doesn't work, try yang. If power and control don't work, try yin. Whatever it is you're doing, reserve the capability to do the other.

BE SPECIFIC

> We are what we repeatedly do.
> —Aristotle

As we all know, stress can wreak havoc on our bodies, our cognition, and our behavior. And on bad days, it just seems to make everything worse. Hammered by cortisol, we stumble through life, sometimes finding the right combination but mostly making a mess of things. Our typical responses to stress feel awkward, dysfunctional, and counterproductive. As some observers have put it, stress makes us stupid.

But sometimes, and for some of us, things do come together. In fact, some high-performing people seem to turn the whole thing around. Instead of being distracted or derailed by stress, they actually seem to feed off it. The greater the stress, the greater their focus and the higher their performance. We might describe this as a "paradoxical stress response" or a "mastery response." In the modern world, we think of athletes, especially today's high-risk adventure athletes who actually seem to become calmer when their lives are on the line. We also think of high-performing musicians, speakers, and others who seem to thrive under pressure. The higher the stakes, the greater their focus.

Modern examples are easy to find, but this must surely be an ancient human aptitude. Imagine a master hunter in the

Paleolithic period, well honed by years of experience in the bush. He's seen plenty of tigers in his day, and he understands something of their ways. And so, when the carnivore wanders into camp or even follows him in the bush, he doesn't panic. He takes a breath, increases his focus, and keeps his wits.

PRACTICE: THE OPEN SECRET

When we witness these amazing feats of focus and performance, many of us are quick to suppose that it's all a result of the aptitude and fortitude of the individual in question. He's just an amazing person; she has the right stuff; they were born that way. We're in awe—and rightly so—but the reality is hidden deep behind layers of practice and experience. These performers are good at dealing with tigers precisely because they have had a lot of experience dealing with tigers.

The formula has been pretty well worked out by now. A recent series of books makes the case that "experts are made, not born." *The Talent Code: Greatness Isn't Born, It's Grown* by Daniel Coyle and *Talent Is Overrated: What Really Separates World-Class Performers from Everybody Else* by Geoff Colvin tell us most of what we need to know. Coyle advocates for "deep practice," while Colvin writes about "deliberate practice," but these are simply different labels for the same act: total immersion and engagement in a disciplined process. If you really want to rewire your nervous system to feed off stress and pressure, you're going to have to do the work, and this means hours of highly focused concentration.

WHAT WE CAN LEARN FROM PARACHUTE JUMPERS

All of which tells us something very interesting about stress and mastery. As we watch the high performers at work, it's tempting to suppose that they've figured out a way to transcend their stress, to somehow magically make it disappear. They look perfectly relaxed, and we envy their composure. In some cases, they even look oblivious to the tigers in their lives.

But we're wrong about all of this. Master-level performers are well aware of the pressure; they can feel it in every cell in their bodies. The difference is that they've found a way to contain it, to coexist, to keep it at bay just a little longer than the rest of us. A telling example comes from the world of parachute jumping, where researchers took heart-rate readings from groups of beginning and advanced jumpers.

Both groups showed similar peaks in their stress response, but there was a notable difference. The beginner's stress response began well before the jump itself—even days before—and persisted long afterward, also for days. For the advanced jumpers, there was a last-minute activation, a spike with the jump itself, and then a quick, almost immediate, return to baseline. In other words, experience and practice allowed the advanced jumpers to contain or compartmentalize their stress.[15]

This is an important lesson for all of us because it knocks the elite performers down to size. They're not superhuman, and they really aren't much different from the rest of us. They still feel the pressure of the big match, the finals, the public presentation, or the time on camera, but they've put in the time, the practice, and the preparation. Any of us could do likewise.

THE SAID PRINCIPLE

Naturally, all of this depends on context. Our advanced parachute jumpers learned how to compartmentalize their stress when jumping out of an airplane, but there's no guarantee that their autonomic skills would translate into another domain. How would they do if forced to scuba dive in rough conditions or speak in front of a highly critical audience? In all likelihood, they'd do no better than any other novice. That's because the body understands context, and our learning—including autonomic learning—is highly specific to circumstance.

This kind of thinking is all the rage in the world of athletic training and physical therapy, where coaches often talk about the power of the SAID principle: Specific Adaptations to Imposed Demands. The idea is simple: no matter what you throw at it, the body will do everything it can to remodel itself to make future encounters with that experience easier. Challenge the body with strength training, and it will immediately go to work growing muscle fibers, tendons, ligaments, and nervous system support. Challenge the body with endurance activity, and you'll see microscopic tissue-level changes, perfectly specific to that kind of experience.

The body—especially the nervous system—is constantly building new pathways and structures to meet whatever demands it encounters. This is why trainers everywhere are always on the lookout for ways to simulate real-world challenges. Coaches don't just give their athletes random drills; they study the detailed demands of the upcoming season, including the challenges of competition and the playoffs, then craft their training accordingly. The more precise, the better.

All of this makes sense at the level of athletic training and rehabilitation, but what most of us fail to realize is that this process of specific adaptation takes place continuously throughout our lives, no matter what kind of adaptations we're seeking. Challenge the body to do a particular task and it'll do its best to make that happen. In a sense, the body is really not that smart. It can't predict the future, so it simply assumes that tomorrow will be pretty much like today. So, it builds and remodels itself, all based on the experience of now.

The thing to remember is that the adaptations are unbelievably specific and precise, all the way down to the molecular level. The body tries to give us exactly what we ask of it, no more and no less. This is why modern trainers put so much effort into crafting challenges that mimic real-world conditions. In medical school, trainers attempt to create precise simulations of surgery, emergency room encounters, and other clinical practices, even going so far as to build detailed mock-ups of the physical surroundings. In the military, trainers prepare special-op teams for combat by constructing actual full-scale buildings to mimic conditions they expect to encounter in the field. Every detail of the operation is practiced in advance; the more specific the training, the better the adaptation and ultimate performance. The closer you can get in training, the better your chances of doing the right thing in real life.

The SAID principle suggests a simple set of safe assumptions: We get good at dealing with stressful circumstances by practicing in just those circumstances. We get good at dealing with ambiguity by putting ourselves in contact with ambiguity. There's no surprise to any of this. There are no magic tricks or shortcuts. We get good at dealing with tigers by dealing with tigers.

This also sheds some light on our conventional assumptions about stress relief. In the popular imagination, we suppose that the solution to stress is escape—that if we retreat to a luxurious spa in a remote location, we can finally relax and feel better. And to be sure, some of us do find relief in such an experience; there really is something to be said for relaxation, good food, and beautiful surroundings. But if you really want to learn how to adapt and deal with stressful conditions, the spa and retreat model makes little sense. The spa is an artificial paradise that is intentionally designed to be separate and apart from the challenges that we typically face. And in that sense, it's a poor form of training. The body has little or no incentive to adapt, and as a consequence, no learning takes place.

If you're learning how to climb a mountain, you've got to climb mountains. If you're learning how to deal with ambiguity and stress, you've got to expose yourself to ambiguity and stress. From an educational or training standpoint, going to a spa or retreat to hone one's stress skills is very close to being a waste of time. You may feel better for a while, but on your return to your "normal" stress environment, you'll be no better off than before.

So, we've got to be specific. According to the standard narrative, stress is just stress and all tigers are the same. It's unpleasant and icky, so let's try to make it go away. But all tigers are not the same. From the mind-body point of view, there's a world of difference between the stress of falling behind at the office and the stress of a romantic relationship gone bad. There's a world of difference between the stress of public speaking and the stress of piloting an aircraft in bad weather. The body knows this.

That's why we need precision. It's not good enough to simply train and hope for success with all kinds of stressors. We need to say exactly what we're trying to do. In turn, this suggests that we make distinctions between physical stress, cognitive stress, social and relational stress, moral and ethical stress, political stress, creative stress, occupational stress, and, of course, financial stress. Each is a different tiger, each demanding its own kind of experience and training. What kind of stress do you want to master? Make a list and use it to inform your practice.

BUILD A CULTURE OF MASTERY

In a sense, none of this comes as much of a surprise. All of us have heard about the power of practice, and this understanding probably goes all the way back to our Paleolithic ancestors. We can be sure that experienced hunters understood the value of repetition and focus in tracking animals and preparing poison for arrowheads. And in Eastern cultures, an ethic of deep, deliberate practice is baked into yoga, martial arts, craft, cooking, music, and calligraphy. Anything worth doing is worth mastering.

So, why then is such deep, deliberate practice so rare in modern culture? Why do we struggle so mightily in trying to learn fundamentals, and why are we so often intimidated and even crippled by the prospect of stressful competition, presentation, and engagement?

The answer lies in the creeping advance of distraction, exacerbated by a culture of convenience, amplified by electronic devices. In today's hyperactive market economy, producers and advertisers do everything possible to cater to the consumer's every whim. We want things and we want them now, and somebody out there is happy to step in and deliver. We've been trained to expect instant gratification, and in this environment, the prospect of deep and deliberate practice begins to feel increasingly unacceptable. Who wants to put in the legendary ten thousand hours for mastery when somebody's promising an instant solution to whatever ails us?

In the process, we've become weaker. The inevitable consequence of hyperconvenience is that no one wants to put in the time. When gratification is just a click away, we wind up with a shallow, antimastery culture, and in this kind of setting, stress looms even larger. Untrained, distracted students fail to develop the resilience and grit that comes with sustained engagement, and as a result, they become increasingly fragile and vulnerable to stress.

What we need is a return to immersive learning environments, intentionally created and managed to promote focus and concentration. Imagine the traditional martial art dojo, a place where deep, deliberate practice is honored and respected. This is an ideal model. Whether you're engaged with a school, a university, a workplace, a clinic, or an athletic training facility, resist the creeping fragmentation of attention. Insulate yourself and your students from distraction culture; protect the experience of deep, deliberate practice. Practice is a sacred time and these are sacred spaces.

As for your own practice, keep it deep and focused. Work works; put in the time and you will improve. Like the parachute jumpers, you're going to get better with each repetition. Feel it or not, your body will be learning and adapting with precision. The stress will still be there, but you'll be stronger and, after a while, you'll hardly even notice that you're jumping out of a perfectly good airplane.

KEEP ADAPTING

> In times of profound change, the learners inherit the earth, while the learned find themselves beautifully equipped to deal with a world that no longer exists.
> —Eric Hoffer

When it comes to living with stress, there's a paradox that lies at the heart of our efforts: When faced with difficult circumstances, our bodies begin to adapt immediately with extremely specific tissue-level changes that—if all goes well—will make future encounters more successful. After a few weeks or months of exposure and tissue remodeling, the difficult circumstances begin to feel more manageable and maybe even exhilarating; at this point, we've adapted. If conditions remain substantially the same, we'll be functional and maybe even happy, but if anything about our environment changes, the whole enterprise can fall apart in a hurry and, you guessed it, we'll feel stressed.

This distinction is extremely important for all of us, but it's particularly noticeable in the world of athletic training, where specific physical adaptation is both a key to success *and* a potential liability. The hypertrained athlete can succeed if his challenge remains constant, but if anything changes, things can collapse in short order. This is why modern athletes are encouraged to think and train bigger. Coaches are asking, Are you *adapted* or *adaptable*? And for many, this becomes a Zen koan that reorients both their training and even the trajectory of their lives.

This question poses an essential challenge for all of us modern humans. Like today's athlete, many of us—most of us, really—are in serious danger of becoming too narrowly adapted. The modern world channels us into particular skills and specializations, and before long, most of us are doing essentially the same things each day: habitual patterns of food, transportation, living arrangements, screen time, and communication, all of it standardized and driven by routine—all of which became even more deeply entrenched during the COVID-19 pandemic of 2020. After a few decades of living the standard American lifestyle, most of us are deeply adapted, not adaptable.

But this is an incredibly dangerous position to be in, especially in a rapidly accelerating, hockey-stick world that's on the brink of radical change. If there's one thing we can count on in this moment, it's that tomorrow's challenges are going to be far different—in both kind and magnitude—from what we're experiencing today. In this kind of world, the adapted will struggle and maybe even perish, while the adaptable will go on to create something new and viable.

This also tells us something crucial about stress. In a static world, those who are highly adapted can function at a high level, but when the world shifts, narrow specializations become increasingly out of sync, vulnerable, and brittle. This is what so many of us are feeling today, consciously or otherwise. We specialize and adapt, but lurking in the background is the possibility—even the probability—that our expertise may soon become irrelevant. And then what? We've spent our entire lives becoming adapted to a particular set of circumstances, skills, and values, all of which may soon be left out in the cold. It's no wonder we're so on edge.

BE LIKE WATER

When being *adapted* is a potential liability, being *adaptable* becomes an essential skill, a psychophysical metaskill for today's world. When we're adapted, our training process is essentially complete; the work is finished. The body has done its work at the tissue level, engineering precise changes to fit with prevailing conditions. We're good at what we do. End of story.

But to remain adaptable, we have to maintain our fluidity and move gracefully from one environment to the next. This challenges the mind, spirit, and body to transform continuously, on the fly, as it moves from one domain to the next. And in the process, we become more adept at dealing with the stress of novelty.

So, how do we do it? How do we become less adapted and more adaptable? This might seem like a bit of a puzzle, but in fact, we already know because the SAID principle tells us so. We become more adaptable by practicing precisely this very thing. We become more adaptable by putting ourselves in new situations that force us to adjust on the fly.

There's really no mystery to this, but it does call for a unique kind of training, one that will be counterintuitive for most of us. Instead of trying to perfect particular skills or capabilities in a particular setting, we practice moving fluidly from one domain to another. Build some capability, then switch. Gain some mastery, then go back to being a beginner in some new art. As soon as you're feeling competent, switch again. You'll never become great at any one thing, but you will develop something even more vital—the psychospiritual ability to move into new situations, confident that your body and mind will eventually figure out what to do.

In practice, we build our adaptability by engaging in novel circumstances, by leaping into the unknown and doing something different. Intentionally put yourself into circumstances in which you have no prior experience, skill, or understanding. Travel to new destinations, try new sports, new crafts, new social settings, new languages, new professions. All of these will demand and develop our adaptability.

Of course, your mind is likely to rebel at the prospect. The known is a comfortable place to inhabit, and we're happy to live there, especially when we're stressed. But that comfort comes at a cost in the form of increased vulnerability in the face of change. So, we must take the risk, try the new thing, and embrace the discomfort.

In turn, this suggests a powerful reframing of disruptive life experiences. When turmoil comes into our lives and forces us into new circumstances, we're quick to resist and dig in our heels. We suffer a divorce, a job loss, a health problem, or other apparent catastrophe, and we're quick to push back against our situation. We've been building our lives in one way, and now we're forced into a circumstance that, on the face of it, seems completely unacceptable.

But seen from another perspective, the crisis is simply an opportunity to practice our adaptability. It's just another form of training, a challenge to your mind and body's plasticity. Of course, it's going to be unpleasant at first, and maybe even for quite a while. The good news is that you're almost certainly more adaptable than you think. Put your body into a new circumstance and it'll start producing fresh tissue-level and nervous-system adaptations immediately. You may not feel the transformation, but the process is in motion; your body is rising to the challenge.

Along the way, take inspiration from a master of the adaptive mindset, Pablo Picasso: "I am always doing that which I cannot do, in order that I may learn how to do it . . . Each time I undertake to paint a picture I have a sensation of leaping into space. I never know whether I shall fall on my feet."[16]

Embrace the novelty. Trust your body. You're a lot more resilient than you think.

CHAPTER 3

SURROUNDED
BY TIGERS

We all know what stress feels like and, for the most part, we don't like it. The tension, the racing mind, the anxiety, and the insomnia—it's all bad news. As the story goes, stress will ruin your health, your cognition, and even your future. It's going to kill nerve cells, impair your judgment, compromise your athletic performance, and hold back your career. But the question remains: Where does all this stress come from?

The standard narrative tells us that stress comes from our own personal circumstances: having too much work and too little time, maybe from conflicts with coworkers and family members, or maybe from a death in the family or a divorce. But this is stress as usual for most of us. It's local stress in the here and now, the garden-variety stress that we're all familiar with. But for human primates in the modern world, there are far more stressors at work on our bodies and psyches than most of us realize.

In fact, our experience of stress is inevitably shaped by powerful forces that operate beyond our individual bodies and lives: our evolutionary mismatch with the modern world, the radical acceleration of modern life, the destruction of the natural world, our increasing separation from our most basic life support systems, the collapse of community, narrative dysfunction, and social ambiguity. These are the megafauna of our time, the deeply powerful, systemic, biological, cultural, and historical forces that afflict us to our core, often without our conscious awareness. In fact, we have ample cause to be stressed, and we're right to feel the way we do.

MISMATCH: THE PRIMATE'S PREDICAMENT

> [H]umans have dragged a body with a long hominid history into an overfed, malnourished, sedentary, sunlight-deficient, sleep-deprived, competitive, inequitable, and socially-isolating environment with dire consequences.
> —Sebastian Junger, *Tribe: On Homecoming and Belonging*

The story of stress begins with an understanding of prehistory. Not so long ago, we were healthy, wild animals living in intimate contact with our natural habitat and one another. Life on the grassland was stressful in its own way, but those stresses were occasional and episodic, and they always made sense in context. A lion or hyena might attack you or your people, but it was their habitat too, and once you learned their behaviors and inclinations, you could even get along after a fashion. And if you succeeded with hunting and gathering, life could actually be pretty sweet.

But today, we're struggling to adapt—in an evolutionary blink of an eye—to some radically novel conditions. Things are different now, not just because of the fact that we have new tools, technologies, knowledge, and social arrangements but also in the way that our bodies experience the world. And it's happened almost overnight. From a big-history perspective, our transformation to modernity has been almost instantaneous. If our ancestors traveled forward in time to today's world, they'd be mystified, shocked, and even repelled by the magnitude of the change. In essence, we are refugees from the deep past, trying to make a go of it in a world we can scarcely understand.[17]

The story of the human body stretches back millions of years. Over the course of thousands of generations, every detail of our anatomy, physiology, and psychology has been sculpted for survival and reproductive success in wild, natural, outdoor environments. Our skeletal, muscular, circulatory, nervous, and hormonal systems are the way they are because they enhanced our survival prospects in natural, ancestral habitats. Every cell, organ, feedback loop, and mental inclination has been shaped by our experience as hunters, gatherers, and scavengers. We're here today because our bodies are good at surviving in ancestral conditions.

In contrast, our bodies are almost entirely unprepared for a world of cars, couches, computers, and concrete. We're just not suited for lives of sedentary work, chronic stress, technological acceleration, social injustice, and looming planetary catastrophe. Our normal, evolutionary impulses clash with modern reality, setting us up for stress, addictions, and other dysfunctions.

In essence, we are animals attempting to live outside our normal ecological range. We're round, hunter-gatherer pegs trying to fit into square, industrial-technological holes. If we try really hard, we can force the pegs to fit, but damage is inevitable. This is the paradox of our time: we are misfits in a world of our own creation.

This is known as the problem of mismatch, sometimes described as "the evolutionary discordance hypothesis." And while it may sound like just another academic curiosity, it's actually one of the most urgent and consequential problems of our age. Far from being a mere hypothesis, the effects on our bodies and our spirits are very real and sometimes catastrophic.

THE GOLD STANDARD FOR UNDERSTANDING OURSELVES

Sadly, mismatch doesn't get the attention it deserves. In casual conversation, most of us are content to pigeonhole our ancestors under the heading of "sweaty, brutish cave dwellers" and to let it go at that. But our prehistoric ancestry is such an overwhelming percentage of human history that we have no choice but to take it seriously.

The proportions speak for themselves. Consider the fact that *Homo sapiens* has inhabited this planet for three hundred thousand years, and if we include our nearly human, hominid ancestors, human history spans something like six million years. In contrast, agricultural civilization has been our way of life for less than ten thousand years, and even more to the point, animal-powered agriculture—the truly pivotal change in the human relationship with the world—didn't take place until some five thousand years ago. Even then, the truly drastic changes that mark our hyperstressful modern world didn't appear until a few hundred years ago. In other words, the modern world constitutes only a tiny fraction of human experience.[18]

From this perspective, we begin to realize that the Paleolithic period (the "old Stone Age") should be considered the reference era for all our conversations about human life, medicine, education, training, and behavior. The word *Paleo* has a couple of definitions, but for our purposes, such differences are trivial, because, no matter how we define it, the Paleo encompasses a vast expanse of time, one that dwarfs the existence of the modern world.

In fact, the Paleo is such an overwhelming percentage of human experience that it must be held as the gold standard for understanding the way our brains and bodies work.[19] In 1973, the evolutionary biologist Theodosius Dobzhansky famously declared that "nothing in biology makes sense except in the light of evolution." Well said, but we might also say that "nothing in human biology and behavior makes sense except in the light of the Paleo." Or to put it yet another way, we might say that talking about human biology, behavior, education, or training *without* referring to the Paleo is nothing more than a shot in the dark. For a meaningful study of the human animal, the Paleo must be taken as normal until proven otherwise.[20]

OUR COLLECTIVE TRAUMA

To be sure, some people adapt easily to the modern world, and with a few adjustments, many of us remain happy and healthy. But for many others, the contrast is too great, the stresses of the alien environment too overwhelming to manage. Recognize it or not, our bodies feel the pull of the Paleo in every minute of every day, a frustrated longing for movement, physicality, and contact with other human beings and the living world. In this sense, mismatch must be considered a genuine form of trauma and should be treated as such.

Likewise, we might well describe mismatch as a low-grade form of PTSD, or at least a precursor. The trauma may not be as acute as that of combat or domestic violence, but the effects are just as real. When people are prevented from exercising their ancestral life ways and are separated from the continuities that support their health, they're far more likely to experience anxiety, depression, addictions, and other dysfunctions. Going further, we can accurately describe mismatch as a preexisting medical condition for nearly every human being on the planet, a condition that compromises our health in myriad ways. In other words, most of us are prestressed even before we come in contact with dangerous microbes, inflammatory processes, poisonous foods, and other disease-causing agents. This is the unrecognized public health crisis of our age. Millions of people are suffering and yet we fail to acknowledge the origins of their affliction. We pin the blame on personal behavior or flaws in physiology, but we ignore the bigger picture.

All of which adds up to a rather bleak prognosis. All of us, even the most well adapted, have one foot deep in the Paleo and another in the modern world. But with each new round of innovation and sophistication, the modern world becomes even more alienating, increasingly divorced from the ancestral conditions that support our health and sanity. New technologies, new constraints on behavior, new social arrangements— each of these "developments" pulls us further away from our origins. And with one foot in each world, the stresses on the human mind and body will only increase. It's no surprise that so many of us feel like we're being torn apart.

OUR COLLECTIVE CHALLENGE

Mismatch may well sound like a wicked, intractable problem, but the good news is that our understanding can give us fresh insight into our individual psychophysical afflictions. In the process, our stress, depression, anxiety, and physical unhappiness begin to feel less like personal failings and more like the inevitable consequence of out-of-context living.

In our hyperindividualized culture, we're accustomed to blaming ourselves when our bodies and our lives go sideways: *I feel bad—there must be something wrong with me* goes the typical refrain. But seen through the lens of mismatch, we come to see our afflictions as part of a larger whole. That is, our psychophysical angst is simply the result of trying to live outside our normal ecological range.

In fact, aside from occasional diseases and injuries, there's probably nothing wrong with you at all. And even more to the point, many of your "symptoms" can be seen as the normal response of a healthy, wild animal attempting to live in profoundly abnormal circumstances—all of which would be perfectly obvious to any veterinarian.

Even better, the human behavior we see around us no longer seems so arbitrary, inexplicable, and infuriating. In the conventional view, we're quick to suppose that bad behavior, aggression, extremism, and narcissism are simply a consequence of poor character and ignorance. We're quick to level accusations, point fingers of blame, and even bring criminal charges against the perpetrators. But with our new understanding, we begin to see these behaviors as a nearly inevitable consequence of living in an alien environment. When you build an industrial civilization that's fundamentally at odds with the deep nature of the human body, you're bound to see some serious misbehavior.

Ultimately, our struggles with mismatch should be seen as the *normal* response of wild animals to domestication and incarceration. In other words, our anxiety, depression, physical weakness, and other afflictions are really no surprise. Everyone around us is struggling. Some of us manage to adapt, some of the time, but in general, what we're seeing is the public health consequence of civilization itself.

In turn, this understanding leads us to greater compassion, patience, and tolerance, as well as to a simple life lesson:

treat everyone around you like they've been traumatized. They may not show overt signs of psychophysical dysfunction or mismatch-induced trauma, but everyone is struggling with the challenge. We're all in this together.

OUR CONFUSED NERVOUS SYSTEMS

The problem of mismatch goes deeper as the complexity of the modern world puts our bodies into a state of psychophysical distress, a condition we might call "autonomic confusion." Almost everywhere we go in today's world, our bodies are under siege by random, often irrelevant or conflicting stimuli. The deep, primal nervous system suffers under an onslaught of mixed messages, mostly electronic and digital. We flit wildly from the fight-flight response to rest-and-digest, often independent of the actual facts on the ground.

Just imagine you're sitting on a park bench on a warm spring day. Nature is waking up in all her glory, and your habitat is telling you to relax into rest-and-digest or feed-and-breed. This should be a calming, even healing, moment, a time for integration and coherence. But your phone is chirping out a series of alerts, alarms, and notifications about events and demands from the great elsewhere, sending your autonomic nervous system into fight-flight. Your habitat says relax, but your phone says panic.

If this happened only occasionally, it would simply be a minor nuisance, an annoyance of no real significance. But today, the disconnect has become radical and ubiquitous. Everywhere we go, from our homes to our vehicles to our workplaces, we're flooded with autonomic influences that have no connection to place, no relationship to the body's actual lived experience. In essence, the deep functions of our body are being remotely stimulated and controlled by actors, agents, and forces far away. Our nervous systems have no idea what to do, so they swing wildly back and forth, one minute working to heal the body, the next minute prepping for the worst. It's no wonder we suffer so much anxiety. When your body is in one place but your sensory influence comes from somewhere else, you're bound to be confused.

YOUR BRAIN ON NOISE

Closely related to our autonomic confusion is the modern onslaught of noise that assaults our senses and raises our stress levels. Motor vehicles, aircraft, trains, construction, and leaf blowers assault our ears at nearly every hour of the day and night. Far from being a mere annoyance, this acoustic pollution has significant health consequences for the human animal. Research has shown increases in hearing loss, high blood pressure, cardiovascular disease, injuries, and, of course, interrupted sleep. It also increases our impatience and our general state of anxiety.

The contrast with our original, normal, Paleo experience is immense. Just imagine that you're sitting on a hill in East Africa, tens of thousands of years ago. If you'd time traveled to this point, you'd be awestruck, not just by the vista of plants and animals before you but also by the silence. No vehicles, no aircraft, no construction crews, no car alarms. The only sounds are the voices of your friends, the calls of the animals, and the wind in the grass. Inevitably, you'd find this silence calming in a profound way. The so-called normal stresses of your modern life would dissolve, and you'd sink into a state of relaxation.

But today, we live on a planet of noise, only some of it acoustic. The world has become a twenty-four-hour distraction machine, a conspiracy against focused attention, and every day is a blizzard of beeps, buzzers, hypernormal colors, and flashing lights, all intruding into our lives at almost every moment.

This presents an unprecedented challenge to our cognitive resources and our ability to pay attention.

For the most part, we endure, like frogs in warming water, but this is far more than a simple annoyance. Acoustic and cognitive noise is highly destructive to the human animal's ability to focus and concentrate. It decreases our work and school performance, but even more to the point, it compromises our ability to hear and feel the primal, vital messages that come from ancestry, habitat, people, and our bodies. How are we supposed to feel the Earth when we're under acoustic assault? How are we supposed to hear and feel the life experiences of one another?

It's also important to remember that noise doesn't just impact human life. It's also destructive to nonhuman animals and habitat as a whole. When noise becomes ubiquitous, birds have trouble hearing one another's calls and are forced to either sing louder or migrate to a quieter habitat, if such a thing can be found. It's safe to assume that noise impacts other organisms as well.

The rising cacophony of noise erodes our powers of concentration just when we need them most. And for those of us who've managed to retain a sensitivity to the natural world, noise is beginning to feel like a kind of violence—against habitat, against our neighbors, and against ourselves. It's a double-barreled stressor that simultaneously erodes our concentration as it degrades our ability to hear, sense, and feel the systems that ultimately keep us alive. In this sense, noise is far more than a public health issue; it's a very real threat to our ability to create a functional future.

THE END OF RHYTHM AS WE KNOW IT

The challenge of mismatch takes many forms, but without question, one of the most vexing is the progressive obliteration

of our most basic, primal life rhythms. In short, we're attempting to impose stasis on a system that's inherently dynamic. To
say that this is stressful to us as individuals doesn't even begin
to describe it. In effect, we are literally stressing the entire biosphere, damping down the oscillations that are essential to all
of life. And when the whole is stressed, so are all the parts of
that whole.

The most obvious example is the widespread, indiscrim-
inate use of artificial light in almost every human dwelling,
workplace, and outdoor setting. In the span of just a century,
we've radically altered the most fundamental rhythm on
planet Earth, the day-night cycle. But that's just the beginning.
As globalization of commerce spreads across every time zone,
workers are expected to ignore the primal rhythms of their
bodies and be ready to work anytime, anywhere. If a customer
or supplier on the other side of the planet has a need, we've got
to be ready to serve that need. In the process, the words *day*
and *night* have begun to lose their meaning. It's all one thing
now, 24/7.

Our new flatline culture is reflected in our devices, which
are frequently advertised as "always on." These systems do not
take breaks but hum along continuously and tirelessly. And
in tandem with always-on technology, many of today's corporations now require employees to be "always contactable."
In other words, the commitment to work never sleeps. As an
employee, you can no longer have your own private life. You
and your body are now subject to "digital serfdom."

Once again, this stands in sharp contrast to human life
in the Paleo. For thousands of generations, we lived in intimate contact with the day-night cycle. Human brains and
bodies evolved with this rhythm, and it's safe to assume that
the deep details of our physiology are attuned to oscillations
of light and dark. But today, all that's changed. According to
the International Dark-Sky Association (darksky.org), night

skies near urban centers are hundreds or even thousands of times brighter than they were two hundred years ago. In other words, the primal signals that once governed the workings of our bodies have been radically disrupted. In short, we are taking our normal, rhythmic, oscillatory experience and replacing it with a flatline state of near-constant illumination. This isn't just stressful; it's destructive to our entire living system.

Some consequences are obvious. People are sleeping less now than in previous decades, and the quality of our sleep has been massively degraded.[21] Insomnia has become one of the most common complaints that people bring to physicians. But this is just the tip of a pathological iceberg. Not only are we sleeping less, we're suffering a host of lifestyle diseases, some of which can be traced back to our modern "darkness deficit." Heart disease and obesity are obvious candidates, but it's likely that many other conditions are exacerbated by circadian disruption. When you mess with a primary driver of human physiology, the entire animal is likely to suffer.

And it's essential to remember that the flood of artificial light doesn't just affect the human animal, it affects *all* forms of life on our planet. Without exception, terrestrial organisms have evolved under regular daily cycles linked to the Earth's rotation. Artificial light affects amphibians, sea turtle hatchlings, many bird species, and, of course, insects. The fatal attraction of artificial light not only impacts insects themselves but also all manner of species that rely on insects for food or pollination.

In the early years, artificial light was celebrated as progress, a grand, symbolic human victory of light over darkness. But today, it's beginning to look like a tragic mistake, a self-inflicted injury to human health and a threat to the biosphere. Like noise, we might well consider artificial light to be a form of violence against habitat, against humans and nonhumans alike. For all creatures, night should be a right.

OUR LIVES IN LOCKDOWN

Modern advertising promises us freedom in all things, but when we look at actual constraints on human movement in the modern world, our condition begins to look and feel less like freedom and more like incarceration. Which brings us to the word of the day: *vagility*, the ability of an individual animal or species to disperse or move from place to place. It's a hot topic in the emerging field of movement ecology: animals have certain movement needs for foraging, and if those needs are compromised, health and behavior consequences are sure to follow.

For ancient humans in the Paleo, vagility was almost unlimited. Our ancestors could walk, run, and hunt wherever they pleased, restricted only by the occasional river, mountain, dense vegetation, or interference from other tribes. No fences, no walls—just walk wherever you want and let terrain be your guide. And of course, our psychic or intellectual vagility would have been uninhibited as well. With no intellectual fences to restrict our imagination, our minds might well have ranged over the entire cosmos.

But today, our natural vagility is inhibited, blocked, restricted, and fenced off, seemingly at every turn. Beginning with agriculture and settled villages, humanity has experienced a vast indoor migration, out of the wild and into a world of boxes. Today, we're walled in, isolated from habitat and even from one another.

Sometimes our incarceration is literal. As often reported by many organizations, the United States has the largest prison population in the world and the highest per-capita incarceration rate. In 2016, over two million Americans were incarcerated in actual jails and prisons. But we're also suffering incarceration in other forms. Some of us are locked down by economic forces, and of course, many have suffered from the pandemic lockdowns of 2020.

But literal incarceration is only the beginning. Many of us are suffering from an inability to move socially, what we might call "social incarceration." Rigid social structures lock inequality in place, making it almost impossible for many of us to advance. And to make matters worse, some of us are suffering from what we might call "intellectual incarceration." As the modern drive for specialization grows ever more demanding, many of us are finding ourselves forced into narrow professions and fields of study. We'd like to learn new things and expand our horizons, but the demands of the job force us to restrict our focus—don't look out the window and, whatever you do, don't get creative.

But no matter it's form, the psychophysical consequences of incarceration can be severe. The human animal wants to move, to explore and adventure. We have a deeply ingrained need to experience a wider world, to see our habitat, and, in the process, to find out what we're made of. Sculpted by evolution for life in wild outdoor settings, it makes sense to suppose that living indoors, locked down and separated from our natural surroundings, would be a challenge for the entire organism, including our minds and spirits.

Disturbingly, we've now begun to see this effect reflected in the actual tissue of our brains. A growing body of evidence has shown that captivity causes literal brain damage in large mammals, most notably elephants.[22] Veterinary researchers have documented thinning of the brain's cortex, thinner capillaries and reduced blood supply, a reduced number of helper glial cells, shorter and fewer nerve cell branches (dendrites), and less-efficient synapses.[23] Presumably, the same processes take place in humans, especially those who live in an impoverished or monotonous environment. And in fact, research in anthropology suggests that the brains of human ancestors may well have been larger than human brains today.[24]

DISPLACEMENT COSTS

There's yet another challenge that comes with mismatch and our struggles with life in the modern world. Even when civilization provides us with sensible, healthy living conditions, it also tends to eclipse our primal attention to the living world. In the language of economics, we'd say that civilization has a displacement cost. That is, for all the time we spend paying attention to modern human innovations, commerce, and culture, that's time we *don't* spend paying attention to the very things that would normally sustain our lives and our sanity: the world of plants, animals, habitat, and weather.

For every hour we're indoors, that's an hour we're not outdoors. For every hour we spend shopping or doing work on the computer, that's an hour we're *not* looking at the living world. And the contrast is stark. In a Paleo setting, people would have spent many hours each day paying close attention to what we now call "nature." But today, many of us go months, years, even entire lifetimes without substantive contact with our living habitat.

This attentional shift is reflected in popular culture. In a study in *Perspectives on Psychological Science*, titled "A Growing Disconnection from Nature Is Evident in Cultural Products," the authors report that "references to nature have been decreasing steadily in fiction books, song lyrics, and film storylines, whereas references to the human-made environment have not."[25]

From a Paleo point of view, this is a tragedy in and of itself, but it's also likely to have immense downstream consequences for our health and our world at large. As the study authors state, "these findings are cause for concern, not only because they imply foregone physical and psychological benefits from engagement with nature, but also because cultural products are agents of socialization that can evoke curiosity, respect, and concern for the natural world."

In other words, this attentional shift puts us in a nasty positive feedback loop of displaced attention and diminishing interest in the natural world. All of which makes it even easier to exploit and tyrannize our last remaining wild places. And the more that nature is diminished, the more our resilience is compromised. What we do to the planet, we do to ourselves.

WILDNESS AT RISK

One foot in the Paleo, one foot in the modern urban world. It's a delicate balancing act, and to make it work, many of us are called upon to deny our animal nature, to suppress our wildness, and to give ourselves over to the regimented, artificial world of professional conduct.

Some of us manage this without particular difficulty, but for many, the chasm is too wide and our Paleo roots too deep. We might function for a time, but the body cannot be ignored or left behind forever. Some wild animals can be partially domesticated, but what about humans? Can we suppress our wildness and still remain healthy and sane?

The problem of domestication is that it systematically devitalizes the human spirit as it sucks the life out of the human animal. Domestication holds out the promise of wealth, security, power, and comfort, all at the cost of our animal vitality, our spirit, and our vagility. On the face of it, this might sound like a good deal, but little by little, we give away our animal nature and our wildness—sometimes by economic necessity and sometimes through habit, laziness, peer pressure, and conformity.

The end result is that our wildness has become critically endangered, and just as with any other extinction event, the loss would be irreversible, the consequences catastrophic. Wildness is our conduit to the history and exuberance of life herself. It's our connection to an incredible, ancient power.

In short, our wildness *is* our resilience. Destroy one and you destroy the other.

RELAX, YOU'RE PERFECTLY NORMAL

Mismatch imposes a daunting, sometimes crushing, burden on our animal bodies and spirits. Recognize it or not, understand it or not, this is something that all of us are struggling with each day; it's a background stressor that saps our energy, weakens our focus, and depletes our resilience. And to make matters even more challenging, we have no curriculum to meet this challenge. It's unlikely that any educational institution in the modern world teaches a course in How to Navigate Mismatch.

All of which leads us to an essential lesson for life in the modern world. If you're suffering anxiety about modern life, there's almost certainly nothing wrong with you. You're simply a wild animal attempting to live in a mismatched condition, outside your normal range. Of course you're stressed; this is how wild animals respond to captivity. In all probability, you're not suffering from a neurotransmitter deficiency, a medical condition, or a character flaw. The stress you're feeling is the simple consequence of living in this strange, furious, and exhausting world. All of us are mismatched, all of us are struggling to adapt, and most of us are stressed because of it. So, give yourself and the people around you a break. Exercise some compassion and some forgiveness. We are animals, after all.

THE POWER RATCHET

> If you don't understand the past, you won't have a future.
> —Cherokee saying

Living in a highly individualized society as we do, we're likely to imagine that stress begins and ends with our own personal circumstances, attitudes, and behavior. It may well feel like a personal matter, but in fact, there's a lot of history working in the background, below the level of conscious awareness. To get the picture, imagine that you're living deep in prehistory, as part of a hunting-and-gathering tribe somewhere in what is today North Africa or the Middle East. At that time, the entire region was lush, covered with verdant hills, forests, and grasslands thick with game animals. Hunter-gatherers could make a good living off the land and probably had ample time to relax, gossip, and make up stories around the fire. We may well over-romanticize it, but this might have been a sort of utopia—a garden of Eden.

But now for a question: "Imagine a group of tribes living within reach of one another. If all choose the way of peace, then all may live in peace. But what if all but one choose peace, and that one is ambitious for expansion and conquest?"

This is the question posed by Andrew Bard Schmookler in his landmark book *The Parable of the Tribes*. As he saw it, the natural state of humanity was mostly peaceful and relatively stress free. People enjoyed an idyllic state of living, with lots of time for casual gathering around camp and observing the natural world. In this setting, life was good, but one aggressive tribe could change everything.

Suppose that your tribe suffers a violent surprise attack from a neighboring tribe, resulting in chaos, injury, and casualties. Shocked by the event, your people resolve not to be ambushed in the future, and in the months and years to come, you begin taking countermeasures that include weapons, vigilance, and even a new warrior culture. You declare your preparations necessary, proportional, and just, but over time, your culture slowly becomes more militant and defense oriented. As Schmookler put it, "successful defense against a power-maximizing aggressor requires a society to become more like the society that threatens it . . . the defensive society will have to transform itself into something more like its foe in order to resist the external force."

It's easy to see how this condition would multiply, ripple, and cascade across entire regions and, eventually, the entire globe. Power operates like a ratchet; defensiveness spreads through the system, and life never returns to its original, mostly peaceful state. As tribes become more militarized, a warrior culture emerges, and people place increasing value on weapons, strategy, and deterrence.

Over time, the process spreads from one generation to the next, completely transforming not just culture but even what we consider to be "human nature." What started with spears and arrows eventually escalates into a global arms race, apocalyptic weapons, cyber warfare, and a strategy of mutually assured destruction. Eye for an eye, limb for a limb, blood for blood. The easy, stress-free living of early humans is forgotten, replaced by chronic stress, xenophobia, and paranoia. According to this narrative, humanity has spent the last six thousand years on a war footing; humans red in tooth and claw.

THE AGE OF SEPARATION

This story dovetails perfectly with work by author Steve Taylor in his book *The Fall: The Insanity of the Ego in Human History and the Dawning of a New Era*. For Taylor, a fundamental shift in human consciousness and culture took place in tandem with ecological changes that began in the Middle East and central Asia. This is the story of Saharasia—a vast area that stretches from North Africa through the Middle East and into central Asia.

Until around 4000 BCE, this was a fertile, semiforested grassland, with ample lakes, rivers, and human and animal life.

But the abrupt transition to defense and militarism sparked a fundamental shift in human consciousness, from interdependence to xenophobia, power, ego, and narcissism. As Taylor describes it, "for the last 6,000 years, human beings have been suffering from a kind of collective psychosis. For almost all of recorded history human beings have been—at least to some degree—insane." He calls this transformation "the ego explosion" and describes it as "the most momentous event in the history of the human race." As individuality exploded, the mind became a separate entity, and our original participation in the cosmos gave way to an alienated, nonparticipating consciousness and, in turn, a deeply embedded sense of anxiety and stress.

The consequences of this shift are immense, although rarely recognized as such. Because of the widespread selection for power, we are very nearly compelled to participate in a vast, competitive, power-maximizing culture with deep historical roots, one that puts us at odds with our hunting and gathering ancestry—our true nature. In other words, the way we're living now is completely abnormal. The stress that we feel from the brinksmanship, posturing, and militarization of the planet is unprecedented in our history.

BONOBOS GONE BAD?

All of which reminds us of the ongoing conversation in pop primatology about our ultimate human nature: Are we more like aggressive and patriarchal chimpanzees, or are we more like the peace- and sex-loving bonobos? Did the power shift of six thousand years ago fundamentally alter our original primate character?

As Taylor's story suggests, maybe we really are more like peaceful bonobos at the core. Our animal bodies want to play, lounge, hunt a little, and have lots of sex, but the ratcheting of power has transformed us into more chimp-like creatures: highly aggressive, militant, and male dominated. It's a disturbing and highly stressful thought in its own right.

So, what's to be done? For most of us, it's difficult if not impossible to escape the power ratcheting that's taken place over the last six thousand years. We're surrounded by the entrenched layers of defense, vigilance, power, and ego, and we're compelled to participate to some degree. Like it or not, it's a game that many of us are forced to play.

Nevertheless, we are not powerless. At the very least, we can stop amplifying the ratcheting of power. We can stop glorifying it, stop worshipping it, and stop identifying with it. Your true nature is peaceful, and there's really no need to be so afraid. Just imagine your natural ancestry—start behaving more like a bonobo and less like a chimp.

RADICAL ACCELERATION

> It is a mistake to think that moving fast is the
> same as actually going somewhere.
> —Steve Goodier, *Lessons of the Turtle:
> Living Right Side Up*

Mismatch challenges us in myriad ways, many of them invisible to our naked eyes. Domestication and incarceration are hard on our bodies and our spirits, but when we get right down to it, one of the most problematic features of modern life is the brutal pace of change and acceleration, depicted most famously by the hockey-stick graph of exponential growth.

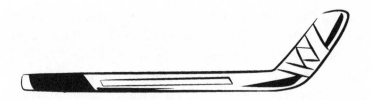

All of us have seen the hockey stick depicted in graphs of population growth and atmospheric heating, but today, we're seeing acceleration almost everywhere we look—habitat destruction, fresh-water depletion, species extinction, and technological innovation. In fact, it's hard to identify *any* dimension of modern life that isn't changing at an accelerating pace. The pace of change is so radical that we can take almost nothing for granted; yesterday's innovations may well become obsolete by tomorrow.

Fully immersed in this process, we adjust. Many of us have come to think of this pace of social and technological change as familiar and even unremarkable; that's just the way the world is now. New products, services, and methods appear every day, seemingly out of nowhere, and we jump to adapt. Another day, another novelty.

But in fact, this state of acceleration is unprecedented in human history. Throughout the Paleo, the pace of social, cultural, and technological change was so slow as to be undetectable by any one individual or generation. Hunters and gatherers remained as hunters and gatherers from one generation to the next. The lifeways of your parents would become your lifeways, and you could reasonably expect that your children would inherit a world basically indistinguishable from your own. Seasons would come and go, animals would migrate in and out of your region, water holes would dry out and fill again, but beyond these familiar, natural variations, nothing much would change at all.

But then, beginning with the ancient Greeks and accelerating with the scientific revolution, human invention exploded on the scene and, suddenly, everything was in flux. The rise in experimental science, objectivity, the printing press, the steam engine—each of these developments fed the others to create a wave of radical change. In big-history terms, this transition to the modern world was almost instantaneous. As educator and cultural critic Neil Postman famously put it, "change changed." No longer could humanity count on the predictability of the future; everything was suddenly up for grabs.

OUR BRAINS ON CHANGE

Today, the hockey stick poses an immense challenge to human life, equanimity, and mental health. As we navigate our daily challenges, the brain wonders, *Is my world stable?* When the answer is yes, we relax into rest-and-digest. We're patient and comfortable. The body has time to metabolize information and experience. We can mull things over. We don't need to mobilize, take action, or fire the fight-flight response. But when the answer is no, our minds and spirits go on full alert. Our predictions may be worthless; anything could happen and we must be ready. Cortisol surges and the body prepares for combat.

Throughout prehistory, life on the semi-wooded grassland was generally stable; conditions might well have been harsh, even life-threatening, but the fundamental challenges of finding food, water, and shelter were mostly predictable. But today, almost everything looks and feels tenuous and fragile. Hockey sticks are everywhere and nothing feels reliable. Tomorrow will almost certainly be different from today. And who can plan for a future when things are so sketchy? Who can relax? It's no wonder that so many of us are having trouble with the basic demands of living; we don't even know what the world will look like a year from now.

In short, we are "future shocked," from the title of the 1970 book by futurist Alvin Toffler. Defined as "too much change in too short a period of time" and "a state of distress or disorientation due to rapid social or technological change," this is a dead ringer for life in the twenty-first century. And in turn, it begs the questions: How much change can the human animal handle? How much change can a culture sustain before it blows apart?

This is where we come up against a powerful paradox. We are a hypercreative species, but that creativity has a powerful tendency to feed back onto itself, creating a vicious cycle of invention and change. One innovation leads to another, and together they combine to create new, disruptive industries that overturn stable existing methods, processes, and relationships. This state holds its shape for a time and might even serve humanity in some way, but eager consultants and "visionaries" call for more innovation as a cure for everything that ails us. Innovators step up with new ideas, products, and processes and the whole cycle of disruption starts anew. This may well provide some of us with slick new toys, but it's really hard on the human animal. Maybe what we really need is *unnovation*, a return to simpler methods on a human scale.

LINGER, SAVOR, PAUSE

On a gut level, all of us know that hockey-stick acceleration isn't sustainable. Even children understand that exponential change can't go on forever. This is just how nature works. In highly interdependent systems like bodies and ecosystems, exponential change is always punished, dampened, or beaten back by some other force or agent. In the long run, homeostasis rules the day. Nothing in a natural system accelerates forever; this is how health works. Blood sugar, cancer cells, exploding insect and animal populations—all are eventually dampened by regulatory forces and actors. Most of us know this intuitively, which is why the hockey stick makes us so uncomfortable.

Heraclitus would be both vindicated and perplexed. "You can't step into the same river twice," he famously taught. But what if that river is accelerating, sweeping us downstream faster and faster each day? Like it or not, there's going to be a post-hockey-stick era of some kind. A crash perhaps, a return to some simpler time, an end to civilized life as we know it? There's no way to know the details, but we do know that it stresses us in ways that our Paleolithic ancestors couldn't have imagined.

We'll find out soon enough, but in the meantime, there are things we can do: Do less of everything and take more time doing it. Don't be in such a rush to be productive. Drive slower, talk slower, work slower. Ignore the constant pressure to "get more done in less time." Don't be seduced by products and services that promise ever-greater speed and efficiency. Focus on the long qualities of life, the stable and consistent themes that animate the biosphere. Linger. Savor the ordinary moments, even the stressful times. Focus on the long-wave dynamics of seasons, habitat, and the great turnings of the night sky.

And remember—the hockey-stick acceleration of the modern world is wickedly abnormal. If you're feeling anxious about the breakneck pace of change, you're perfectly normal. Take a deep breath and relax.

WORLD OF WOUNDS

> It may well be that more and more of what people bring before doctors and therapists for treatment—agonies of body and spirit— are symptoms of the biospheric emergency

registering at the most intimate levels of life.
The Earth hurts, and we hurt with it.
—Theodore Roszak, *The Voice of the Earth*

Hockey sticks are bad enough. Acceleration across the modern world challenges our minds, bodies, and spirits, bringing an escalating threat of instability and future shock. But an even bigger stress looms large, consciously or not, in the human psyche. As we look at the deteriorating state of the planet, now described in intricate, excruciating detail by sober scientists around the world, an intimidating picture comes into focus: the undeniable fact of the devastating human impact on the biosphere and the widespread destruction of our life-supporting systems.

Of course, not everyone sees it. Or to be precise, many people dodge this reality by simple denial and contracted attention. It's not really happening, they say, but even if it is happening, these things are far away; and besides, there's always a green, technological solution just over the horizon that'll allow us to carry on with culture as usual. All is well and humans will continue to reign supreme.

But ever since Rachel Carson's monumental 1962 work *Silent Spring*, scientific and ecological education has crept into the classroom and popular consciousness. People are beginning to understand the interdependence of the living world, the web of life, and the importance of biodiversity. It's a step forward, but paradoxically, there are profound psychospiritual consequences that come with this increased awareness. Suddenly, as if viewing the destruction of the biosphere with fresh eyes, we become aware of the damage we are causing to every living system, from the deepest oceans to the highest reaches of the atmosphere. As the great conservationist Aldo Leopold famously wrote in his 1949 classic *A Sand County*

Almanac, "one of the penalties of an ecological education is that one lives alone in a world of wounds."[26]

This realization is an extreme stressor, unprecedented in human history. To be sure, we've always seen damage to the natural world, some of it caused by our own hand: wildfires, floods, pestilence, and war. But the magnitude of the damage before us today is orders of magnitude greater than anything faced by our ancestors. We are literally looking at the ecological overshoot of civilization and the collapse of the only living world we know. The devastation of habitat now extends around the planet and shows no sign of slowing. Forests, wetlands, rivers, and oceans are, in the language of individual human experience, traumatized, and many are desperately clinging to life.[27]

We've seen it with our own eyes. Most of us have traveled by air, and we've seen the clear-cuts, the mining, the malignant spread of development, roads, factories, and sprawl. Children assume that it's always been this way, but the elders know differently—habitat destroyed almost everywhere we look, the open fields of our youth obliterated by layers of concrete, asphalt, steel, and plastic. Plants and animals gone. Creeks and streams gone. Coral reefs gone. Fish gone. When we witness these things, it feels as if parts of our own bodies have been torn away, chunks of skin ripped to the bone, limbs amputated. What we do to the Earth, we do to ourselves, body and spirit. As philosopher and historian Thomas Berry put it, "physical degradation of the natural world is also the degradation of the interior world of the human."[28]

To call this a "stressor" just doesn't go far enough. There's a desperate finality to our predicament now, one that goes far beyond any acute illness, trauma, or injury that might be suffered by any single individual. In fact, many of us, young people in particular, are coming to the realization that our future as a people, a culture, and even a species may well be over.

THE DARK NARRATIVE

And so, an ominous new narrative has emerged, a story of doom and collapse—a looming apocalypse of human and nonhuman suffering. This perspective is reflected in a strange new word that's now being spoken in whispered conversations around campfires and even in academic conference rooms: *WASF*, short for *we are so fucked*. In other words, we have no functional future to look forward to. The human jig is up.

It's an easy conclusion to draw. The drumbeat of ominous reports has become incessant, each one telling a story of disappearing habitats, the loss of biodiversity, more warming, more sea-level rise, and more feedback loops that promise cataclysm and collapse. In early 2021, a prominent paper by the world's leading ecologists warned of a "ghastly future" looming just over the horizon.[29]

But WASF really brings us right to the end of our psychospiritual rope. Why do anything at all? Why fight back against the forces that are wrecking the world? Why even try to build better relations with the planet and with one another? No matter what we do, it's all going away. This is a spiritual crisis on a planetary, even a cosmic, scale.

The WASF narrative is an epic stressor, even when we do our best to ignore it, and even for denialists who try to wish it away. Not only are our individual lives threatened, our entire civilization is now at risk, as well as the life-supporting conditions that humans need to sustain themselves. Coping with this realization will soon become the biggest mental health challenge of our age, if it's not already.

To be sure, end-of-the-world predictions have been common throughout human history, but this one carries the weight of solid scientific evidence and unambiguous, measurable fact. Even for people who don't believe in the scientific method, the daily stream of bad news weighs on the spirit and the body. Images of deforestation, dead coral reefs, orphaned animals,

and desperate humans rock us to the core. Even the naysay-
ers and techno-optimists suspect that something is very, very
wrong.

This is a recipe for a monstrous stress response in the
human mind-body, a worst-case cortisol tsunami. All the classic triggers are there: As individuals, few of us have power or
control over the course of planetary events. Personal actions
like recycling are worth doing but feel inconsequential, even
farcical. Faced with a hockey stick of radical change, we have
almost no sense of predictability, and the trajectories point to
worsening conditions. And so, we feel helpless, stranded in the
mother of all stress quagmires.

But other reference points are possible, and the stress
may not be inevitable. We could, for example, put our attention on the biosphere herself and attach our identity to the
living world. Suddenly, new insights emerge: When we study
the vast scope of biological history, we're struck by the fact
that the biosphere is enormously, outrageously resilient. She's
suffered near-fatal wounds in five prior extinction events—
asteroid strikes, oxygen holocausts, rising and falling sea levels, and tectonic shifts—but she's always rebounded with new
diversity and new health. In this sense, we aren't fucked at all.
The planet may become increasingly inhospitable for humans
in the near future, but life on Earth is going to be just fine. Life
will find a way.

THE FIGHT IS RIGHT

It's easy to get sucked into the WASF narrative, but it's a
fatal mistake and a dangerous way to live. Over time, WASF
depletes our resilience and renders us powerless. It makes us
more vulnerable to stress and depression and makes us ineffective agents of change. In short, WASF makes us weak and
irrelevant, precisely when we need to be strong and active. As

a narrative, WASF fails because it ties our spirits to a predetermined outcome and lays claim to defeat before the game has run its course. The outcome is sealed, so there's no point in even trying.

But try we must, no matter the odds. Yes, there's no question that we live in a world of wounds. There's no question that the projections are daunting. But we cannot and must not allow WASF to dominate our consciousness. There is vital work to be done, sacred work. Regardless of the odds, there's meaning in the effort and value in this fight. In fact, the fight itself can make us stronger, regardless of the result.

Spiritual teachers, tribal elders, and high performers in a wide variety of arts have long taught that it's a mistake to tie our efforts to outcomes, to persist only for the promise of some kind of reward at the end. Focus on the journey, they tell us, not the destination. Focus on the pleasures and the challenges of the work in front of us. When we tie our efforts to outcomes and then fail, we are shattered, then depressed. But when we focus on the intrinsic values of our work, we become more powerful; outcomes are less relevant and maybe even beside the point.

So, engage the fight in any way you can. Take action against the planet-hostile forces that are destroying our future. Fight for the forests, the oceans, the atmosphere, and the biosphere, and take pleasure in the process. Take pleasure in your collaborations, your research, your lifestyle tweaks, and your teaching, even if they seem to lead nowhere. Stop worrying about outcomes and worry more about the intrinsic value of simply doing good work. As Czech dissident and president Václav Havel has said, "hope is not the conviction that something will turn out well, but the certainty that something is worth doing no matter how it turns out." Or as author and activist Chris Hedges has put it, "I don't fight because I think I'm going to win. I fight because it's the right thing to do."

SEPARATION ANXIETY

We do as we have been done by.
—John Bowlby

While stress comes in myriad forms, there's a single, under-lying need that makes us vulnerable to all of it. That is, our deep, ancestral bodies want connection and they want to be attached. And if that attachment fails for some reason, we're going to suffer.

This all becomes clear when we imagine ourselves back in prehistory, anywhere on the mosaic grassland of Africa. Suppose you're part of an ancient hominid band, not yet fully human but highly intelligent and capable nonetheless. The past few generations have been a time of prosperity and rela-tive abundance, the climate has been friendly, the hunting and gathering have been good, and there's plenty of protein to go around.

It's good news for everyone's health, but there's a surpris-ing side effect. As brains and heads have grown larger over the generations, childbirth has become increasingly dangerous, and sadly, many women and children have perished. But you are one of the lucky ones. Your brain and head are large, but by the luck of genes and a few mutations, your mother goes into labor early. Strictly speaking, your body isn't really ready for survival in a wild, outdoor habitat, but there's no fighting the process; suddenly, you've arrived in the world, premature and incompetent, but ready to make a go of it.

At this point, you've got some serious limitations. You can't walk, hunt, speak, or perform any of the functions necessary to make your way in the world. If left on your own, your life expectancy would be mere hours, so you've got to get some social life support right away. Specifically, you've got to attach to a caregiver as soon as possible. Usually, it's Mom, but any warm, caring human will do, someone who will keep you safe from danger, touch you, feed you, and keep you alive until you're fully developed. Attachment, in other words, is absolutely vital for your survival and development.

ATTACHMENT THEORY AND STRESS

Back in today's modern world, you probably haven't given much thought to the nature of your birth, but your need for attachment remains and will have profound consequences that will reverberate for the rest of your life. Secure attachment to a caregiver isn't just important in infancy; it's a major predictor of how successful you'll be as an adult. If you're securely attached as a child, you'll have a good shot at a successful career, good health, and strong social relations.[30]

A powerful body of research, beginning with British psychoanalyst John Bowlby and validated by American psychologist Mary Ainsworth, demonstrates that secure attachment is a better predictor of success than conventional measures such as IQ. And of course, insecure attachment goes the other way; children who grow up without secure attachment are more likely to fall into dysfunctional behavior and disease in adulthood.

All of which has been brilliantly demonstrated by research via the "infant strange test." In short, mothers with young infants are invited into a playroom complete with toys and art supplies. Mom hands her infant over to the caregiver/ researcher and then disappears for a time. The child plays, Mom returns, and the researcher notes the reaction. If the child embraces Mommy and then returns to play, this is noted as "secure attachment." If the child desperately clings to Mommy or ignores her return, this is labeled as "insecure attachment."

In turn, this becomes the basis for long-term study. As we might expect, those children who demonstrate secure attachment in infancy go on to have largely successful careers, relationships, and health outcomes, while those with insecure attachment are far more likely to struggle. It's also safe to assume that those with secure attachment are more resilient and stress resistant.

In short, attachment is a critical fork in the road for the developing human body, mind, and spirit. If the process is successful, the young animal body concludes that the world is mostly friendly and switches on a host of metabolic and growth functions that continue through life. But if attachment fails, the body begins to suspect that the world is unfriendly and prepares for defense. Stress hormones begin remodeling the brain, and the mind crosses over into a state of vigilance or even hypervigilance. The body prepares for a life of danger and immediate action. The fight-flight response is primed for action.

AN ERA OF ALIENATION

It's easy to understand how the young human infant, born premature and incompetent into the wild, would need and benefit from attachment to a primary caregiver. But the process actually goes much further. As vulnerable creatures in an ambiguous and sometimes dangerous world, the human animal craves attachment in general. Our bodies have a deep and compelling need to connect, not just with primary human caregivers but also with habitat, tribe, and culture. These points of contact sustain us, protect us from stress, and keep us whole. Both literally and metaphorically, we need to touch and be touched.

But tragically, attachment is failing across the modern world. In fact, we might well describe the arc of modern history as a progressive and catastrophic erosion of normal human attachment. We are losing our primary points of contact, and we feel ourselves adrift, disconnected, and, in turn, massively stressed.

For some of us, attachment fails right at the outset. For whatever reason, the mother-infant bond just doesn't form, and the infant is left groping for connection. In turn, this sets the tone for everything that follows. In other words, the first human contact becomes the relational prototype. The young animal begins to wonder and doubt: *The world may not be friendly. The world may not sustain me. The world cannot be trusted. I am alone.*

Even worse, our historically normal attachment to habitat has also largely failed. For native people, identification with habitat was taken for granted. *I am the land, the land is me. I am the forest, the forest is me. I am the river, the river is me.* Without exception, this body-habitat connection and attachment is a central feature of indigenous life, all across the planet. It's safe to assume that this attachment gave people a sense of comfort and resilience in the face of stress.

But sadly, modern people have lost this connection as well. Most of us have no idea where our food comes from, and we're more likely to identify with brands than with the plants and animals of our local bioregions. Lost in our species-level narcissism, we no longer converse with the habitat that keeps us alive. As Thomas Berry put it, "we are talking only to ourselves. We are not talking to the rivers, we are not listening to the wind and stars. We have broken the great conversation."[31]

As for our third point of attachment, this seems to be at risk as well. In historically normal, indigenous circumstances, we're quick to bond with the tribe, ritual, and mother culture, but today, our social connections feel scattered, ambiguous, unreliable, and uncertain. Everyone seems to be pulling in different directions, and we're failing to agree on a unifying cultural narrative; are we going forward to technological utopia, or should we be going backward to something ancestral and familiar? Society is splintering, and many people report feeling that they don't really belong. What was once a reliable source of comfort and security has been stretched thin and we feel it—in our bodies and our spirits.

CONTACT IS FUNDAMENTAL

When our primary points of contact fail, we're left groping and grasping, desperate to attach to something, anything. And thus, our search for substitutes and our epidemics of dysfunction and addiction are the result. We'll try anything to get back into contact with life. Substances of all varieties, sex and pornography, workaholism and achievement—the usual suspects. But sadly, none of it seems to work. What we really want is reunification and intimacy with our primary, primal forms of life support.

All of this leaves many of us feeling adrift. We are, like the insecurely attached children in the infant strange test, disconnected and alienated from the very things we need to protect us and keep us whole. Without some solid points of attachment, we begin to feel as if we're literally lost in space. As Carl Jung put it in *The Earth Has a Soul*, "man feels himself isolated in the cosmos. He is no longer involved in nature and has lost his emotional participation in natural events."

Sadly, we're only just beginning to realize the depth of our alienation and estrangement, and we've mostly failed to recognize the immense psychic, physical, and social harm that comes from failed attachment. But time is short and the need is urgent. The time has come to reweave ourselves back into the natural world and help one another find the secure attachment that is so often missing. The point is to close the emotional and spiritual gap between ourselves and the living world.

As Henry David Thoreau put it, the key ingredient is contact.[32] That is, there's got to be an emotional experience of connection; we've got to *feel* it. It's not enough to simply have a passive, superficial contact with nature or the people around us. As we've seen, the path to high performance requires deep or deliberate practice. Shallow experience might be pleasant and it might be valuable in other ways, but it won't drive the changes that we seek. For meaningful, transformative change, we need engagement, concentration, commitment, imagination, curiosity, and inquiry. We need to bring the whole human animal to the experience.

So yes, of course, go outside and spend time in nature. But don't expect it to transform you automatically or passively, without effort. The pleasant sensations are all well and good, but it's essential that we go deeper. Imagine the continuities that exist between your body and the life around you. Sit quietly under a tree and feel your kinship with life. Forget the modern world and let your mind drift back in time, millions of years to a point of ancestral unity. Listen and feel the life around you and in you. It's all one thing.

And yes, of course, spend more time with family and friends, the people you really care about. But don't expect the experience to build continuity automatically and without effort. Do it intentionally. Imagine the continuities between your life and the people around you—the shared ancestry, values, history, and stories. These aren't just people you're familiar with and mostly enjoy. This is your social life-support system; these people sustain you. It's all one thing.

HARDENING OF THE SELF

> I live in a kingdom of one.
> —Rakesh Satyal, *Blue Boy*

In the standard narrative, stress is something that happens to individuals. You're under stress, I'm under stress, and we need to engage in certain practices that will bring relief. But what if individualism itself is the source of our troubles? If that's the case, then the conventional stress narrative begins to look less like a solution and more like a reflection of our problem.

This all becomes clear when we take a big-history perspective. For Paleo human life, tribal living was the norm. People banded together naturally because it was the most effective way to stay safe in a predator-rich environment. Stay in the circle and you'll be OK; stay together and you'll have companionship and the sense that, yes, the world is friendly, controllable, and at least somewhat predictable. But if you get separated from the circle, your body will react immediately, and cortisol will begin to flow. Your body knows that it's dangerous to be alone.

But today, this sense of aloneness is precisely what we've created. Our historically normal tribal life has been fragmented and replaced by a sense of radical individualism, especially in America and Western Europe but also, increasingly, the world over. People are encouraged to think for themselves and forge their own path. Traditional support structures have largely broken down, often replaced by a massively stressful and historically abnormal every-man-for-himself approach. In modern society, the individual has now become the basic, isolated unit of humanity.

THE PERILS OF SELF-AWARENESS

There are, no doubt, many forces that drove this shift to individuality, but one of the most notable was the invention of cameras and the widespread production of mirrors, beginning in the nineteenth century. Almost overnight, people in modern economies could see themselves in detail. Each of these encounters would have been a reminder of the self, an abrupt jolt out of world consciousness into self-consciousness. Over the course of the next century, human attention was radically transformed, narcissism began to rise, and culture began to morph into what *New York Times* columnist David Brooks has called "the Big Me." In other words, selfie culture.

The consequences have been radically disruptive. Today, it's considered perfectly normal to obsess over one's self: the way we look, dress, talk, perform, and behave. Even our language reflects this new obsession, and an entirely new self-based lexicon has taken shape:

self-consciousness
self-discovery
self-awareness
self-acceptance
self-confidence
self-esteem
self-help
self-assurance
self-realization
self-actualization
self-mastery
self-control
self-love
self-care
self-worth
self-improvement
self-sufficiency
self-talk

Modern people take these words for granted and feel comfortable using them, but they are historically strange and culturally abnormal. Across the entire expanse of human history, it's unlikely that there's ever been such an unabashed, all-consuming focus on the self.

Likewise, entire industries are now devoted to optimizing the individual: personal training, personal wellness, personalized diets and medicine, genetic testing, personal shoppers, and personal branding. These services sometimes offer genuine value, but in a historical sense, they, too, are profoundly abnormal. And from a Paleo and indigenous perspective, this naked focus on the individual is considered self-indulgent—which is to say, it's bad manners, even shameful. In a Paleo setting, narcissists might well be thrown out of the tribe entirely.

FROM WE TO ME

This transition in identity from *we* to *me* can be described as a shift from historically normal "interdependent selves" to our modern, abnormal "independent selves." As Steve Taylor puts it in *The Fall*:

> The basic difference between us and native peoples is that we have a *stronger* sense of ego . . . The Fall was, and is, the intensification of the human sense of "I" or individuality . . . Our sharply developed sense of ego gives us a sense of being trapped inside our own heads, of being an "I" inside our skulls with the rest of the universe and all other human beings on the other side. As a result, we feel a basic sense of *aloneness* . . . Our sharpened sense of ego means that we're *dis*connected from the world around us, from other creatures and even other people. In a way, we live in solitary confinement.[33]

Quite obviously, this is a massive stress load, one that's unique and culturally inflicted. More self-consciousness equals more alienation, more disconnection, and, in turn, an extremely stressful, even terrifying, sense of being alone in the cosmos. It's no wonder that modern people suffer so much anxiety, depression, and mental illness. Our culture makes it nearly inevitable.

We express our rugged narcissism in ever more outrageous ways. Bodybuilders stand onstage to demonstrate their perfect forms, while adventure athletes embark on audacious solo ventures, sometimes crossing major oceans and polar ice caps without support. Mountain climbers climb major peaks unaided, a trend exemplified by Alex Honnold's 2017 ropeless solo climb of El Capitan in Yosemite Valley, vividly depicted in the movie *Free Solo*.

To compound the problem, we glorify the solo entrepreneur and the coffee shop millionaire who writes his own code and sells it to the highest bidder. We tell our young people to strive for financial independence (sometimes called "fuck you money") so that they'll never have to depend on anyone else. This, too, is profoundly abnormal.

All of which puts us into a vicious spiral of social dysfunction and yet more stress. As the Buddhist monk Matthieu Ricard has said, "our grasping to the perception of a 'self' as a separate entity leads to an increasing feeling of vulnerability and insecurity . . . This imagined self becomes the constant victim hit by life's events."[34] When we—as individuals—feel separated, alone, and fearful, we're likely to cling to the familiar, our sense of individualism. But this separates us even further from the very experience that's likely to feel better, and worse yet, it makes other people feel rejected, isolated, and alone, which of course inspires them to revert to their familiar focus on the self, and so on. In the process, individualism cascades through the system and intensifies, leaving a society of independent, self-interested particles—which is to say, no society at all.

A SOFTER SENSE OF SELF

All of which makes us wonder about the modern prescriptions and cures we hear so much about, including popular remedies for stress. Living in a radically individualistic culture, many of us are told to look inward in times of trouble. If you feel bad, afflicted, stressed, or anxious, there's something wrong with you that needs to be fixed, so we double down on self-examination, self-reflection, and self-interest. But in the process, we only manage to intensify our suffering and our alienation. Maybe a better way out is to let go, to abandon the self, to give up on the individualism and just live.

This is not to say that we should give up on personal care or let the world walk all over us. This is not to say that we should just dissolve into the larger social matrix and give up on our own individual welfare. Obviously, there's good reason to care for ourselves and protect our core interests. It is to say that individualism—especially the extreme, almost militant form we practice today—is a dangerous and self-defeating path. Biology teaches us clearly that human beings are not stand-alone organisms. Not only are we completely dependent on habitat and other humans for our survival, even our individual bodies are massively networked with the microbial life that exists in us and on us. We are literally continuous with habitat and one another.

So, maybe it's time to expand our identity and soften our focus on the self. Our individualism isn't doing us much good as it is, and even worse, it distracts us from the primal relationships that sustain us. So, look around. Put your attention back where it belongs—on relationship. Stop thinking about yourself and your suffering for a while and you'll feel a whole lot better. Let go of the chronic introspection, the self-examination, and the self-improvement. Spend less time agonizing over your weaknesses. Maybe you're OK just the way you are. Remember, individualism is a cultural creation and is therefore optional. There's nothing to say that you must think of yourself as a stand-alone organism. In actual fact, you're bigger than that.

PYRAMID SCHEME

> The object of power is power.
> —George Orwell, *1984*

Another major stressor in the modern human experience comes in the form of geometry, specifically the triumph of pyramid-shaped social structures over the circular orientation of historically normal human life. In the Paleo, our original human culture, people lived according to the circle. Across the planet, from Africa to Australia to North and South America, our ancestors lived in participation with nature, and in this kind of world, everything connects, everything participates, everything has a role to play. Nothing is an island, nothing is apart, and nothing is superior.

As Black Elk of the Oglala Lakota people put it,

> Everything the Power of the World does is done in a circle. The sky is round, and I have heard that the earth is round like a ball, and so are all the stars. The wind, in its greatest power whirls. Birds make their nest in circles, for theirs is the same religion as ours. The sun comes forth and goes down again in a circle. The moon does the same and both are round.

> Even the seasons form a great circle in their changing, and always come back again to where they were. The life of a man is a circle from childhood to childhood, and so it is in everything where power moves. Our tepees were round like the nests of birds, and these were always set in a circle, the nation's hoop.[35]

It's a reassuring philosophy, and we can be certain that this circular view had a calming, stress-reducing effect on people. When everyone has a part to play and all are roughly equal, it's a lot easier to bear the slings and arrows of life in the wild. Even death itself seems inconsequential. After all, if everything is part of the grand circle of life, there must be continuity, even in death, so relax. No matter your physical form, you're always part of the whole.

But then came agriculture, the declared ownership of habitat, followed by hierarchy, power, imperialism, and social stratification. Civilized people began to assemble themselves in a new order, and over the next few thousand years, the pyramid grew ever higher and steeper, and, today, it's nearly impossible to escape. Access to the highest ranks is almost impossible and influence is extremely unlikely. With a massively interconnected world of eight billion people, most of it dominated by corporate power, there's nowhere else to go. The pyramid dominates our lives. In short, the vertical has triumphed over the horizontal.

STRESSED BY THE PYRAMID

There's no question that our pyramid-shaped social arrangement is inherently stressogenic. For hypersocial animals that evolved to live in small, roughly equal tribal groups, rigid hierarchy triggers unease, distress, and even full-blown trauma. We simply aren't accustomed to living this way; it feels unnatural, uncomfortable, jarring. We want to relate as human beings on the horizontal axis of equality, but we're forced to work on the vertical axis of power and rank. Our bodies and minds rebel, but many of us are locked in place with nowhere to go.

In particular, we're distressed by the "reverse Robin Hood" practices that are baked into the system. Power gathers more power, and affluence gathers more affluence, sucking up wealth like a giant vacuum from the less powerful and the less fortunate. It's expensive to be poor, and it pays to be wealthy. In effect, money flows up the pyramid, while cortisol flows down.

And for people of lower rank, the ever-present threat of exclusion lurks in every transaction and relationship. The incessant comparison, judgment, and competition are historically abnormal and contrary to everything we know and feel about our true nature. We evolved on the horizontal, but today, we live and die on the vertical. Our socioeconomic vagility is highly restricted, and in turn, we feel massively stressed.

Some of this is, or should be, obvious. People without resources have little in the way of power and control and often live lives of struggle, even desperation. But the surprise here is that pyramids are stressful for almost *everyone* involved, even those of privilege. This is the point of *The Spirit Level: Why More Equal Societies Almost Always Do Better*. Authors Richard Wilkinson and Kate Pickett argue that there are "pernicious effects that inequality has on societies: eroding trust, increasing anxiety and illness, (and) encouraging excessive consumption." They claim that, for each of eleven different health and social problems—physical health, mental health, drug abuse, education, imprisonment, obesity, social mobility, trust and community life, violence, teenage pregnancies, and child well-being—outcomes are significantly worse in more unequal countries, whether rich or poor. In other words, the top of the pyramid isn't really the refuge that it appears to be.

No matter how affluent you happen to be, you're still part of a larger whole.

THE STATUS SYNDROME

Not surprisingly, the stress of pyramid-shaped inequality is reflected in the state of our bodies, a fact that's been amply documented by epidemiologist Michael Marmot in *The Status Syndrome.* Marmot has compiled thirty years of evidence demonstrating the crucial importance of social rank to our health and well-being and concludes that "health follows a social gradient."

In reviewing hundreds of studies from around the world, Marmot found that social inequalities are powerful determinants of human health. "Wherever we are in the social hierarchy, our health is likely to be better than those below us and worse than those above us." This holds true not just for one particular kind of illness but for all forms of human affliction. "Being low in the hierarchy means a greater susceptibility to just about every disease that's going."

Marmot spent almost three decades studying the health of British civil servants. His team followed thousands of workers, all classified according to their ranking in the occupational hierarchy. The findings showed a dramatic social gradient in mortality for most major causes of death: disease of the cardiovascular, renal, gastrointestinal, and respiratory systems; most cancers; and even accidental deaths and violent deaths. His conclusion was that "subtle differences in social ranking can lead to dramatic differences in health."

All of which presents our health and medical system with some profoundly disruptive and inconvenient implications. That is, we may well be chasing the wrong causalities in our approach to lifestyle disease. In conventional thinking, we're quick to seize on the standard explanation: afflictions such as obesity, diabetes, and heart disease are simply the result of a failure to exercise and eat the right foods; they're problems of impulse control and even character. But suddenly, this kind of explanation seems rather weak and misguided because it ignores the health-negative effects of social inequality. In fact, it may well be the case that the pyramid is far more influential in human health than previously thought. And there's something slightly perverse about telling people of low social standing to exercise more and eat better; maybe what their bodies really need is more opportunity, mobility, and power.

THE PALEO SOLUTION

To make matters worse, the pyramid is sustained by a highly destructive and false mythology. As the story goes, one's position in the hierarchy is simply a matter of effort and performance—in other words, merit. It's a fair and just system, we're told. Those at the top are where they are because they're better performers—which is to say, they're better people. They're smarter and they work harder. They made good choices and took advantage of opportunities. Anyone could do the same. It's really a level playing field, and if you're not living at a high level, it simply means that you're not particularly smart or, well, just lazy.

But this myth is not just untrue, it's positively cynical and destructive. It's a cover story, honed and propagated by the aristocracy. Naturally, people at the top are happy to embrace this narrative of implicit superiority but, tragically, so are many at the bottom. The powerful are where they are because they're smart and resourceful, but we are where we are because we're slow, undisciplined, and unworthy, none of which is actually the case.

So, what are we to do about the pathologies of power and the onerous, stressogenic nature of the pyramid? Once again, we take a lesson from the Paleo. Native and indigenous people have long understood the problem of hierarchy, pride and ego, and the way a pyramid can overwhelm the circle. As an antidote, they devised some clever cultural practices. For example, anthropologist Christopher Boehm has studied hunter-gatherers and discovered they maintained equality through a practice he labeled "reverse dominance."

In a standard, pyramidal hierarchy, a few individuals dominate the many, but in a system of reverse dominance, the many act in unison to deflate the ego of anyone who tries to dominate them. In this kind of system, people use leveling mechanisms to ensure the "domination of leaders by their own followers."[36]

Instead of glorifying power as we often do in the modern world, Paleolithic people sought to bring one another down to a level of shared equality. Imagine the scene when a hunting party returns to camp: A hunter has made a good kill of a large, meaty animal, but instead of bragging, he minimizes his accomplishment, a practice known as "dishonoring the meat." He understates the importance of his achievement and describes it as "a poor kill." This practice stands in marked contrast to modern cultures in which self-promotion is not only considered acceptable but is celebrated as an essential path to advancement and success.

Today, reverse dominance lives on in the world of comedy, and most comedians are quick to take aim at the top of the pyramid, using a "kick up, kiss down" approach. This ridicule of power is good entertainment, but even better, it's absolutely essential to a functional society and a working democracy. Kicking up and kissing down levels the hierarchy and minimizes the pathologies of power. It's healthy behavior.

MORE HORIZONTAL, LESS VERTICAL

The trouble with the pyramid, particularly in a globalized world with billions of people, is that it's almost impossible to do anything creative or worthwhile without some sort of organizing structure. But there's no need for the pyramid to be so steep, so high, so impervious, or so destructive. Modern creativity experts and business consultants encourage people to "think outside the box," but what we really need to do is "think outside the pyramid."

As teachers, coaches, and trainers, we can remind our students and clients about the old ways of circular equality. As individuals, we can spend more time working the horizontal axis: one human animal speaking to another human animal, without concern for rank, power, or status. Above all, don't internalize your rank or accept what the pyramid might suggest about your capabilities or value. Stop assuming that pyramids are the only way to organize people. Stop believing that people in power are somehow better. Stop believing that they're more important or smarter. Some of them are just lucky, and most are no smarter than you or me, and many of them are less smart. In short, there is no correlation between rank and value.

They are not more.

You are not less.

INFORMATION OVERLOAD

> [A] wealth of information creates a poverty of attention.
> —Herbert A. Simon

Of all the stressors that modern humans complain about, the one that seems to grind us down most relentlessly is the endless pressure of tasks, work, decisions, and information overload, all of which usually take place in an atmosphere of temporal poverty—which is to say, urgency. No matter your industry, profession, occupation, or situation, you're probably up to your eyeballs in things that need to be studied, sorted, evaluated, tracked, managed, and manipulated. Everyone's to-do list stretches to the horizon, and there's not enough time to do any of it.

We can get a vivid sense of our predicament by comparing imaginary to-do lists of the Kalahari bushmen of Southern Africa with the typical American modern. For the bushmen (and -women), life was (and is) pretty simple:

- Hunt and gather food (which requires only a few hours each day)
- Prepare food and eat
- Hang out and gossip around the fire
- Watch the animals and the sky
- Do an occasional trance-dance ceremony to enter the spirit world and bring success in the hunt

Taken together, this amounts to a modest stress load and a sensible, relaxed way to live. This is why anthropologists have described this kind of culture as "the original affluent society." In contrast, the modern to-do list is intimidating, even preposterous:

- Get into a good primary school
- Excel at basic academic and social skills
- Start building a resume with lots of sporting success and volunteer activity
- Master a wide range of academic subjects and the various technologies of our day
- Get into an elite college and excel at the right major

- Get letters of recommendation and get accepted into grad school
- Get a good car
- Find a reliable, high-functioning mate
- Develop a powerful social network
- Start making money and building a credit history
- Find a place to live and start fixing it up
- Land a good job and develop more skills
- Pay off college loans
- Find health insurance and/or pray you don't get sick
- Start and raise a family
- Write books and give presentations to advance your professional standing
- Secure your retirement
- Master the intricacies of wills and trusts to pass your wealth to your offspring

The contrast is striking. If we take the Kalahari to-do list as the touchstone for the human experience, we're struck by the extremity and absurdity of our age. Evolution has sculpted our minds, bodies, and spirits to do a few simple things with lots of free time in between. In fact, for the vast, overwhelming majority of human history, there were no cognitive tasks to be performed whatsoever. No numbers, no letters or words, no websites, no passwords, no pdfs, no special codes, no programming, no homework. Just basic, analog living. Watch the animals, gossip with your friends, find food, and enjoy your life.

But today, we're confronted with an immense boulder of tasks that—according to someone—must be attended to. We've got to keep pushing the boulder up the hill, but whenever we seem to be getting to the top, the gods conspire to roll it back down again. It's no surprise that so many of us are suffering; we're asking ourselves to do something that's historically unprecedented and brutally abnormal. If you're feeling completely overwhelmed at the moment, you're absolutely normal.

TOO MUCH HOMEWORK

Everywhere we turn, there's too much to do, too much to study, too much to manage. We work all day and hope for a refuge when we get home, but our houses don't sleep. There's always something to be cleaned up, repaired, adjusted, remodeled, insured, replaced, or decorated. And each of these things requires—you guessed it—more homework, research, and study. In the process, our minds are becoming more and more like the spinning "pizza wheels" on our frozen computers.

We like to use the "drinking from the fire hose" metaphor when describing this cognitive flood, but we might also liken it to a swarm of malicious, distracting insects buzzing around our heads. Mostly, they're false stressors that can be safely ignored, but if we fail to pay attention, some of them will morph into full-scale tigers with razor-sharp teeth. Miss one mouse click on an important document and it might come back to bite you days or years later with an outrageous, incomprehensible bill and the threat of a lawsuit.

Nothing is simple. Every decision requires additional homework, scanning, filing, and record keeping. Even the simplest consumer product comes with dozens of pages of documentation, written in ten languages, in the smallest possible typeface, thick with incomprehensible detail, all of which, inexplicably, is supposed to make our lives easier. Even recycling has become a monstrously annoying homework project. *Is this piece of "paper" in my hand actually made of paper, or is it impregnated with plastic? Will I contaminate an entire load of material if I throw the wrong item in the bin? I'd like to get on with my day, but now I'm gripped by indecision and yet another thing that needs to be researched.* And the flood never stops.

DROWNING IN CHOICE

Closely related to cognitive overload is the modern explosion of choice. Marketing experts have long assumed that consumers want greater selection; it's not enough to have one or two breakfast cereals, one or two insurance plans, one or two entrée options at dinner. Consumers want more, so the reasoning goes, and now we have a thousand of just about everything.

In his book *The Paradox of Choice: Why More Is Less*, psychologist Barry Schwartz describes how "the culture of abundance robs us of satisfaction." He might well have said "how a culture of cognitive overload stresses us to the gills and destroys the quality of our lives." As he sees it, excess choice swamps our cognitive machinery and forces us into a pattern of continuous vigilance and mental labor. We spend more of our psychophysical resources to keep up with the options, all the while stalked by the fear that we might make the wrong choice. According to research by Schwartz, this inclines us toward anxiety, depression, and, of course, exhaustion.

This might all be tolerable or at least manageable if we had the time to ponder and metabolize the myriad choices we're faced with each day. Under historically normal circumstances, we'd simply sit down under a tree in camp, take all afternoon or even a couple of days to read all the fine print on our latest project, and make some good decisions. We'd process the information, reflect on the large-scale and long-range consequences of our action, mull it over some more, and do the right thing in due course.

But the modern world will have none of it. Decisions must be made right now, if not sooner. If we slow our pace of decision-making for even a bit, the cognitive flood will keep on coming, and then we'll be even further behind. This explains the tragic fact that modern people often fail to take their rightful vacation time each year. People are simply afraid of falling further behind. Better to skip the vacation and retain some measure of control.

The problem with this kind of ultra-high-urgency culture is that it takes the body, the gut, and the slow-motion circuitry of the brain out of the process. The human animal simply isn't cut out to make high-speed decisions in every moment of the day. Urgency narrows our attention, and when our attention narrows, we're less likely to make wise decisions that honor the integrity of the whole. Sapience takes time, but sadly, modern culture will have none of it.

SPECIALIZE OR DIE

When we combine it all—cognitive overload, excessive choice, and temporal poverty—the whole experience starts to look like a psychology experiment gone bad. The great researcher in the sky is wondering just how much stress the human animal can take. How much overload can he inflict before the subject buckles or becomes ill?

Early in our careers, the challenge of cognitive and task overload seemed temporary and therefore manageable. In freshman year of college, professors heaped an astounding amount of work on our plates, and we struggled to catch up, running full tilt until the end of the semester. We told ourselves that the grind would stop on graduation day, but it only got worse. The work just seemed to propagate, the papers on our desks reproducing without limit in a never-ending onslaught of things that must be done. And computers only make it worse, offering up the promise of control, only to break our hearts and our brains with an avalanche of new programs to learn, upgrades to be performed, crashes to be managed, and malware to be eliminated.

The problem is particularly acute in the world of academia, medicine, and the professions. In a simpler time, professionals could keep up with their field by reading a few journal articles each year. But today, publication is incessant and overwhelming, and the only recourse is to narrow our scope of attention—which is to say, we've got to specialize to survive. And so, our inquiries get narrower and narrower, each specialization taking on a smaller and smaller piece of reality. This may well feel like sensible self-defense, but the consequences are severe for individuals and our culture. The more we specialize, the more we lose sight of the whole.

The cognitive demands keep escalating and we keep adapting, like frogs in warming water. We devise cognitive shortcuts and work-arounds to stay ahead of it all. We triage like crazy, but it's never enough. Every day there's one more layer of demand, one more calculation that must be performed, one more hour of homework to make sure that we're making the right choice. After a few years, cognition and calculation begin to dominate our experience, and we forget our ancestral heritage and our bodies. Our animal nature is left in the dust.

BE SATISFIED

Most of us feel trapped and even helpless in the face of it all, but there is a way out of the quagmire. When Barry Schwartz investigated the challenge of excessive choice and cognitive overload, he researched the decision-making styles of two groups. The perfectionists (the "maximizers") did lots of homework and attempted to make the best possible decision, sometimes agonizing over the details. These people read every report, clicked on every link, and followed every lead in their effort to make the best possible decision. The other group (the "satisficers") did a little homework but didn't agonize over the details. They surveyed their choices, concluded that they were all "pretty good," and picked one that was "good enough." In the long run, these people were happier, less stressed, and less depressed than the perfectionists.

This suggests a path forward and a way to ease our stress. We don't have to make a perfect decision every time, and it's OK to let most of it go. It's OK to focus hard on your biggest priorities and let the rest of it slide. Good enough is good enough, and in the long run, good enough might really be an ideal way to live.

FEAR MEDIA

> We become what we behold. We shape our
> tools, and thereafter our tools shape us.
> —Marshall McLuhan[37]

Some tigers are made of flesh and blood, claws and teeth. If they catch us unaware in the bush, they can bring our lives to an abrupt and terrifying end. But in the modern world, a new species of tiger has come on to the scene—ghostly apparitions that appear on our screens, threatening us in strange, abstract ways. When these tigers catch us unaware, they spike our cortisol levels and send us into fits of anxiety, rage, and polarization, all of which feeds back on itself in an endless cycle of stress.

Many of us understand the dangers of this digital media predicament and we'd like to look away, but the dilemma is obvious: to live in a functional society, we need to pay attention to important events, but excessive attention to modern media can also drive us into anxiety, exhaustion, anger, and bitterness. Excessive consumption of social media has been associated with a host of negative mental health consequences, most notoriously depression. When we see other people succeeding and gathering attention for their great works, their astounding beauty, their magical voices, or their incredible athletic feats, our lives feel small and pathetic by comparison. Or agitated by the surge in vitriolic speech, we go the other way, into chronic anger, bitterness, and cynicism.

SURROUNDED BY TIGERS

The problem is that, taken together, this thing we call "the media" traffics indiscriminately in false and real tigers. Minor, inconsequential stories are often given as much or even more attention than genuine, planetary-scale threats to our future.

All of which begs the questions: Who (or, increasingly, *what*) writes the headlines that we read and hear? And what kind of standard do they (or, increasingly, *it*) use? If it's simple shock value, that brings us right back to false tigers. There are plenty of stories out there that lack substantive consequence but that carry a big emotional punch. The problem is that if you're a big media producer, your first duty is to go after eyeballs and ears. Emotionally hot topics are always a good choice, no matter whether they're based on substantive threats or not. The point is to attract viewers and listeners, not to help people distinguish between the trivial and the consequential. This is why minor political battles tend to get solid press coverage while climate, biodiversity, habitat, and water get treated as if they're sideshows.

The end result is that modern digital media, with its furious and relentless focus on anything that's even vaguely threatening, coupled with our natural negativity bias, gives us the impression that our world is saturated with tigers. Danger is everywhere, in a million forms. The more we listen and watch, the more "evidence" we accumulate, confirming our suspicions that the world is a very unfriendly place.

Even more problematic is the way that modern media increases our sense of powerlessness, just at the very moment when we need all the strength we can muster. The information that comes into our feeds often consists of reports of wicked, systemic problems that the average individual can do absolutely nothing about. The metastory sounds like this: "Here are ten thousand issues that you have absolutely no control over."

Computer hacks and data breaches, revolutions and violence in faraway places, complex threats to health, large-scale economic issues—these stories may inform us in some way, but the psychological effect is to diminish our sense of power and control in the world. In other words, they make us more vulnerable to stressors while they decrease our resilience. And when we hear a cascade of such stories, day after day for years, the net effect is to make us weaker and more frightened. In this, our TVs, computers, and phones operate as stress amplifiers and resilience reducers, leaving us quivering, angry, disempowered, and frustrated.

Ideally, media should help us distinguish false tigers from real ones, but in practice, that's not how things work. Public radio and TV sometimes get it right, but in corporate, profit-driven media, there's little incentive to educate or even to tell the truth. On the contrary, the primary objective is to cater to advertisers and that means attracting ears and eyeballs by any means necessary. And if that means presenting false threats as real tigers, so be it. If that means whipping up the viewership or listenership into a frenzy of unnecessary stress, so be it. It's often said that "sex sells," but it's equally true that "stress sells." Perk up people's eyes and ears with danger, conflict, and ambiguity and they'll tune in.

THE TYRANNY OF COGNITION

> It is certain that I, that is to say my mind . . . is
> entirely and truly distinct from my body, and
> may exist without it.
> —René Descartes, *Meditations on First
> Philosophy*

Of all the stressors faced by modern humans, one of the most destructive is the domination of the body by cognition, calculation, and abstraction—which is to say, the head. The working of the mind is now held in the highest esteem, while the wonders of the body are demoted, ignored, and pigeonholed into subservience. Across the modern world, physical education lies at the bottom of the academic totem pole, and many don't even consider it a discipline at all.

In Hollywood terms, cognition is the star of the modern show, while the body is merely a supporting actor, a locomotor device for the head. In essence, the head/brain is now imperializing the body, in much the same way that modern Western European cultures have dominated indigenous peoples and lands for the last several hundred years. In short, our culture has become top-heavy. Cognition *über alles.*

To call this a stressor doesn't even begin to describe the damage done. This value system tears the human mind-body apart and, worse yet, rejects the animal ancestry that makes us who we are. It's a kind of auto-alienation, a monstrously destructive separation at our root. For many, the body now lives in exile, a dim memory of power and vitality. If this is not a major stressor, nothing else is.

Journey back in time to the Paleo and you'll understand. For the vast majority of human history, the body reigned supreme. Integration of mind, body, and spirit was routine, normal, and unremarkable. Thoughts would come and go, and early language no doubt made for some interesting evenings around the campfire, but most of this cognitive activity was a distant second to our whole-organism experience. On any typical day, our hunting and gathering was guided by sensation, imagination, and, especially, the ability of the body to understand habitat. The raw physical animal was a sponge, soaking up everything it could about plants, animals, soils, and weather. No clipboards or iPads, no calculation or data gathering, no scanning, no sensors, no spreadsheets, no distractions from the primary purpose of learning habitat and finding food. In a modern sense, there was no independent mind at all. The head was a participant, not the driver.

THE BODY LEFT BEHIND

But all that began to change with agriculture, written language, and early feats of cognition, especially the geometry of Euclid and Pythagoras. Suddenly, a new form of knowledge appeared, one that promised to be absolutely reliable and true, no matter the conditions on the ground. A triangle *always* behaves the same way, anywhere in the universe. And not only is this knowledge rock solid, new knowledge can be obtained, deduced, or proved simply by the operation of the mind alone. Today, we don't think much about the marvels of geometry, but in its day, it must have staggered the imaginations of early adopters. Suddenly, the potential of the mind was revealed, and the body was pushed into the background.

Next, Plato went further, imagining that there existed perfect "forms" of all earthly objects—ideal models on which everything else was based. These forms could be accessed by the mind, above and beyond the experience of the body. In this, we begin to see early hints of white-collar elitism; those who work with their brains are held to be superior to those who work with their bodies.

In turn, Aristotle gave us the syllogism and the laws of rational thought. Like geometry, the syllogism promised reliable and unassailable knowledge, a perfect product of the mind. If you got your premises right and followed the proper form, you could be certain of the result. Once again, the mind came out on top and the body was all but forgotten.

This was all very intriguing for the aristocracy and helped promote hierarchy and social class, but it went mostly unnoticed for the next thousand years or so, until the scientific revolution. In the process, the mind and the products of the mind became increasingly exalted. Reason, logic, and experimental proof came to be seen as the *only* avenues to truth and knowledge. Subjective experience came to be seen as merely "anecdotal," unreliable and untrustworthy.

Not to be outdone, philosopher René Descartes dealt the final death blow to the integrated human animal. As legend has it, the young Descartes aspired to be a great philosopher and was determined to get to the ultimate root of human knowledge. He resolved to doubt everything and even went so far as to doubt the physical sensations from his own body. After all, he mused, there might be an unseen evil demon at work, pumping false sensory information into his brain—and how would he ever know? His brain might very well be floating in a vat of liquid, subject to the inputs of a mad operator with a hidden agenda; there was simply no way to tell.

So, for Descartes, sensation was off the table as a reliable source of knowledge. And since the body was not to be trusted, all that was left was the mind, and in turn, this became his ultimate touchstone and identity. "I think, therefore I am," he famously declared. The body became irrelevant, except as a life-support system for his prodigious feats of cognition.

Descartes's work was profoundly influential in his day, and he eventually came to be recognized as an icon of Western civilization. We have thoroughly incorporated his philosophy into our culture and our institutions, and today, we honor the mind while neglecting the body. We think, therefore we are; we are physical, therefore we are not. In effect, Descartes amputated the body and the emotions from the human experience in what physicians might call a "bodyectomy." This had profound downstream effects on modern culture, perfectly exemplified by Sherlock Holmes's disturbing declaration: "I am a brain, my dear Watson, and the rest of me is a mere appendage."

But when you take away the body, you also take away the heart, both metaphorically and maybe even literally. The heart, after all, is more than just a dumb pump. It's surrounded by dense clusters of neurons, which makes it a kind of brain in its own right. The same goes for the gut, the so-called enteric nervous system. So, at best, the Cartesian method uses just a fraction of the body's total intelligence. Which seems odd, or worse. When you're trying to understand an outrageously rich and complex world, wouldn't you want every possible advantage? Wouldn't you want the entire body and all its ancestry working for you?

Indigenous people would have found Descartes's ideas to be not just strange but abhorrent. Why would anyone ever want to doubt the sensations coming from his or her body? What good could possibly come from such an exercise? The body is our primary connection to habitat and survival; it would be folly of the highest order to doubt or reject one's physical intelligence. On the contrary, the whole point of practice in hunting and gathering is to sharpen your sensitivity and learn to trust what your body is telling you. In a Paleo setting, Descartes would have been laughed out of the tribe in short order. And even in a modern therapy setting, anyone who entered a counseling office declaring a complete and total separation of mind and body might well be diagnosed with a psychological disorder. In other words, Descartes wouldn't be celebrated; he'd be medicated.

And yet, in spite of the fact that he's been dead for over three hundred years, Descartes remains the biggest man on the university campus. We honor the students of the mind and devalue those who study human physicality. We accept and promote an outdated mind-over-body caste system handed to us centuries ago, a system that now appears increasingly archaic, unhealthy, and even absurd.

Unfortunately, there's a huge price to be paid for this value system. When we put the body at the bottom of our hierarchy, we shouldn't be surprised to find a sedentary population completely out of touch with their physicality. We shouldn't be surprised to find an epidemic of physical apathy, lifestyle disease, and psychological distress. The mind and the body want to be united, but when this is denied, trouble is bound to follow.

Even worse, the values of the university cascade downward through the rest of our educational system: high schools mimic colleges, elementary schools mimic high schools. In the process, the body becomes devalued across the board. If resources are tight and something needs to be cut, physical education is always the first to go. Test scores are vital, we're told, but the body is expendable.

The tragic irony is that the Cartesian mind-body split has been soundly refuted by a hundred years of solid scientific research, especially in the neurosciences. We now know without question that the mind and body are indivisible.[38] The conversation between tissue and cognition is complementary and reciprocal; the mind drives the body, and the body drives the mind. And if the body is denied, stress is sure to follow. When the body is no longer trusted, our unity is literally torn to pieces. And worse yet, we throw away the ancient half of who we are. In the process, we create anxiety, depression, and, perhaps worst of all, disempowerment. At best, we are fragments of our former selves.

THE MIND-BODY RECONNECT

Some of us understand the problem of this modern mind-body disconnect and resolve to make things right with something we call "exercise." If we can just "get in shape," maybe we'll be whole again. But the problem isn't just our adipose tissue or our high blood-sugar levels. The problem is that we've lost touch with our physicality, the very essence of who we are. And sadly, a couple of hours each week on the treadmill aren't going to change that.

What we really need is a new kind of culture and identity, one that gives the body its due, one that honors all forms of physicality, one that trusts the body to learn and know the world. Cognition is all well and good, but as a stand-alone aptitude, it's limited, weak, and also extremely dangerous. Until and unless we put our bodies back to work, learning habitat and navigating the natural world, cognition will continue to lead us astray. So, maybe it's time to revise the academic hierarchy and put the body back at the center of our studies. The head has had its day in the sun and has been found wanting. Remember, the brain is, and always will be, a subset of the body.

I move, therefore I am.

I feel, therefore I am.

I breathe, therefore I am.

I am an animal, therefore I am.

NARRATIVE DYSFUNCTION

There's nothing fundamentally wrong with people. Given a story to enact that puts them in accord with the world, they will live in accord with the world. But given a story to enact that puts them at odds with the world,

as yours does, they will live at odds with the
world. Given a story to enact in which they are
the lords of the world, they will act like lords
of the world.
—Daniel Quinn, *Ishmael*

In the standard narrative, most of the conversation about
stress focuses on the individual who's suffering. There's lots of
talk about stress hormones and the role of the body, and we're
encouraged to breathe, relax, and accept our circumstances.
Stretch out, our teachers tell us—relinquish your attachment
and let go. This is all well and good, but what often goes missing is the pivotal power of story and what it means for our
experience. As you'll see, story can be both the cause and the
solution for much of the stress we experience.

Our first problem is simply narrative noise. From the time
we get up in the morning until the time we go to sleep, the
modern human animal is assaulted with a fire hose of stories,
ideas, explanations, books, magazines, reports, and papers
that all purport to offer some kind of narrative window on the
world. Some are valuable, many are worthless, but it's the sheer
volume that causes us so much distress.

Every day we're bombarded with mixed messages, each of
them pushing or pulling us in one direction or another. We're
encouraged to "be strong" but "get along." We're told to "stand
up for yourself" and "be a team player." The valuable and the
trivial are all mixed up in one vast, incomprehensible hodge-
podge of genuine life lessons, triviality, and, of course, highly
sophisticated neuromarketing. No one can possibly keep up
with it all, and in the din, we find ourselves losing touch with
the primal narratives of sun and earth, wind and sky, bodies
and people. As a people, we're not even sure we *have* a unifying
narrative.

All of which stands in radical contrast to our Paleolithic ancestry. Sitting around the campfire each night, how many stories would you have heard? A handful perhaps, some old favorites, maybe some new tales of the hunt or the comic relief of someone's misadventure. But in the main, the narrative arc of your tribal culture would have been easy to track and remember. By modern standards, we would have found it simplistic or even boring, but it also would have been comforting and reassuring. We would have known who we are.

LOST IN THE MYTH GAP

But today, we've lost our focus and we're struggling to find our way. We're like a party of hikers, deep in the mountains, suddenly aware that we've lost our landmarks and our sense of direction. Some people argue that we should continue on, toward the promise of a green, technological utopia. Others say that the only sensible course is to return to our primal origins and our historical roots. We can't agree, so we stand there arguing until the light fades and our food runs out.

We're starving for a functional explanation. Our dominant narrative of progress, "man over nature," and infinite growth staggers on, but many of us no longer believe its promise. Religious narratives no longer carry the influence they once did, and an increasing number of young people identify themselves as "nones"—which is to say, they have no affiliation or interest in the subject. Futurists try to whip up enthusiasm for a technological utopia, but many of us remain skeptical of that narrative as well. Even our nationalistic narratives are breaking down as biologically educated people begin to realize that most political boundaries have nothing to do with the flora and fauna of a particular region: viruses, water, weather, and animals care nothing about human-generated political boundaries. And how can a nationalistic narrative be truly useful and meaningful when it's disconnected from biological, life-supporting facts on the ground?

To put it another way, author Alex Evans says we're experiencing a "myth gap." As a former political adviser with the British government and the United Nations, Evans advises scientists on how to be better storytellers and mythmakers:

> In this time of global crisis and transition—mass migration, inequality, resource scarcity and climate change—it is only by finding new myths, those that speak to us of renewal and restoration, that we will navigate our way to a better future. It is stories, rather than facts and pie-charts, that have the power to animate us and bring us together to change the world.[39]

The problem with the myth gap is that it leaves us exposed to distraction, division, and toxic explanations that erode our health, our lives, and our future. Without a functional story, we become vulnerable to whatever messaging happens to be making the rounds at the moment, putting us at the mercy of whoever's got the biggest megaphone.

To make matters worse, many of our traditional, guiding narratives have been replaced by synthetic commercial narratives that have come to dominate modern consciousness. Today, we no longer talk about Paleo themes of habitat, hunting, or the spirits that inhabit the world—we talk about brands. We design stories to sell lifestyles to sell stuff. All of which is profoundly abnormal.

In fact, today's synthetic narratives are so far removed from their original, organic form that they're best described as "plastic narratives" or "narrative products." Like food products, these narratives are refined, distilled, and stripped of their original nutrients and meaning. They're intentionally produced not to reveal, express, explain, or enlighten but to manipulate and exploit. The objective is to produce a certain kind of behavior in the consumer, usually in the form of clicking the "Buy Now" button.

Even worse, synthetic narratives don't just lure us into buying particular products and services; they also manipulate us into living in particular ways. Lifestyle narratives tell us who to admire, what to eat, what to value, and how to succeed. And above it all is the master commercial narrative that tells us that we can buy our way to beauty, happiness, power, and control. Health, adventure, romance, and transcendence can all be yours with a click or a swipe.[40]

Just as excess consumption of food products eventually compromises our health, the chronic consumption of synthetic narratives ultimately degrades our ability to think clearly and exercise our own judgment. The threat is subtle and insidious. Narrative products sound like real stories and are highly palatable, but the danger is real, to individuals and to our culture as a whole. Try to get by on a diet of synthetic narratives and you'll eventually lose contact with your identity, your history, and your purpose. You'll simply exist as a character in someone else's story. In the process, you'll degrade your personal health and our chance for a functional future.

TELL A BETTER STORY

Story works best when it's coherent and consistent with reality, when it solves problems, and when it helps us navigate the world; healthy narratives tell us the truth and help us find our way. Even fiction serves this purpose when it reveals important truths about the human experience and relationships. But problems arise when our narrative map doesn't fit the territory we're trying to navigate. Ideally, the stories o childhood—the stories provided by culture—should be accurate representations of the reality that we're likely to face. When this happens, things usually go smoothly. But when there's a narrative mismatch, we often find ourselves annoyed, shocked, angry, and stressed. A narrative that doesn't fit with reality can rightly be called dysfunctional.

But sadly, this quest for map-territory coherence seems to be falling apart in our internet age of "anything goes" storytelling. Social media generates and spreads narratives indiscriminately, with no consideration of terrain whatsoever: conspiracy theories, wild speculation, utter fabrications, rumors, and gossip—free-floating ideas with no foundation, and no connection to reality whatsoever. No cross-checking, no grounding in research or history, no peer review, and, above all, no revision in the event of error. This is narrative dysfunction at its worst.

Attempting to navigate the world with these hyperfictional narratives is bound to generate an immense amount of stress. It's like trying to navigate a modern city with a map derived from *The Lord of the Rings*. Inevitably, the end result is confusion and a crushing sense of anxiety that only promises to get worse. As humans, our natural inclination is to turn to story in times of trouble, but when our narrative environment is chaotic, unreliable, and toxic, the cortisol begins to flow.

This is precisely why some of us turn to science. The entire point of the scientific enterprise is to generate stories that track as closely to reality as possible, to produce accurate maps of the world. The method is both simple and elegant: compare the map and the territory. If there's a discrepancy, change the map, change the narrative. The territory is never wrong. Reality is never wrong. If you keep revising the map with an eye toward coherence, you'll eventually come closer to the truth. This is why science has given us the most accurate maps the world has ever known. It's also why science is (or was) held in such high esteem.

In any case, the challenge is clear. To ease our stress, we need a sense of narrative coherence and hygiene. We've got to tell better stories, stories that are true, relevant, and meaningful. The words that come out of our mouths and flow from our keyboards literally create the future. So pause before speaking. Pause before writing. And above all, pause before posting. For humans, language is a deadly serious business. Can you improve upon the silence?

SOCIAL AMBIGUITY

> We seldom realize that our most private thoughts and emotions are not actually our own. For we think in terms of languages and images which we did not invent, but which were given to us by our society.
> —Alan Watts

If you lived in the Paleo—any time in prehistory—you lived in a tribe. Maybe a small tribe with an extended family, or maybe a large, dispersed tribe with a hundred or more individuals, but in any case, you knew your people and you saw them most every day. Maybe you were a hunter yourself or maybe you just helped out with the gathering, but you were always a member, no matter your age, your appearance, your history, or your abilities. As a hypersocial animal, tribe was the norm, your daily life.

And it was a perfect fit. Your brain and body were finely tuned by thousands of generations of evolution for just this kind of life, so it's no surprise that it felt comfortable. In this kind of setting, your people were familiar, and contact with strangers was rare. Everyone in your tribe was in contact with people of all ages, from infants to tribal elders. In a typical year, you'd see people being born, flourishing, aging, and dying, the entire human life span playing out in your awareness. Gossip and storytelling would have been a daily pleasure, your family and friends constantly gabbing about their adventures. Time around the campfire would have been a special time to connect, laugh, tell stories, and wonder.

But today, our tribal life has been mangled almost beyond recognition. We live where we can afford to live, matched up with one another by work, by necessity, or by chance. Our social lives are in constant flux, everyone breaking up and making up, often by text or email. We're stratified in dozens of ways, included in some groups, excluded from others.

Unless you live in an isolated town, contact with strangers is routine, almost constant. And there's a good chance that you're locked into a single age category; unless they're part of your immediate family, you might never come in contact with the very young or the very old. And as for the gossip, storytelling, and laughter around the campfire, it's all been displaced by the synthetic chatter that flickers across our screens. In short, our social lives are historically abnormal and stressful in ways that our ancestors would scarcely recognize, much less accept.

WINNER TAKES ALL?

Competition makes everything worse. From the moment we enter kindergarten, we're conditioned to the idea that competition is simply the natural order of things; life is simply a zero-sum game: your gain is my loss and vice versa. Like it or not, that's just the way human life is. The way to get ahead is to get ahead.

You don't have to be a social scientist or psychologist to see that this might be a real systemic stressor. Pervasive, institutionalized competition creates an atmosphere in which we're constantly being judged and measured, an atmosphere of artificial scarcity, not abundance. It creates distance between people, increases individualism, and breaks up circular social cohesion. It emphasizes product over process—which is to say, the destination becomes more important than the journey. It turns sports and play into work, and even contributes to a sense of xenophobia and paranoia, all based on the understanding that someone is always out there, trying to beat us.

As sophisticated modern people, we tend to assume that competition is the natural and obvious order of things, but when we take a historical perspective—as we must—we get an entirely different picture. A quick thought experiment makes the point: Imagine your life anywhere in the Paleo. You're living in a predator-rich environment and you're vulnerable, but there's no possible way you can survive on your own. As an individual, you have no prior knowledge of your habitat, no way to make sense of the plants and animals around you. In short, the only way you can survive is as part of a functional tribe with an oral tradition. Cooperation is how you stay alive. Cooperation is the status quo for humanity.

But all that began to change some six thousand years ago as power began to ratchet up in North Africa and the Middle East. As we saw in *The Parable of the Tribes* and Steve Taylor's *The Fall*, early tribes were probably mostly peaceful and egalitarian and competition was probably rare. But with the rise of militarism, defensiveness, ego, and warrior cultures, competition spread like wildfire. Taylor describes the effect:

> As with personal property, competition goes against the communal principles of pre-Fall cultures. As soon as a person makes himself more important than everybody else, the balance and harmony of the community is disturbed. Even the great artists of unfallen cultures seem strangely ego-less from our

point of view, and rarely state personal author-
ship of their work . . . In view of this it's not
surprising that things never went smoothly
when European colonists tried to introduce
their competitive sports to the natives. In New
Guinea, boys were forced to play football in
mission schools, but instead of going all out to
win by as many goals as possible, they usually
carried on until scores were level. Football was
also opposed to the community sensibility of
the Aborigines. They found the idea of "beat-
ing" members of their own community incomprehensible, and couldn't bring themselves to
show the kind of aggression and confrontation
that the game requires.[41]

Of course, advocates of competition persist, often citing
a radical misinterpretation of Darwin and natural selection,
particularly the idea of "social Darwinism," the notion that
those at the top of the social hierarchy are somehow better
than those at the bottom. But this is all nonsense. In fact,
Darwin's entire thesis rests on the principle of reproductive
success, and there's a million ways to achieve that. If you can
find a way to leave behind large numbers of viable offspring,
you win. Competition might play an occasional role in the
process, but cooperation is just as likely to succeed. In other
words, our entire assumption that competition is somehow
"natural" is completely misguided.

JUDGMENT NEVER SLEEPS

Closely related to competition is the fact that we're being
judged almost constantly. From school to the workplace,
and even in our homes, our performance is constantly being

tracked, evaluated, measured, and recorded. For many of us, there's no slack in the system. Every minute of our day is now under scrutiny, by cameras, keyboard trackers, fitness monitors, and the like.

Historically speaking, this is wickedly abnormal. In a Paleo world, people observed one another and were probably judgmental about it too, but no one was keeping a record of your hunting and gathering performance, no one was writing down the details of your fire-building skills or your ability to dig for roots. There was plenty of time to simply be. But today, many of us feel judged in every waking moment, and for monotheists who worship a judgmental God, the process continues even after death. The stress of perpetual judgment never ends.

In this kind of hypercompetitive, hyperjudgmental environment, it's no surprise that we've become socially and culturally polarized. But it's not just the contrast of differing philosophies that turns on our stress responses, it's the rise of *negative* polarization across society. That is, a substantial number of us are now motivated not by being *for* any particular thing, issue, or idea but simply by being *against* the opposing side: *I don't really know what I'm for, but those people on the other side are evil and must be stopped.* The obvious consequence of this hate-based stance is that people are increasingly afraid to talk to one another, particularly those who have the "look and feel" of people in the other camp. Even if the effect is minor—which it isn't—the downstream effects are profound. A society in which people are afraid to talk to one another is no society at all.

THE HUMANITY VACUUM

In a normal, healthy society, people have a primal need for communication and conversation. Regardless of culture, race, or history, everyone wants the basic human acknowledgments:

we want to be seen, heard, felt, understood, and respected. This is ground zero for healthy human interaction and is a true human universal. People of every age, culture, origin, and status need and crave this experience. Even the Na'vi, the indigenous people of Pandora depicted in the movie *Avatar*, address one another with the honorific *I see you*. When these qualities are present, people can get along, even in the face of sharp differences in philosophy or politics.

This is not a "nice to have" experience nor is it "frosting on the cake" to be layered on top of other content or educational experiences. This is rock-solid biology that goes all the way to the deepest levels of physiology and nervous-system function. Our need to feel felt is as real as our need for food and water. When the body feels recognized and appreciated, the organism feels safe, and in turn, the autonomic nervous system goes into action, repairing tissues and opening up our cognition and creativity. Without question, this experience is a powerful and inexpensive form of medicine in its own right.

But tragically, the experience of feeling felt, heard, seen, understood, and respected is rapidly disappearing from our modern cultural landscape. In the very domains where we would most desire and expect a personal and humane connection—medicine and education in particular—it's often absent, eclipsed by administrative and technical urgencies. As we race from one task to another, our communications become increasingly superficial, and we neglect this most fundamental human need. Many of our students, clients, and patients go years without feeling felt, heard, and seen, and some of us never experience these things at all.

As a culture, we've lost sight of the primal, human fundamentals. Perversely, we take something that is (or was) intrinsically human and professionalize it. We wrap humane social experience in technical language and hand it over to an expert class of psychologists and therapists. Today, if you really want to feel felt, you might have to pay an expert to do something that an average, nonexpert person should be able to do without any training whatsoever. This professionalization of our humanity is sometimes presented as a solution to our mental and spiritual distress, but it's really a reflection of our alienation and our failure to master the fundamentals of being good social animals.

"SHOOT ME AN EMAIL"

To make matters worse, technological communication spreads and dilutes our social attention across vast reaches of space and time. In historically normal human settings, communication takes place in real time and is mediated by the body. This process includes all manner of nuance, gesture, tone of voice, pacing, and expression. This is rich communication.

But our modern form of technological "communication" is shallow and tenuous at best, and maddening at its worst. The more technology that exists between two parties, the lower the chances that genuine, rich communication will take place. If I "speak" to someone via email, I may get a response right away, maybe a day later, maybe a month later, or maybe never. This "conversation"—if we can call it that—is asynchronous; that is, the dialogue is fragmented. It's abnormal and wickedly laborious because it forces us to maintain attention across time. Digital communication requires us to keep conversations active in our minds indefinitely, until something conclusive happens. We call this "efficient," but it actually increases our mental workload; in other words, it's a stressor.[42]

To make matters worse, everyone seems to have their own personal channel, and many of us will only respond on one platform. "If you want to talk, contact me on Facebook," people say. Or Twitter. Or Instagram. Everyone wants their friends and contacts to dance to the tune of their personal electronic habits. If you happen to choose the "wrong" channel, nothing happens. This fragmentation of human communication is hugely destructive and alienating.

Closely related is the epidemic of "ghosting," the increasingly common practice of disappearing in online conversations and, now, in real-world conversations as well. Not so long ago, it was considered rude to simply exit a conversation without explanation or transition, but today, such behavior has been normalized. If you don't like what your conversational partner is saying or you get bored, just move on. There's always another conversation, just a click away. But ghosting isn't just bad manners; it breaks continuity and leaves the ghosted party feeling torn, the relationship ruptured.

AUTOMATION AND DEHUMANIZATION

Our social experience is distorted and corrupted in yet another way. As innovation increases across nearly every profession and industry and speed is forced on us at every turn, we're often required (or choose) to rely on templates, automation, boilerplate, and technology to maintain order and get our work done. In the beginning, such changes seem beneficial or, at least, benign as they free us up to focus on "more important matters." Our businesses and professions become more streamlined and efficient and we deliver better service, so the narrative goes. We move things along as quickly as possible: Don't call, email. Don't talk, text. Don't ask people for verbal, human feedback; force them to provide digital survey data. It's easy and fast, but it obliterates the human connection. A Google advertisement for an automated 3D-printing device brags "No human, no problem," implying, of course, that humans are the problem.

This automated approach to managing humanity reaches its peak (or nadir) in modern phone applications that allow us to reject (or occasionally accept) one another with effortless gestures. Want someone to go away? Just swipe left. The notorious dating app Tinder promotes "Swipe Life" as a solution to the complexities of modern relationships—the tag line tells us to just "match, chat, date." It's never been easier to make someone go away. People are nothing more than pictures on a screen. Disposable humans, swipe left.

Today, we see the automation of transactions and relationships in almost every domain. Everyone's a technician now, offering up carefully scripted and premeditated words, pitches, and information. The modern world runs on boilerplate, we speak in boilerplate, and many of us even think in boilerplate. It's becoming harder and harder to have an authentic, human conversation with anyone. This becomes a massive stressor, especially for those on the receiving end of these dehumanized, denatured interactions. When people don't feel felt, heard, or seen, they're just not sure what to make of the relationship. And if they feel controlled, manipulated, or processed, the stress is even worse.

This overreliance on automation and boilerplate is becoming standard practice in many domains. In the world of medicine, office visits and procedures are often conducted by rote, with minimal participation by the patient. Conversation is discouraged because that would interfere with efficiency. In the world of education, teachers deliver canned curriculums, created by invisible people thousands of miles away from their classrooms. In the world of law, legal advice is carefully parceled out by strict procedural rules. And in the world of business, especially big corporate business, the human element is completely eclipsed by computer-driven "behaviors," often delivered by people on the other side of the planet.

It's no wonder we feel so alienated. People are saying words to us, but they're not really talking to us. As recipients in such transactions, we begin to feel distinctly less human. At best, we feel like recording devices, dutifully absorbing the data that comes our way. The information has been transmitted to our nervous systems, and thus, the legal requirements have been met, but we don't feel touched, felt, or heard. If anything, we feel manipulated, processed, ignored, and even abused.

A MONEY-PRIMED WORLD

If we asked a group of modern people to point to the biggest stressors in their lives, we can be certain that many would point to challenges of finance, credit, and debt—which is to say, money. Everyone complains about it and we're quick to identify it as a major stressor, but most of our woes are about scarcity. That is, money is a stressor because we don't have enough of it.

But it's important to take a step back and think about money *itself* and the ways it's transformed our lives, our culture, our consciousness, and our happiness. As it turns out, money is a systemic social stressor for all of society, regardless of how much you might happen to have. And the problem is worse than you might think.

As usual, it's essential that we take the long, historical view. When we do, it won't be long before we realize that money as we know it is a relatively new, unproven concept. Our Paleolithic ancestors had virtually no possessions, no bank accounts, no credit, and no cash. Their consciousness was focused on habitat, one another, and the cosmos at large. In good years, habitat *was* their affluence. The land was their wealth. And in most years, that was enough.[43]

In contrast, modern people spend much, if not most, of their time obsessing over all things financial and money related. We complain about the stress, but this is far more than a minor lifestyle annoyance. Research demonstrates that money is a profoundly disruptive, antitribal, even antihuman force. In one particularly striking example, Kathleen Vohs at the University of Minnesota primed subjects with reminders of economics, finance, prices, and costs and discovered that "money-primed people behave more selfishly and show a greater reluctance to be involved with others . . . Even in intimate relationships and collectivistic cultures, reminders of money weaken sociomoral responses."[44]

Likewise, in a 2015 review of money-priming experiments, Vohs found two major effects: "Compared to neutral primes, people reminded of money are less interpersonally attuned. They are not prosocial, caring, or warm. They eschew interdependence. Second, people reminded of money shift into professional, business, and work mentality."[45]

These findings, described by the Nobel Prize winner Daniel Kahneman in *Thinking, Fast and Slow*, are profoundly disturbing and inconvenient to our culture as usual. Obviously, people who live in the modern world are massively and continuously "money primed." Immersed in a world of twenty-four-hour commerce, advertising, special offers, and discount pricing, we're reminded of money hundreds of times each day—in our cars, our workplaces, and even in our homes. If these priming events incline us even slightly away from our historically normal protribal, prosocial orientation, the overall effect is destructive on a planetary scale. In effect, money is a corrosive agent, an acid that dissolves normal human relationships and communities. Is it any wonder that so many of our modern social relations are so strained?

THE TRUST APOCALYPSE

All of this dysfunction adds up to a growing, unprecedented unwillingness to rely on the words and behavior of the people around us. *New York Times* columnist David Brooks calls this "the social trust apocalypse." An increasing number of people don't trust government, corporations, science, media, neighbors, or businesses. We see cons everywhere we look, everyone is lying, everyone is trying to cheat us. We don't trust our tribes, our communities, our institutions, or our leaders.[46]

All of which has a direct and profoundly destructive effect on the functioning of the human animal, especially on the autonomic nervous system. The system asks, Is my social world reliable? But increasingly, the answer is no. And if you can't trust your social world, things start to go downhill fast. We become more vigilant and suspicious, which, in turn, makes us less likely to enter into the genuine, authentic relationships that would ordinarily sustain us. And if we can't trust the people around us, where will we turn when the stress really hits the fan?

BE A GOOD SOCIAL ANIMAL

If you feel the stress of social ambiguity—and you almost certainly do—the first thing to remember is that there's nothing wrong with you. You almost surely don't have a neurotransmitter deficiency, a neurosis, or a personality disorder. Given the social ambiguity of our era, your distress is absolutely explicable, understandable, and forgivable. So, take a breath and relax. Remember, you're responding the way any animal would in the face of social ambiguity and chaos.

In the meantime, we have a lot of work ahead of us, nothing less than to repair the social fabric of the modern world. Incredibly enough, many of us will have to relearn basic social skills that we once took for granted, ancient skills that were an intrinsic part of the human repertoire. Start with authentic conversation, rich communication, practiced face to face in real time. And remember, people need to feel felt, heard, seen, respected, and understood. The process is inefficient, time consuming, and sometimes difficult, but absolutely essential.

CHAPTER 4

HUMANS UNDER PRESSURE

Meet the first beginnings. Look to the budding
mischief before it has time to ripen to maturity.
—Shakespeare

As we've seen, the human animal is suffering from a host of large-scale stressors—historical, systemic, cultural, and ecological tigers that afflict our bodies, minds, and spirits. So, how do we respond to the pressure? How are we holding up under the combined weight of mismatch, separation anxiety, cognitive overload, and cultural dysfunction? The short answer is "Not well."

As you'll see, there's a lot that can go sideways when the tigers come around. We humans have a staggering range of dysfunctional responses to ambiguity, chaos, and pressure. We fight and flee, we freeze and hide, contract and hoard, distort and complain. We get addicted and we fall ill. We suffer, repeat our mistakes, and then dig our holes deeper. It sounds like a lot of bad news all the way around, but once we become aware of our tendencies, we're better equipped to chart a more functional course. When we see our inclinations in advance, we've got a chance to act early, before the budding mischief has time to wreak havoc on our lives.

FIGHTING AND FLEEING

When it comes to stress, everyone talks about the classic fight-flight response, and we're quick to imagine ourselves running away from predators on the savanna or battling lions that are invading our camp. Danger is imminent and it's time to mobilize our bodies for action. The body dumps glucose into the bloodstream, muscles become energized, and the nervous system perks up for maximum responsiveness.

This is all well and good when the danger is palpable and real. When the predator is a flesh-and-blood presence within striking range, it makes sense to fire up our adrenal glands and start pumping stress hormones. But what happens when the danger is diffuse, abstract, or imaginary? What happens when the predators are remote, digital, or ideological? We feel threatened and fire up our neurobiology for physical action, but where or what is the target?

This is precisely the problem that we see across the modern world with increasingly random acts of hostility, anger, polarization, and adversarial energy. Danger is in the air, amplified by our always-on media. Warning! Real tigers, false tigers, ghost tigers coming to your neighborhood! Click here for more info! All of which whips us into a frenzy, desperate for something to fight against or, if that fails, flee from. Our brains and bodies tell us that predators are near, but we can't really see them or touch them. We're not sure what to do, but we sure feel like we've got to do *something*.

RANDOM ACTS OF FIGHT-FLIGHT

The fundamental problem is that we just can't seem to agree on what's dangerous. In the modern world, there's simply no consensus on what we ought to be afraid of. When are we supposed to engage our autonomic nervous systems? When should we fight or flee?

Back in the Paleo, no such confusion existed. Everyone in your tribe—even children—would have agreed that predators, large animals, wildfires, gravity, and fast water in the local rivers posed genuine danger. In other words, everyone in your tribe was on the same autonomic page. At any moment, everyone around you would have been in roughly the same psychophysical state: either fight-flight or rest-and-digest. This synchrony made it easy to reach consensus and get along.

In contrast, modern people seem to have little or no agreement as to what's really dangerous. Do a man-on-the-street poll and you'll get hundreds of different answers to the question "What's dangerous?" People might talk about urban violence, immigration, economic problems, rampaging viruses, plastic, disinformation, carbon in the atmosphere, or someone's ideology. And to make matters worse, we fail to teach any of this; it's unlikely that anyone you know has ever taken a class on Dangerous Things.

The result is that our fight-flight responses are often arbitrary, individualized, and untethered to any shared reality. In other words, we're *not* on the same autonomic page. At any given moment, you might be in feed-and-breed while the person next to you is exercising a full-blown fight-flight response. This makes it far more difficult to reach consensus and get things done. If we can't agree on what's dangerous, our bodies won't be able to agree on how to build a functional future.

Common sense would suggest that we would take the time to dig deeper, do our homework, consult the research, exercise some personal introspection, and find out precisely what's threatening us. But that's not what we do. We're irrational animals under stress, so we pick whatever's handy: a political party, a prominent individual, an organization, institution, substance, or ideology. The reality of the situation doesn't matter much; what matters is that we've got a target, an outlet for our anxiety and unease.

And of course, all of this impulsive fighting and fleeing amplifies our stress even further. Misplaced acts of hostility and free-floating adversarial energy only serve to put everyone else on edge and feed an atmosphere of suspicion and distrust, which lowers the threshold for yet more fighting and fleeing. When everyone's primed for combat, it's hard to get anything done.

FREEZING AND HIDING

Fight-flight is the classic response to stress, but it's not the only option. In some situations, and for some species, the smart move might be no movement at all. In other words, freeze. This is a common response in many prey animals, but here in the modern world, freezing in place implies more than the physical act of staying still. It's a psychosocial effort to become invisible, to blend in, and, above all, to not attract attention.

This surely explains a good deal of modern human behavior. We don't literally "freeze" on the sidewalk, in our homes, or the workplace, but we do try to blend into whatever social setting we inhabit. We seek the mainstream and follow convention. Don't rock the boat, don't make waves, don't draw attention to yourself. In short, try to remain invisible and stick to the status quo, whatever it might happen to be. Conditions might well be calling—even screaming—for change, but that would be risky. Taking action on climate, habitat destruction, or social inequality would mean exposure and vulnerability, so it's better to stay with the familiar.

Most notoriously, we hide out in obedience. We do as we're told and we follow directions. This may well feel like a safe strategy, but it can backfire catastrophically in the long run. Obedience, famously described by Stanley Milgram in his legendary *Obedience to Authority*, sets us up for inhumane behavior, even atrocity. We comply as instructed, even to the point of destroying the biosphere and one another. As the notorious street artist Banksy observed, "the greatest crimes in the world are not committed by people breaking the rules but by people following the rules."[47]

Equally troubling is the problem of conformity, famously explored by Solomon Asch in the 1950s. His experiments demonstrated that a sizable percentage of people are willing to adjust their personal sensory perceptions to fit the dominant estimates of the group.[48] In other words, a lot of us are willing to reject our own judgment for the sake of getting along, even in the face of glaring, contradictory evidence.

And thus, our dilemma. Big systemic tigers are everywhere now, screaming for change, but we're afraid to act. The world feels exceedingly dangerous and the risks are overwhelming, so we freeze up. We think that blending in will make us safe, but ultimately, we're not safe at all. When everyone obeys and conforms, the status quo triumphs and nothing changes. In times like these, standing up and standing out becomes the most sensible path. To save the whole, it's sometimes necessary to risk, to act, and above all, to differ.

CONTRACTION

In all animals—mammals, primates, and humans alike—the natural, healthy tendency is toward curiosity, exploration, and even adventure. The animal wants to know the world and will seek out new experiences whenever possible. We desire engagement, contact, and relationship. We want to touch and be touched by the world. But when stress hits the fan, it all goes the other way and the entire mind-body-spirit begins to withdraw and contract.

The most obvious manifestation is in the way we experience our bodies. When stress becomes chronic, we begin to stand and sit differently. Gravity prevails over exhausted muscles and we slump. Posture begins to favor flexion over extension as the body collapses in on itself, defeated by conditions. This is precisely what we see in the epidemic of flexion across the modern world. Chained to our desks and devices, suffering under cognitive overload, we bend forward, bodies collapsed in on themselves as we grind out our digital duties. The result is that the head moves forward, breathing is suppressed, and the spirit suffers. This is the distinctive psychophysical expression of depression.

Stress also drives us into cognitive contraction. Working at our limit, we take on fewer intellectual challenges and protect ourselves from novelty. We stick with what we know and reject whatever we can get away with. New ideas, new problems, and new interests fall by the wayside. Our minds—and probably our brains themselves—become smaller.

Likewise, we fall into behavioral contraction. Our responses to the world become stereotyped and repetitive. We double down on the familiar and retreat into established habits, no matter how functional or dysfunctional they might be. Most of this happens unconsciously, below the level of awareness. Our repertoires become narrower as we repeat whatever we did yesterday. We may be dimly aware of this tendency, and we might well prefer to strike out into some new behavioral territory, but our stress and exhaustion limits our capacity for change.

We also contract socially as we avoid new engagements and withdraw into our individual lives and interests. We see other people as challenging, annoying, or threatening, and we're less likely to take risks with those whom we perceive as different. But of course, this does us no good. As our social world contracts, we become even more vulnerable to loneliness and the stress that goes with it—a perfect setup for a vicious spiral.

As stress escalates, even our narratives contract. The vast, sprawling stories that were natural in childhood begin to shrink. Our explanations for how the world works become more simplistic, our stories reduced to polar opposition, broad-brush generalizations, cliché, and stereotypes. As our stories shrink, our imaginations go along for the ride, and the world becomes smaller, duller, and less interesting.

And of course, we also experience a spiritual contraction. As stress escalates, our curiosity wanes, and our vision of the cosmos and the future begins to shrink. In a relaxed, healthy human animal, there's a sense of continuity with people, habitat, and the larger world, but when stress escalates, this sense of kinship starts to break down; we begin to experience ourselves as isolated, stranded individuals. Possibility narrows and we start to experience compassion and empathy fatigue.

Much of this will feel familiar, as most of us have experienced it firsthand. But it's also essential to remember that similar contractions play out at the larger levels of organizations, governments, society, and culture. When stress escalates, we're likely to see cognitive contraction, as organizations and governments double down on routine and familiar methods; behavioral contraction, as societies revert to what they've done in the past; and social contraction, as groups shrink into familiar circles and networks. There's even a kind of narrative contraction, as ideas with big potential are rejected out of hand in favor of simplistic stories for organizational success.

All of which ultimately degenerates into a siege mentality: *the world is against me, so I must defend myself at all costs.* Tigers are on the prowl, so we erect a psychophysical fortress. We build walls, dig a moat around the perimeter, and fill it with sharp spikes. We position archers at every arrow slit and set cauldrons of boiling oil on top of every wall. Inside, we lay in a stockpile of provisions to last months or even years. In short, life is a sustained, chronic battle, stretching all the way to the horizon. Defense is everything.

But the effects are corrosive on a planetary scale. The more we dig in, the more we "otherize" the world. Fearing for our welfare, we go all-in on paranoia and xenophobia. Our sense of continuity with the world dissolves, ego becomes dominant, and we become increasingly selfish, vigilant, and antisocial.

In *Behave: The Biology of Humans at Our Best and Worst,* Robert Sapolsky sums up the research about moral decision-making after a social stressor: "Stress made people give more egoistic answers about emotionally intense moral decisions; the more glucocorticoid levels rose, the more egoistic the answers." The fortress promises safety, but it ultimately back-fires. The more we defend, the more isolated we become. And the more isolated we become, the greater our fear.

HOARDING

Not surprisingly, stress also shifts our perspective away from abundance and toward scarcity. When we're pumping corti-sol, it feels like there's less of everything: less wealth, less time, and fewer resources to work with. We're more likely to see life and society as a competitive, zero-sum game. Hoarding behavior—by individuals and organizations—becomes increasingly common. There's only so much to go around, so we'd better get what we can, when we can.

This becomes the paradox of our age. Compared to our hunting and gathering ancestors, we live in an era of spectacular, unimaginable affluence. Most of us have heat in the winter, fairly reliable access to food, and at least some medical care. Objectively speaking, we are wildly, outrageously rich. But because we're so stressed, we rarely feel it. And if you can't feel it, you're likely to want even more.

All of which drives some truly outrageous behaviors by both individuals and corporations. If you can't feel your wealth and abundance, nothing is ever going to satisfy you; nothing will ever be enough. And so, our default behavior in the modern world is to get more of everything. More money, more territory, more power, and more control. And of course, this puts us into perpetual conflict with one another. If everyone's stressed, no one feels the abundance, and everyone wants more, things are not going to end well.

DEPLETED WILLPOWER

Scarcity consciousness isn't just about things; it's also about our sense of time. When we're stressed, we get impatient, anxiety surges, and we start looking for quick solutions. Maybe if we speed up, we can get to somewhere safer and more comfortable. Let's go fast and get this over with!

In essence, the stress of the modern world causes us to fail the famous "marshmallow test." Almost everyone knows the story. Young children are offered a simple choice: "You can have one marshmallow right now, but if you can wait a few minutes, you can have two." Researchers recorded the results and tracked the kids over the course of decades. Ultimately, the findings were clear: the kids who could delay gratification with marshmallows went on to enjoy significantly greater success in their careers, their health, and their relationships.[49]

The problem is that stress literally degrades our ability to delay gratification. Stress hormones erode the circuitry of the prefrontal cortex, which, in turn, opens the gates for greater impulsivity. In a healthy, nonstressed brain, the prefrontal cortex serves an inhibitory function, operating as a neurological brake on deeper emotional impulses. But when we're stressed, the prefrontal cortex is more likely to go "off-line."[50]

In other words, stress turns off the brakes and increases the odds that we'll reach for the single marshmallow right now. But if you want to succeed in today's world, you've got to have a fully functioning prefrontal cortex. In other words, you've got to be able to wait, and you've got to be able to delay gratification, step by step, first through high school, then through college, and all the way into some kind of profession. You've got to exercise, eat right, save, plan for the future, and, above all, keep your impulses under control. Wait for the marshmallow and you can succeed. But stress puts us into a vicious cycle. It makes us more impulsive, but impulsivity leads to bad decisions and—you guessed it—more stress. Unless something or someone intervenes, our lives can well go off the rails.

This is all pretty clear in our personal lives, but we see it on a larger scale as well. In fact, the arc of recent modern history shows a progressive erosion of inhibition. Early human civilizations were literally built on delayed gratification. It's no easy thing to build great pyramids, temples, road systems, and irrigation canals. You've got to have a long, intergenerational view, and you've got to be able to wait. By analogy, we might well say that early human civilizations had a functional prefrontal cortex, a value system that put the brakes on impulsivity. The tribal elders of the day counseled patience in all things; this was sapience in action.

But today, stress surges through our social system, eroding our collective sense of inhibition and turning off the brakes. So now, we don't just want two marshmallows, we want the whole bag, ordered with a swipe and delivered by drone. In fact, entire industries are hard at work making sure that we can do just that. A former Google employee reportedly warned that "there are a thousand people on the other side of the screen whose job it is to break down your self-regulation."[51] Instant gratification at the push of a button, all of which undermines the very basis of our society and, more generally, any society. As author Jason Hickel tweeted: "A civilization that is incapable of self-limitation in its relationship to the living world can hardly be described as a civilization at all."

DISORDERED THINKING

Stress also has a corrosive effect on our ability to appreciate the totality of systems, relationships, and life at large. Specifically, and most tragically, stress warps our ability to "see whole," to grok the entire picture of interdependent realities. We lose our appreciation for the circle, we exaggerate some qualities, and we lose sight of others. We lose our sense of proportion.

Most notorious is our mountains-out-of-molehills reaction. We focus on some small annoyance or trivial event in life and blow it out of proportion. To put it another way, we take false tigers and treat them like they're life-threatening carnivores, complete with claws and razor-sharp teeth. And in the process, we say nasty things to the people around us, things that we're certain to regret in a few hours or days. Hair on fire, we go ballistic on our friends, our coworkers, and whoever's on the other side of a digital conversation. Our inflamed minds and spirits go berserk. We catastrophize and go directly to the most outrageous worst-case outcomes. Humans seem to have an almost unlimited capacity in this regard; when we're in the grip of cortisol intoxication, nothing is too small to threaten the fate of the entire world.

All of which compromises our ability to see and appreciate the functional interdependence of whole systems. Consider the familiar bicycle wheel. As every bicycle mechanic knows, a good wheel is built on balanced qualities of length and tension across the system. The structure is interdependent and integration is the ultimate goal. It simply won't do to focus on one spoke at a time. If you want the wheel to roll true, you've got to make your adjustments in keeping with the totality.

But when we're stressed, our attention narrows and our sense of the whole disappears. In our myopia, we focus on a single element while ignoring the cascading effect on the rest of the system. Ideally, a good mechanic would alternate his attention rhythmically as whole-part-whole: Look at the total wheel and make an assessment, focus and adjust the single offending part, then return your attention to the whole for a reevaluation. Then repeat. This is a time-honored method in all sorts of disciplines, but it breaks down when we're stressed. Overwhelmed by time pressure, fear, or complexity, we lose the rhythm and focus exclusively on component parts. We focus on a single spoke while we lose sight of the whole wheel.

PERFECTIONISM

When stress surges, the world begins to feel like it's falling apart. We feel ourselves losing control, and without thinking, we seek out anything that will help us get back in charge. We double down on work, tools, technologies, programs, and anything else that promises to make the feelings of insecurity go away.

And so begins our personal and cultural perfectionism, the quest to get every last detail right. If we succeed—so our inner narrative tells us—we won't have to suffer criticism, rejection, or, presumably, death. In our flawless performance, we'll be safe, invulnerable, and, if all goes well, desirable. We might even transcend this messy, earthly realm and become one with the Creator.

But the curious thing about perfectionism is that it's both a result of stress and a cause of stress. We feel stressed, so we try to compensate by trying to be perfect, which of course ultimately fails and causes us even more stress. In turn, this creates a vicious, positive feedback cycle that spirals, tighter and tighter, into a knot of chronic effort, doubt, fear, and even more stress. Perfectionism may well seem like a solution, but it's really more of a symptom, a marker of our inability to live in the world as it is.

At its core, perfectionism is a fear-based strategy that attempts to force order on to a messy and often incomprehensible world. Like so many other defensive strategies, it's an attempt to be invulnerable. After all, if you're perfect, you'll never have to suffer criticism or rejection. And in our perfection, we can finally "be someone" and get the recognition that we crave. As the writer Anne Lamott put it, "I think perfectionism is based on the obsessive belief that if you run carefully enough, hitting each stepping stone just right, you won't have to die."

Perfectionism is the ultimate all-or-nothing psychology. We tell ourselves *either I'm perfect or I'm nothing* and *I'm going to fix things, once and for all.* Naturally, this puts us into a predicament of maximum stress. When you're up against these self-imposed ultimatums, your fight-flight system is going to be on a hair trigger. Rest-and-digest will come to be seen not as a beneficial healing state but as a shameful lapse of will and control. This sets up a powerful internal duality: *it's me versus my own lazy self.* As everyone knows, perfectionists are their own harshest critics. In fact, they're preemptive critics, judging their own performance before anyone else can step in and do the job.

The paradox of perfectionism is that, even if it were to succeed, it would only succeed in creating separation and distance from the vast, messy, complex, and incomprehensible universe we inhabit. You'd be living on a perfect island—your own personal planet—divorced from reality, alone, or perhaps living with a bunch of other perfectionists, which of course is one of the most stressful things we could imagine.

STRESS HARDENING

When we're stressed, danger is in the air; we feel exposed, vulnerable. We try to cope with our anxiety by being perfect, a quest that even extends to the way we hold, move, and experience our bodies. In the process, we harden our minds and bodies to resist our predicament. The world closes in, so we try harder, and harder still. We may even respond to the experience of chronic stress by working ourselves to death.

Epidemiologist and public health researcher Sherman James coined the term *John Henryism* to describe this behavior. In his investigation of racial health disparities between blacks and others in the American South, he observed that some people coped with prolonged exposure to stress by expending high levels of sustained effort. The label refers to the folk hero John Henry, an African American who worked hard enough to compete with a steam-powered machine, but died as a result.

James developed the John Henryism Scale for Active Coping. Three themes were considered:

- Efficacious mental and physical vigor

- A strong commitment to hard work
- A single-minded determination to succeed

Scoring was based on agreement with a series of statements, such as: "When things don't go the way I want them to, that just makes me work even harder" and "I've always felt that I could make of my life pretty much what I wanted to make of it."

James's research suggested that people who adopt a John Henry approach to life and stress are more likely to experience hypertension and other health problems as they age, none of which should come as a surprise. After all, chronic effort, as much as chronic stress itself, is historically and physiologically abnormal. You don't have to be an epidemiologist to conclude that such an approach to life would be hard on the body, as well as on the people around us.

But modern culture drives and rewards this behavior relentlessly. We promote this "chronic work ethic," often without realizing it. We praise the worker who pushes him- or herself to the limit, saying "he's like a machine." Likewise, we use metaphors of invulnerability in our sporting events and in our aspirations for the tissue of our bodies—think Ironman triathlon. And conversely, we abuse those who work at a modest, human, sustainable pace, calling them "slackers," and worse.

But it's a dead-end strategy. When hard work and effort become chronic, we become little more than one-trick ponies. No matter the stressor, we try harder. False tigers, real tigers— it doesn't much matter; we just increase our effort. We may succeed for a time and even attract attention for our achievements, but the body knows better. To use the language of ecology, such an approach isn't even close to being sustainable. In short, John Henryism is flatlining. It has no waxing and waning, no bounce, no rhythm, no oscillation, and no dance. In other words, no life.

DRAMA

When all is well in our lives, it's easy to be patient, fair, and reflective, but when we're under stress, it all goes out the window. Gradually or suddenly, our judgment becomes distorted, and we shift from a healthy, creative orientation to blaming, complaining, faultfinding, and desperate bids for rescue.

We hear it everywhere now: *It's all his fault! It's all their fault! I'm not to blame! Please come and fix me. Make my life work again.* These refrains are common across the modern world, and we hear them dozens of times each day in one form or another. They're so common in fact that young people might even suppose that they're normal human expressions; this is just how people talk.

But in fact, this is *not* how healthy people talk. All these sentiments are symptoms of a dysfunctional attitude and relational pathology, first described by psychologist Stephen Karpman in 1968. Often used as a tool in counseling and psychotherapy, this "drama triangle" has powerful applications across the entire range of human experience.[52]

The trouble begins when a person identifies himself as a powerless victim in the face of circumstance. According to the victim's narrative, the source of his unhappiness lies with other people, agents, forces, and events. He pins the blame for his predicament on a persecutor, or if that doesn't work, he goes in search of a rescuer, someone or something that will extract him from his predicament and save the day.

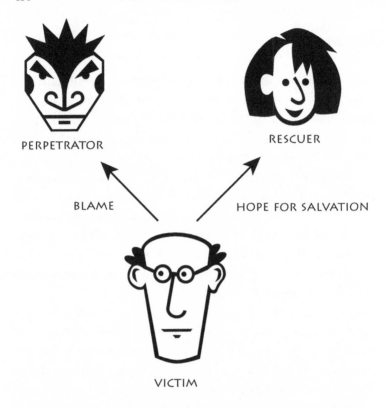

PERPETRATOR

RESCUER

BLAME

HOPE FOR SALVATION

VICTIM

Of course, it's essential to remember there *are* genuine victims in this world and, just as obviously, authentic persecutors who deserve justice. Likewise, there are times when we can and should reach out to others for support. But the drama triangle is something different; it's about attitude, identity, and orientations. What roles are we claiming in the world? Who is creating our lives? These are questions of agency and responsibility.

The drama begins when we're stressed, when we stumble, get hurt, or fail to get what we desire. Looking for a way out of our unhappiness, we claim victim status. *It's someone else's fault that I'm suffering.* We blame our parents, our genes, our childhood, our jobs, our bosses, and our partners. We blame humanity, society, government policy, the opposition party, stress, and overwork. These accusations may well contain elements of truth, but this is beside the point. The real issue is our orientation. By claiming the role of victim, we give away our power. No longer are we acting in the world—the world is acting on us. We're triggered by external forces.

Going to the other point of the triangle—toward rescue—is not much better. In our unhappiness, we look for people, substances, ideas, or organizations to bail us out of our predicament, but once again, we give away our power. Rescuers can sometimes comfort us, agree with us that the perpetrators are horrible, and maybe even go to battle and solve our problems for us. But none of this really helps in the long run; the more we seek to be propped up by the world, the weaker we become.

Many of us have heard this story before, and it's easy to assume that the victim orientation is something reserved for the dark underbelly of society; hardened alcoholics, drug addicts, and criminals come to mind. But victimhood is alive and well at every level of society, and no one is immune. That's because it's an easy, seductive trap. There's always plenty of blame to go around, perps are everywhere, and excuses are always handy: The economy is in recession, our parents were flawed, our neighborhood was in turmoil. Immigrants took our jobs, bullies abused us, the schools failed us, the system didn't provide the kind of opportunities we deserved. That's why complaining has become a national sport, with entire media empires dedicated to round-the-clock finger-pointing, otherwise known as "blamestorming." When things aren't going well, there's always a handy perpetrator we can blame, right across the aisle or down the street.

It gets worse. When we're highly stressed, it becomes easier and easier to cast blame on others, and in the process, we become susceptible to any passing narrative, no matter how preposterous, as long as it suits our purposes. No conspiracy theory is too outrageous, no leap of faith too extreme, no story too outlandish. If it helps us build a case against our chosen perpetrator, we're all in. And before long, we stop cross-checking, stop seeking truth, and stop asking deeper questions about evidence, sources, facts, and history. It takes a good deal of cognitive labor and strength of character to examine propositions in detail, to fact check, to dig for scientific truth and revise our understandings, but when we're stressed and exhausted, we have no energy for such projects. It's easier to simply blame whoever's handy.

Even worse, the attitude is contagious. When we see people around us blaming perpetrators and running for rescue, the behavior becomes normalized. We come to believe that's just how it's done in human society, and before long, millions of people are working the drama triangle. In theory, we could find our way out of the drama triangle by accepting responsibility and actively creating our lives, but this requires character and resolve, qualities that are in increasingly short supply in our stressed-out world.

ADDICTION

Even for the most casual observer, one of the most obvious consequences of our stress epidemic is the surge in addictions of all varieties, and it's not hard to see where this might be coming from. In the healthy human, early childhood is sustained by strong attachments to a primary caregiver, tribe, habitat, and culture. If all goes well and these connections hold true, the child goes on to live a fulfilling, functional life. But if attachment fails, we feel lost in space, vulnerable to the ambiguity of the world.

Today, many of us suffer from broken continuities at almost every level. Our bodies are barely connected to habitat, barely connected to one another. Our original life-giving continuities have been stretched to the breaking point and it scares us. So we reach for compensatory attachments and artificial substitutes—anything that promises to sustain us. Judgmental observers are quick to condemn this kind of addictive behavior as a moral failing, but these efforts should be seen for what they really are: failed attempts to reunite with our life-supporting systems.

Without a link to primal reality, we attach to anything that's handy: substances, people, ideas, possessions—anything that promises to give us the primal contact we so desperately need. This is precisely the process that Bruce Alexander described in *The Globalization of Addiction: A Study in Poverty of the Spirit*. As he sees it, the prevalence of addiction is increasing around the world: "Globalization of free-market society has produced an unprecedented, worldwide collapse of psychosocial integration."

And inevitably, we get addicted to stress itself. If this sounds surprising, remember the psychophysical effects of stress hormones. At the right doses, they give us a host of powerful, beneficial, and even euphoric effects. It just feels good to be lightly stressed, so we begin to seek it out compulsively, unconsciously. The body begins to crave the stimulation, and the rest of life begins to feel boring by comparison. We become stress junkies, internal drug addicts, mainlining cortisol at every opportunity. If a little stress is good, more must be better, so we keep pushing, keep working, keep exercising, keep doing. After a while, we'll do anything to get that cortisol rush. In fact, our entire modern workaholic culture can be seen in precisely these terms: addiction on a grand scale.

PAIN

Addiction is bad enough, but chronic stress also puts millions of us into chronic and unnecessary pain. The human animal has always experienced pain in a multitude of ways, of course, but today, it looks and feels different. Back pain, neck pain, shoulder pain, knee pain: these conditions are probably normal for humans, primates, and mammals—even dinosaur fossils show evidence of arthritic joints—but never before has pain been so pervasive and debilitating for so many.

A common explanation holds that pain is simply the result of tissue injury and inflammation, but most of us suspect there's a lot more to it than that. Our various pains wax and wane from day to day for no obvious reason, all of it complicated by personal history, disposition, meaning, and, of course, our stress load.

It makes sense to suppose that stress would intensify our pain, but as they say in the research community, the effect is divergent. That is, fear inhibits pain, whereas anxiety enhances it. All of which makes perfect sense. Most of us have had at least one acutely terrifying experience in life, and there's a good chance we remember that the pain was surprisingly absent, until the next day. This is also a common report with combat injuries, where fear is likely to be surging.

But when anxiety nags at our minds and bodies, it all goes the other way. Even minor, nearly nonexistent tissue injuries can flare up and put us into agony. This is what the experts call "stress-induced hyperalgesia." The more sustained the stress, the greater the perception of pain.

All of which makes sense in the context of modern public health. The average American isn't suffering from acute fear so much as chronic, crushing anxiety. Most of us manage to make it through the day without being physically attacked or assaulted, but nearly all of us are laboring under a load of vaguely threatening uncertainty and ambiguity. It's not so much that we're being attacked by real tigers; it's the millions of not-quite-real tigers that wear us down and lower our pain thresholds. What we're experiencing is classic, stress-induced hyperalgesia.

This is precisely what the statistics tell us. In 2011, the US Institute of Medicine published *Relieving Pain in America: A Blueprint for Transforming Prevention, Care, Education, and Research*. Among the findings: "Common chronic pain conditions affect at least 116 million U.S. adults at a cost of $560–635 billion annually in direct medical treatment costs and lost productivity."[53] To put it another way, this is roughly a third of the US population as a whole. And if it's that bad in the United States, it's likely to be equally problematic throughout the rest of the modern world. A report from the business data platform Statista found that "analgesics accounted for 21% of the total over-the-counter pharmaceuticals revenue in 2019. The worldwide revenue of US $25 billion in 2019 is expected to increase to US $32 billion by 2025."[54]

All of which suggests that stress is a much bigger problem than we thought. It's not just about feeling harried at work or having an occasional wave of impatience or unease. This is about the hard-core physical suffering of millions, maybe even billions, of people around the world. If we could reduce people's stress and anxiety across our population—even in some small way—we would also reduce the suffering of millions of people and probably save billions of dollars in the process.

LIFESTYLE DISEASE

Pain is endemic in the modern human animal but so too are the various "diseases of civilization" that we hear about almost every day: obesity, heart disease, diabetes, neurological disorders, and cancer. It's impossible to say exactly how much of this is due to stress, but we can be sure that *all* of these conditions are exacerbated by stress and, in particular, the stress of evolutionary mismatch. When you force an animal to live outside its normal ecological range, you're bound to see psychophysical problems, including disease.

According to the World Health Organization, these so-called noncommunicable diseases are collectively responsible for almost 70 percent of all deaths worldwide.[55] This is plenty bad enough on its face, but when we step back for a wider view, it looks even worse. That is, the spread of lifestyle disease suggests a general weakening of the human animal. It's an impossible thing to measure, but when we compare the outrageous health and physicality of our primate cousins in the wild to what we see in modern human communities, the trend becomes obvious. In other words, lifestyle disease is actually a symptom of a much more serious, species-wide problem. In fact, the general weakening of the human animal ought to be considered a disease state in and of itself.

To be sure, there are plenty of toxic causal agents that are implicated in our afflictions: excess sugar, trans fats, high-fructose corn syrup, pesticides, and toxins—the usual culprits. But mismatch and the proliferation of laborsaving devices, vehicles, and machines has taken away our physical challenge and replaced it with stress, urgency, and ambiguity. We aren't using our physical capability, so we're losing it.

To be sure, lifestyle diseases are afflictions of the human body, but more generally, these are diseases of human resilience. When the resilience reservoir becomes depleted, physical illness is likely to follow soon thereafter. The body no longer has the energy to fight back against toxicities of the modern world, and before long, disease begins to creep into the system.

LEARNED HELPLESSNESS

Episodic, occasional stress and trauma are one thing. The human animal takes a hit, retreats into a safer condition, then gradually bounces back to something resembling normal function. All animals—including humans—have been doing this for millions of years. But what happens when that stress becomes chronic and retreat becomes impossible?

This was the question posed by psychologist Martin Seligman at the University of Pennsylvania. Working with nonhuman animals, mostly dogs, he placed them in situations in which escape from stressful stimuli was impossible. Over time, this led to a condition we now recognize as "learned helplessness." In this state, the organism becomes listless, apathetic, risk averse, and depressed.[56]

None of which should come as a surprise. After all, most of us can appreciate the idea that chronic defeat can wear us down. But what's really surprising is that this effect takes place in *all* animals, not just in people or the "higher," mostly conscious, organisms. When faced with impossible circumstances beyond their control, all animals develop a characteristic set of responses, including sleep and eating disorders, ulcers, and other physical manifestations of depression. Research reported in *Current Biology* (April 2013) even found the same process at work in common houseflies. Flies that experience uncomfortable levels of heat will normally move to escape, but when they realize that the heat is beyond their control and can't be avoided, they stop responding, walking more slowly and taking longer and more frequent rests, as if they were "depressed."[57]

But no matter the particular animal or species, the most unsettling idea is that repeated experiences of inescapable defeat lead individuals, and probably even groups, to *generalize failure.* In other words, animals come to *assume* a lack of power and control over their world, no matter the specific details of a particular challenge. In other words, this becomes a worldview. *There's no point in trying anything because the world is stacked against me. I am powerless.*

It would be one thing if learned helplessness was simply a consequence of physical confinement or a lack of physical vagility. But in the human animal, it's more nuanced. People can feel chronically boxed in and defeated in a thousand ways. Some of us feel perpetually defeated—economically, relationally, professionally, and socially. We redouble our efforts, but the modern world feels like it's stacked against us, especially for those who are part of a marginalized group. And if you feel like there's no escape from your predicament, you're vulnerable.

This is particularly the case for activists working on large-scale systemic problems like social justice, climate, species extinction, oceans, and forests. Dwarfed by corporate power and cultural inertia, it's easy to feel chronically defeated and, in turn, helpless. For social and conservation activists, defeat is common and victory is rare. To put it another way, learned helplessness is an occupational hazard for the modern activist.

All of which bodes poorly for human animals living in modern conditions. We're groping for control, but many of us live in conditions in which we have minimal leverage. Poverty, social exclusion, and health care disparities force many people into "no-win circumstances." Say what you will about the human spirit triumphing over adversity, if the body suffers enough defeat, it will eventually stop trying.

A WORLD OF HURT

In short, stress robs us of our humanity, warps our sense of perspective, wrecks our communities, and diminishes our sapience. Social resources such as trust, reciprocity, and cooperation diminish at the very time we need them most. Our judgment becomes skewed, and we lose sight of big pictures. We become impatient and focus on scarcity; we blame false tigers and become addicted. Our sense of personal power wanes just when we need our strength and courage.

Even worse, the effect is intergenerational. Waves of stress—and all the afflictions that go with them—are passed from fathers to sons, from mothers to daughters. From this point of view, it becomes increasingly obvious that stress is no minor annoyance or lifestyle issue. This is not an individual problem or a matter of personal wellness. This is a vast and highly consequential public health problem on a planetary scale, and it demands our attention. The good news is that there are practical, concrete steps we can take, as individuals and as a people, to ease our stress and find a way forward. Tigers will continue to challenge us, but with some training, practice, and reflection, we can find a way to coexist and even flourish.

CHAPTER 5

STRATEGIES AND ANTIDOTES

Haunted by tigers of a thousand varieties, we're looking for relief and equanimity. The standard narrative gives us some useful suggestions, but we can do better. In the pages to follow, you'll find a series of lessons and ideas about how to make stress work for you. Some of these lessons are remedial, some are fundamental, and some, perhaps, are advanced. But in any case, they're all designed to give you some practical options for dealing with the stressors in your life.

As you'll see, the curriculum is multidisciplinary or, as some might put it, interdisciplinary. That's because no single discipline is up to the task. The human encounter with stress is messy and complex, and we can come at it from almost any direction: physiology, psychology, animal behavior, evolution, even philosophy. And ultimately, there can be no single solution, remedy, or antidote for what ails us. All of us are looking for reliable solutions, but given the diversity of human bodies, minds, and beliefs, the very same practice might be experienced in entirely different ways by people in different cultures. So much depends on who you are and where you stand—your history, your belief systems, and your relationships all make a difference.

Likewise, the lessons you'll find here are not exhaustive. As a study, it would take years, even lifetimes, to chase down all the details of anatomy, physiology, psychology, and philosophy that speak to our experience. Similarly, there can be no sharp division between our individual experience of stress and the stress that courses through our larger tribes, communities, and society. Each touches the other, and the experience is always contagious. And just as personal and systemic stresses feed off one another, so too should the solutions. In other words, our individual and large-scale solutions are, or should be, complementary. What we do for the part, we do for the whole.

PRIMAL REMEDIES

RETURN TO THE SOURCE

> We are not lacking in the dynamic forces needed to create the future. We live immersed in a sea of energy beyond all comprehension.
> —Thomas Berry, *The Great Work: Our Way into the Future*

In the standard narrative, stress is an unwelcome visitor that suddenly appears in our lives, disrupting our equanimity and driving us crazy. It's a problem of unfortunate circumstance, a confluence of toxic forces that converge on our minds and bodies. If we could just manipulate the external world and make it dance to our tune, all would be well.

But why are we so vulnerable to these stresses in the first place? Why do so many of us suffer and even buckle under the strain? Why do we find it so difficult to bounce back when we're struck down? Maybe the deeper problem isn't stress itself but our inability to endure ambiguity, uncertainty, and difficult circumstance.

In fact, we might well describe our problem as a general weakness that stems from a kind of primal amnesia. In the not-so-distant past, we were incredibly robust animals, just as strong and vital as any other primate in the wild. But today, we've forgotten how strong we really are. We've lost our deep connection with the great tree of life, so we struggle mightily, devising all sorts of clever and not-so-clever workarounds to calm our nerves and ease our suffering. But these "solutions" mostly fail and often only serve to increase our sense of alienation and isolation.

In a way, we're very much like the character Jason Bourne in the 2002 action movie *The Bourne Identity*. The protagonist, played by Matt Damon, is found floating in the Mediterranean Sea with two gunshot wounds in his back. On waking, he has no idea who he is or what his history might be, then spends the rest of the movie chasing down his true identity. But Bourne's amnesia is only partial; he retains his physicality, his martial art skills, and his fluency with language, weapons, and technology.

It's a great premise for a movie, but it's also a dead ringer for the modern human predicament. In our amnesia, we've lost contact with our native physicality and our identity as animals. We've forgotten the ancient, primal power that courses through every cell in our bodies, every minute of every day. We're sleepwalking through life, largely unaware of who we are or what we're capable of. It's no wonder we're suffering from so much disease and malaise; this primal amnesia is very much a disease in itself.

WHAT YOU BELIEVE MATTERS

If you want to be strong and resilient, it helps to identify and affiliate with something that's strong and resilient. Most of us, even kids, understand this intuitively. As we grow and develop, we're quick to attach our identity to powerful machines, powerful animals, and, sometimes, the forces of nature. Most obviously, sporting teams identify with robust animals, usually carnivores, predators, and raptors. And in the native and indigenous tradition, people often attach themselves to powerful totem animals and spirits.

So, if we can draw some psychophysical strength from powerful objects and animals around us, why not the totality of life herself? If a sporting team can draw power and resilience from a wolf, a bear, or a cougar, why not from the ecosystems that sustain them? If the Na'vi people depicted in the movie *Avatar* can draw power and resilience from their Hometree, shouldn't we be able to draw some psychophysical inspiration from the immensity of life on *our* Earth?

If we've learned anything from our studies of the placebo effect, it's that *belief matters*. If you believe that a pill, medical procedure, or alternative remedy is going to heal you, you're probably going to feel some relief.[58] If you believe that your body is simply a stand-alone organism with no connection to history and habitat, you're going to experience yourself as exposed, fragile, and vulnerable to every passing stressor. If you believe that your body is deeply, intimately integrated with the very fabric of life, going back billions of years, you're going to feel grounded, strong, and resilient.

In modern classrooms, biology is usually studied strictly as a secular science. Atoms and molecules come together to form organelles, then cells, tissues and organs, organisms, and populations. It's all mechanism, all the way down. But in fact, there are very real psychospiritual and health consequences that flow from the study and observation of life. We might even go so far as to describe biology as a spiritual practice—an exercise in remembering who we are. This is precisely what E. O. Wilson and Stephen R. Kellert suggested with their description of *biophilia*, our innate tendency to affiliate with life.[59]

In his landmark study *On the Origin of Species*, Darwin described the depth, immensity, and power of evolution by natural selection and concluded "there is grandeur in this view of life." But Darwin was being rather modest with his language. It's not just grandeur that we see in the history of plants and animals—it's an astonishing, mind-blowing sense of exuberance, resilience, creativity, and beauty. A unity in diversity, an immensely powerful force with the ability to suffer planet-scale setbacks and return with new forms and new possibilities. As Darwin might have put it, "there's outrageous strength and resilience in this view of life." This is the power that flows through us in every minute of every day.

INTERGENERATIONAL POWER

This all makes even more sense when we look at the way trauma and power can flow across generations. In the world of counseling, therapists understand how the process works. Intergenerational trauma was first identified among the grandchildren of Holocaust survivors.[60] In 1988, a study showed that these children were overrepresented in psychiatric referrals by 300 percent. Research has shown similar effects in indigenous populations.

For our purposes, the precise mechanism doesn't matter much. Intergenerational influence flows through a combination of epigenetic changes, parenting styles, culture, story, and people's sense of identity and meaning. Parents pay attention to the world in particular ways, which inevitably influence their children's learning and even the structure of their brains. Families are biological and psychological systems, and no generation is an island. Influence is inevitable.

But if trauma can be passed to future generations, shouldn't it be the case that a sense of personal and physical power might be passed down? Shouldn't we also be talking about intergenerational resilience? Indeed, a 2017 study published in *Frontiers in Psychology* found "promising results supporting the concept of intergenerational resilience transmission."[61] If parents demonstrate a sense of strength and power, it's likely that their children will as well. And if one generation feels emotionally connected to the power and immensity of life, it's probable that the next generation will too.

JOG YOUR MEMORY

But how would we feel if we suddenly woke up to the immense power that flows through our bodies? What would it be like to suddenly feel the immensity of biological evolution flowing through your spirit and your life? To use a wildly overused word in a perfectly appropriate context, it would be *awesome*. Our bodies would be transformed, awakened, energized. Every living thing would be an ally, every ecosystem a partner. With the totality of biological evolution at our backs, we'd be surfers on a magnificent, living, blue-green wave.

So, how do we do it? How do we refresh our memory and our intimacy with life? Two essential elements are necessary for this remembering to take place: experience and imagination. Or to put it another way, we might say *exposure* and imagination. In other words, we've got to put our bodies in contact with the living world, and we've got to think deeply about the depth of our connection and, above all, feel the natural world around us.

Obviously, going outdoors is an essential prerequisite. But while it's necessary, it's not sufficient. Simply going out for a stroll in the park with your phone might well be pleasant, but it's not going to change much of anything. Instead, we've got to get serious about our outdoor time. Leave your phone behind. Let go of the internal chatter that obscures your sense of plants, animals, soil, and weather. Direct your attention to all things living, and you'll begin to get the feeling. Feel the depth and power of biological history as it flows through even the most modest plants and animals around you. Take your time. Abandon the trivia of the modern world, and you'll be left with the raw, essential experience you're looking for.

FEEL THE AWE

> If I had influence with the good fairy . . . I should ask that her gift to each child in the world be a sense of wonder so indestructible that it would last throughout life.
> —Rachel Carson, *The Sense of Wonder*

When the tigers come around, one of our most natural responses is to get out, find a trail somewhere, and just walk. Surrounded by trees, vistas, and natural features, we relax. After an hour or so or, even better, a few days, we can return to our stressful settings, refreshed and ready to have another go of it. But what is it about nature that helps us feel better? It's the fresh air, of course, the rhythmic movement, the physical contact with the ground, and the room to move, but even more fundamentally, it might be the sense of awe we feel when immersed in the big outside.

It's an intriguing possibility. Work by Professor Dacher Keltner at the University of California, Berkeley, shows that even a mild sense of awe can change attitudes and inspire prosocial behavior.[62] People who watched an awe-inspiring nature video were subsequently more ethical and generous and described themselves as being more connected to others—qualities that are commonplace in indigenous traditions. Keltner's team also found that awe makes people happier and less stressed, even weeks later. Similarly, a study by Jennifer E. Stellar and colleagues found that "positive emotions, especially awe, are associated with lower levels of proinflammatory cytokines."[63]

Research by psychologists at Stanford and the University of Minnesota also shows that awe can increase well-being by giving people the sense that they have more time available, a condition known as "temporal affluence." Keltner and Jonathan Haidt have also argued that awe is the ultimate collective emotion because it motivates people to do things that enhance the greater good.[64] Research reported in the *Journal of Personality and Social Psychology* provides empirical support for this claim.[65] The authors found that awe helps people bind to one another, motivating us to act in collaborative ways that enable strong groups and cohesive communities. Which of course is an ideal quality for both ancestral and modern life.

It sounds like a perfect remedy. Awe activates the parasympathetic nervous system, which works to calm the fight-flight response and dampen the production of toxic stress hormones. It also improves creativity and helps us break out of habitual thinking patterns. In other words, putting ourselves in contact with nature's magnificence is really good for us. We might even say that awe is a form of medicine.

Sadly, modern culture generally fails to appreciate how this works. To be sure, more and more people are going outdoors, and trailheads are often packed with cars and people. But time in nature is often presented and even sold to us as something that's good for our personal, individual health. Go out and take a hike or a bike ride because it'll soothe your personal life, heal your body, and cure whatever ails you. It'll lower your blood pressure, reduce your blood sugar, maintain your muscle mass, and generally make your body work better.

But as usual, this orientation is focused almost entirely on the individual, and in that sense, it might even be described as "nature for narcissism." Go out and experience the natural world because it'll make you stronger, fitter, more attractive, and all the rest. Harness the power of nature to make a better you. Nature—sometimes described as "vitamin N"— becomes just another supplement, an aid to personal growth and development.

This orientation reaches its apex in the world of adventure sport, where nature is simply another thing to be conquered. Nature is just another gym, only bigger. Run, climb, bike, or swim as fast as you possibly can—dominate the terrain, set some records, and be a champion. In this, nature is nothing more than a platform for our personal greatness. Slowing down and actually experiencing the qualities of the natural world are simply out of the question. Performance is the only thing that matters.

All of which is rather grotesque. If nature is simply a vitamin supplement or a backdrop for our own personal grandeur, it only reinforces our sense of self and, in turn, separates us further from the natural world. To really appreciate the totality, the reach, the scope, and the magnificence of the natural world, we've got to be small and we've got to slow down. Nature isn't there *for* us. It's not a tapestry for our personal or species-level greatness. In other words, you can't *feel* the awe if you're trying to *be* the awe. Or as one quip has it, "You climb the mountain to see the world, not so the world can see you."

HUMILITY AND THE AWE GAP

For those of us who've grown up in narcissistic modern cultures, the power of awe may seem perfectly counterintuitive. Most of us like feeling big and celebrating our status as the alpha species or as alpha individuals, but awe in natural settings does its work in reverse. It shrinks the ego and, in turn, leaves more space in our consciousness for the rest of creation. Incredibly, this is actually measurable in research settings. Keltner found that, when test subjects were awe inspired, they actually signed their names smaller and drew themselves smaller. Other researchers have found that people who watched awe-inspiring videos estimated their bodies to be physically smaller than those who watched neutral videos.[66]

All of which should give us pause. When we reflect on the radical differences between ancestral and modern environments, we're struck by what we might call an "awe gap." In a normal, outdoor, Paleo world, the experience of awe would have been commonplace. Our ancestors were in daily contact with the magnificence and enormity of nature; thunderstorms, lightning displays, and animal dramas played out in real time, right before our eyes—life and blood on the grassland, fighting and fleeing just outside our camps. With no light pollution, the night sky would have blazed with an intensity that modern humans can scarcely imagine. And around a tribe's local habitat, vast reaches of unknown territory stretched to the horizon, home to anything a person might imagine. In other words, awe was a daily, health-promoting, prosocial experience.

But today, fewer and fewer of us even go outside, and when we do, most of our parks are highly domesticated, regulated, noisy, and light polluted. Our modern experience of awe— such as it is—mostly derives from our contact with technological devices and spectacular special effects in the movies that we watch. This is massively reinforced by corporate marketing that attempts to attach our sense of awe to various products

and services. In other words, our modern sense of awe is produced and managed—a pale, manufactured imitation of the
real thing.

And of course, pandemic lockdowns made everything
worse. Isolated in our homes, it became almost impossible to
put ourselves in contact with nature's magnificence. Awe—
and the health benefits that come with it—have been increasingly difficult to come by. We might even describe ourselves
as "awe deprived." We don't hear much about this condition
in the popular press, but judging from the research, it's safe to
assume that this is a genuine challenge to public health and a
medical condition in its own right.

The obvious solution is to get outside—way outside. Get
out of yourself and into your habitat, expose yourself to the
outrageous, overwhelming power of sky, earth, wind, and
water. City parks and green spaces are all well and good, but to
really find the awe, you've got to expose your body and spirit
to the enormity of the living earth. Go big. Backpacking, river
rafting, even extended road trips into remote areas are ideal.
Try for one each season, or one every year at least. When it
comes to experiencing the awe of the natural world, more is
almost always better.

Likewise, don't allow yourself to be content with the artificial awe that's forced on us in nearly every waking moment.
Even if you can't get outside, you can still find awe in the study
of human history and the depth and variety of the human
experience. The great sagas of adventure, discovery, and the
search for meaning can give us a sense of the enormity and
magnificence of our world. Then, as soon as you're able, go to
the big places, so you can feel really small. As the legendary
deep ecologist Arnae Naess put it, "the smaller we come to feel
ourselves compared to the mountain, the nearer we come to
participating in its greatness."[67]

BRANCH OUT

> My turn shall also come: I sense the spreading
> of a wing.
>
> —Osip Mandelstam, *The Selected Poems*

As we've seen, our dominant experience of stress is contraction. When the cortisol hits the fan, our minds and spirits narrow to meet the demands of the moment, and even our bodies begin to collapse. Posture becomes chronically flexed and compacted, compressing the abdomen and our ability to breathe comfortably. Our range of curiosity and even our vocabulary begin to shrink as we focus on immediate dangers. Even our social circles begin to contract as we avoid challenging new ideas and unusual people with diverse views. If the process continues long enough, our lives eventually become small, brittle, and even dangerous.

The remedy is expansion and dilation. When we relax, the world gets bigger. Possibilities expand, and options proliferate. Even the body begins to feel bigger. The spaces inside our chest and abdomen feel cavernous as our breath expands. Even the space inside our limbs begins to feel more voluminous. Our hearts literally feel bigger as our sense of empathy and compassion grows. Our attention and curiosity extend to the horizon as we begin to wonder about things that might be. No longer obsessed with predators in the bushes, our imagination soars.

All of which is consistent with everything we know about biological life. That is, it's the very nature of nature to expand, branch, and reach out. In the *Origin of Species*, Darwin wrote beautifully about the "copiously branching bush":

> The affinities of all the beings of the same class have sometimes been represented by a great tree . . . As buds give rise by growth to fresh buds, and these if vigorous, branch out and

overtop on all sides many a feebler branch,
so by generation I believe it has been with the
great Tree of Life, which fills with its dead
and broken branches the crust of the earth,
and covers the surface with its ever branching
and beautiful ramifications.[68]

In other words, our natural inclination, shaped by our ancestry as living creatures, is to reach, branch, and expand. And in this, our guiding principle for stress relief might well come down to three simple words: "Be like life." Imitate the living world and grow.

MEET THE DENDRITIC ARBOR

Expansion, reaching, growing, extending—these are qualities we associate with relaxation, exuberance, learning, and psychospiritual health. But there's a neurological reality to all of this as well, and an intriguing analog to our lived experience. Just imagine what we'd see if we took a microscopic journey inside the human brain: dense clusters of nerve cells, looking and behaving very much like rain forests, branching and connecting in a million directions. Under the right conditions, these nerve fibers, dendrites, and synapses proliferate as the dendritic arbor grows denser and more expansive. In effect, the neural bushes become bushier, establishing ever more powerful webs of communication that link the entire system together into a single vibrant whole.

Not only is this arborization a neurological reality, it also serves as a perfect metaphor for the kind of conditions we're trying to create for the human animal. If we nurture human lives with play, movement, social contact, and enrichment, we stimulate the growth of neurons and the overall function of the human organism. Grow the forest, reach out, expand, branch, and connect. This is a master formula for brains, bodies, and biospheres.

The arborization of the brain is driven by a variety of compounds, hormones, and informational substances. Most famously, advocates for physical exercise point to neurotrophic factors that are produced in response to vigorous physical activity, sometimes described as "Miracle-Gro for the brain." Flood the dendritic arbor with these compounds and you'll get expansion, branching, and growth.[69]

As for the stress hormones, the situation is nuanced and divergent. At low levels, cortisol stimulates the arbor to grow, but once the concentration crosses the tipping point, the very same hormones act like herbicides or defoliants. Flood the brain with these chemicals and you'll get a contraction of the arbor and, in turn, a substantial loss of connectivity in the neural net.

At this point, it's impossible to avoid the comparison on a planetary scale. By relentlessly cutting down tropical rain forests, we are in effect destroying the dendritic arbor of the Earth or, as some might put it, Gaia's brain. It's hard to know precisely what the consequences will be, but the metaphor is ominous. When you cut back the arbor, you cut back essential connectivity and communication and, in turn, impoverish the entire system. This does not bode well for the health of the tropics nor of the planet as a whole.

OUR RESILIENT BRAINS

All this talk about expansion and contraction may give rise to some concern, especially when we think about the neurological consequences of chronic stress. *If cortisol and other stress hormones inhibit the arborization of my brain, what does this mean if I find myself stuck in stressful circumstances beyond my control? What if I'm continuously under assault by tigers? Is this going to damage my brain? Should I be freaking out?* The short answer is almost certainly not. The human brain, like any forest, has immense regenerative powers. Stress hormones can and do beat back the dendritic arbor, but the process is rarely permanent. In fact, this rhythmic cycling of inhibition and growth is a normal part of human life. Branches and dendrites get pruned back during times of stress, but they grow back, especially when nurtured with plenty of sleep, human touch, and good living conditions.

Like the body, the dendritic arbor is resilient. Yes, you'll probably suffer some loss of connectivity during a chronic stress experience, and your performance will probably suffer as a result. But growth will return and connections will reestablish themselves. This is all perfectly normal. Just remember, you are a fantastically resilient animal. Your body and your brain can suffer substantial, even crushing, stress and still find a way to rebound in good order. Even when the brain's arbor is marinating in cortisol, forces of rejuvenation remain and will burst forth as soon as conditions improve. Trust this process; the body knows what it's doing.

EXPERIENTIAL DESIGN

All of this suggests a new kind of job description for teachers, therapists, coaches, trainers, and parents. No matter the specific profession or discipline, your objective is to act as an experiential designer, to create the right kind of conditions for expansion—physical, neurological, and spiritual—to take place. Or to put it another way, set your people up to arborize their brains, bodies, and imagination. Give them an environment where they can reach, expand, branch, and connect.

We do this by creating a sense of safety. Students, clients, patients are going to be challenged, so they should feel that they're going to be supported in the process. Make this clear. Give their bodies some vagility and the ability to move. Give them a chance to maintain continuity with their primal life-supporting systems of tribe and habitat. Dial back on the urgency, and give people time to explore. Give them an opportunity to experience challenge, adventure, and risk in what we might call a "safe emergency." Let them experience some tigers, but do it little by little.

As experiential designers, we'd like to set up our programs and facilities to encourage engagement and expanded curiosity about the world, but sadly, our culture seems to be headed the other way entirely. What we see in many schools and workplaces actually inhibits arborization and expansion. Many elements work in opposition to the branching and expansion we're seeking: chronic anxiety and judgment, social ambiguity and confusion, adventure and risk deprivation.

All of which adds up to what we might call the contraction curriculum of the modern world. If the expansion curriculum is like springtime in the brain, the contraction curriculum is like a tough autumn and winter. The cold is relentless and the dendritic arbors are shrinking back toward the Earth. The human brain and spirit want to expand and grow, but when conditions are hostile, it's unlikely to happen.

AN EXPANSION MEDITATION

The following meditation is written to promote integration, not just within the body but also between the body and the entire range of life on Earth. It's a powerful antidote to the sense of anxiety, separation, and isolation that we often feel in the modern world. It's excellent for yoga classes and good for insomnia as well. If you're alone, just read the list slowly and sink into each image. Or record it to audio and play it back. If you're leading a group, have your people sit comfortably and read the prompts in a soft voice. Take it slow, pausing at the end of each line, and improvise as desired. Give people the chance to feel and connect through their imagination . . .

> Begin by focusing your attention on your breath . . .
> Next, expand your attention to include your entire body in the act of breathing. Every cell in your body is participating in every breath.
> Feel all of this . . .
> If you get distracted, don't worry. Just return to your breath and trust your body. It knows what to do . . .
> Now, widen your attention to include the breath of the people or animals that are near you.
> Breathe with them . . .
> Next, extend your attention to people who are farther away, in the distant reaches of your city, your state, and your country.
> Breathe with them . . .
> Now, broaden your attention further to include the breath of all people, all human beings on the planet.
> You are a part of this . . .
> Next, broaden your attention to include the breath of all the animals of the Earth . . .
> The dogs and cats in your home and your neighborhood . . .
> The coyotes and wolves in your bioregion . . .
> The mice and marmots, the beavers and otters that swim in the lakes and rivers . . .

The deer and elk and antelope grazing in the mountains . . .
The lions and leopards and cougars resting in the shade . . .
The primates, the chimps, the bonobos, the gorillas, and the monkeys, all breathing . . .
You are a part of this . . .
Next, broaden your attention to include the breath of all the marine mammals of the Earth . . .
The orcas and the humpbacks, diving deep and coming up again . . .
The porpoises, the dolphins, the seals, and the sea lions . . .
You are a part of this as well . . .
Next, broaden your attention to include all the plants of the Earth and their waves of respiration . . .
Feel the breath of the great rain forests, the vast canopies, the ferns and vines, and the understory . . .
Feel the grasses around the world, springing forth at every opportunity, reaching out for light and moisture . . .
Feel the soil itself, growing deeper and richer in waves . . .
Even the plankton in the oceans must surely have its breath . . .
You are a part of this as well . . .
Now, broaden your attention to include the water of the planet and its breath-like movement . . .
The evaporation from vast oceans . . .

The condensation into swirling, pulsing
clouds . . .
The rain and snowfall across the Earth . . .
Now, broaden your attention to the breath-
like changes of the seasons in northern and
southern hemispheres . . .
Spring to summer, summer to fall, fall to
winter . . .
Feel the biosphere expanding and con-
tracting in its voyage around the sun . . .
All life breathing, living, thriving . . .
All life is one.
And you are a part of this . . .

SOMATIC SOLUTIONS

MOVE

The body says what words cannot.
—Martha Graham[70]

In conventional prescriptions for stress relief, we're usually
counseled to "get some exercise," and it's generally offered
as a magic bullet that will cure nearly everything that ails
us. And to be sure, there are many perfectly good reasons to
believe that exercise will help us feel better, but unfortunately,
the standard prescription often gets us off on the wrong foot.
That's because "exercise" is actually a modern invention and,
strictly speaking, isn't even part of the original, historically
normal human repertoire.

This may sound like a case of splitting hairs, but in fact,
there's an important reality here. That is, *exercise* is a product

of the modern industrial revolution, something we can tell just by looking: gyms that look suspiciously like factories, with treadmills and machines in perfect rows, people tracking every rep with digital devices. But historically speaking, this is all profoundly abnormal. Prior to the industrial age, people got plenty of physical movement in the course of their daily lives. First by hunting and gathering, walking, and occasionally running and then by dance, agriculture, and craft. For the vast majority of our history, we've been moving our bodies, entirely without the help of gyms, machines, amplified music, or personal trainers.

The same holds true for nonhuman animals. We never observe other mammals doing anything resembling exercise. They hunt, gather, graze, mate, play, fight, and flee, but they never perform repetitive movements for the sake of "staying in shape." They move their bodies for pleasure, to play, to explore, or to stay alive, but otherwise, they eat or rest.

This suggests a broader view and a new appreciation for context. When we exercise, we engage in a physical specialization, but when we move, we put ourselves back into community with every animal that's ever lived. Instead of isolating ourselves in specialized facilities with specialized machines, we're sharing in a common experience with every primate and every mammal, a deep heritage that goes back more than a hundred million years. When we move our bodies, we celebrate our kinship with the natural world and make ourselves part of something much, much larger than ourselves.

And it's movement, not exercise, that keeps us healthy. Across the board, research shows that all forms of physical movement are health promoting and that exercise is only one possibility among many. This realization leads us to a powerful general principle: when it comes to maintaining health, *exercise is optional, but movement is essential.* No one ever died from lack of exercise, but a lack of physical movement is absolutely dangerous to health. As long as we're getting vigorous movement during the course of our days, we might just as well skip the exercise altogether. Instead of setting aside big chunks of time to perform stereotyped exercise in specialized facilities, our challenge is to weave movement back into the fabric of our daily lives. If we can make our lives more vigorous overall, our health will largely take care of itself.

FEEL A SENSE OF CONTROL

In conventional conversations about exercise (aka movement), advocates are quick to list the medical and physiological benefits: decreased blood pressure, improved blood chemistry, increased metabolism, stronger muscles, and improved brain function. But it's actually the damage-and-repair cycle brought on by vigorous movement that really builds our strength and replenishes our reservoirs of resilience.

Physical movement unleashes a flood of waste products and unstable oxygen molecules that compromise cellular function. In the hours that follow, the body begins to repair the damage with anti-inflammatory and cleanup responses. This repair process is incredibly robust and has benefits that extend beyond the original tissue damage. In turn, the physiological rebound makes everything stronger, and since everything in the mind-body is connected, it makes sense to assume that the postexercise recovery will boost our psychological fortitude as well.

These advantages are very real, but there's another dimension to exercise/movement we often fail to appreciate. That is, physical movement has profound psychological benefits in the way it increases our sense of control in the world. It's easy to imagine how this works. Choose an exercise of any type, and think about how it feels in practice. Strength training is the most obvious example: lifting heavy weight builds muscle, bone, and other tissue, but in the very act of lifting, we feel that we are competent, even powerful, actors in the world. We are taking control of our situation and our lives. Cardio does it too, in a slightly different way, but no matter the form, it's all about developing our sense of agency and effectiveness.

HAVE A MOVEMENT SNACK

In conventional circles, we're accustomed to talking about exercise as something that's performed at particular times as part of something called a "workout." But this, too, is a rather abnormal idea; we simply cannot imagine our hunting and gathering ancestors doing anything like it. Why should our animal physicality be concentrated in a single burst, in a single place, at a particular time of day? Something about the whole concept sounds suspiciously modern and even alien.

A better idea is to distribute our movement throughout the day in something we might call "movement snacks." The idea here is to keep updating our connection with the body, to keep refreshing our sense of physicality and control. These movement snacks provide an essential break in the action that can reverse the effects of cognitive overload, chronic postural flexion, and the sedentary blues.

All you need is a small open area and maybe a medicine ball if you've got one. A few simple moves—arm swings, squats, and lunges—for just a few minutes at a time will bring your body-mind back into integration. You'll get your breathing turned on and your metabolism up and running. For best results, repeat often and don't sweat over what your coworkers might happen to think.

Here are some simple shapes to get you started. Don't worry about the details. Just grab a medicine ball and get moving. If you mix and match these shapes with variations in stance, steps, speed, and intensity, you'll find thousands of combinations to keep you moving:

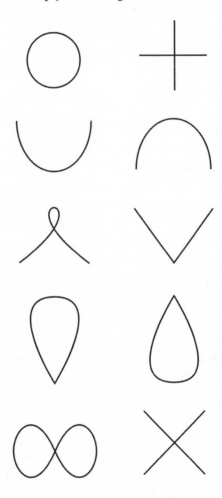

REFRESH YOUR PHYSICALITY

Ultimately, the big idea here is not to "get in shape." The point is not fitness, or even athletic performance. The idea is not to lose weight or make yourself look a certain way. Rather, the point is to remember your animal vitality, your intrinsic resilience, your physical capability, and your exuberance. Everything else is something of a sideshow. The ultimate goal—the primal objective—is to stimulate our physicality, or as the saying goes, "get back into your body." Specifically, reestablish the mind-body unity that's been disrupted by the acute or chronic stress experience of our modern, alien environment.

This changes everything. Suddenly, the details fade away as the animal comes into focus. It doesn't matter how many calories you're burning or what your heart rate happens to be. It doesn't matter what kind of shoes you're wearing, how fast you're going, how much you're lifting, or what your electronic device has to say about it all. What matters is how you *feel*. If you can feel the signal of a strong, vigorous animal body in action, you're doing it right.

All of which leads us to question some of the prevailing thinking about the value of exercise/movement. In some modern quarters, advocates are quick to tell us that exercise/movement will improve our cognitive function and, in turn, make us better students or employees. This may well be true, but it's a fatal distraction from the real objective. That is, the point of moving your body is *not* to score higher on a standardized test or to get a better evaluation on workplace efficiency. The point is to become a better animal.

BREATHE

> All the principles of heaven and earth are living inside you. . . . Everything in heaven and earth breathes. Breath is the thread that ties creation together.
> —Morihei Ueshiba, founder of aikido

When the tigers come around, we get tense. Something big is about to go down, so the body gets ready for action and physical engagement with the world. The autonomic nervous system shifts resources away from what Robert Sapolsky describes as "long-term rebuilding projects" and over to the urgent demands of the moment, especially muscular activation.

In the process, our normal feed-and-breed pattern of deep, rhythmic breathing often gets left behind. In the short term, this is of minor consequence, but when our shallow, fight-flight breathing pattern becomes habitual and chronic, our health and our happiness begin to suffer. And so, the popular recommendation is to work with the breath—to practice deep, diaphragmatic breathing to bring us back into a feed-and-breed state of mind and body.

On the face of it, this sounds like sensible advice that's worth our time. On the other hand, we might well wonder, Isn't this a part of normal animal behavior? Wouldn't this all be obvious to nonhuman animals and people from body-friendly cultures? As animals, we're wired to breathe, and in theory at least, none of us should need instruction of any kind. Other mammals would laugh at our physical ignorance. Even the family dog knows enough to breathe deeply after a high-stress encounter. It's just what animals do.

But here in the modern world, we've drifted from our ancestral ways. Our amnesia is now so deep that we've forgotten even the most basic fundamentals. So yes, some remedial instruction may be called for. The good news is that it's easy and immediately rewarding. Every time we breathe deeply, we tilt the autonomic teeter-totter a little more toward the healing state of rest-and-digest and, in the process, replenish our reservoirs of resilience.

THE DOME IN THE CENTER OF YOUR BODY

This is where it helps to know some anatomy. The breath is powered in large measure by the diaphragm, perhaps the most amazing muscle in the body. It's an incredible structure, a dome between the thoracic cavity and the abdominal cavity. It attaches to your lower ribs all the way around and even to the front of your lumbar spine.

But the diaphragm isn't the only player in the breath; the pattern of muscular activation is yin-yang. That is, muscular agonists and antagonists work in a complementary pattern. On inhalation, the diaphragm contracts and pushes down onto the abdominal organs. But for this to work, the abdominal muscles themselves need to relax. On exhalation, it's just the opposite: the abdominal muscles contract while the diaphragm relaxes.

It's an elegant system, but there's a lot more to it than simply moving air. Every time you contract and relax your diaphragm, you're also massaging your internal organs and moving fluid through your abdominal cavity. This may sound rather strange, as we're accustomed to thinking of massage as something for our backs and limbs, administered by a friendly person in a relaxed setting. But the fact is that organs like it too. The abdomen is packed with neurons and touch sensors, and it makes sense to suppose that a gentle, rhythmic touch of the diaphragm would have big benefits for the whole animal. In essence, every intentional breath is a conversation, a dialogue with the nervous system. This is where the real mind-body action is.

YOUR ATHLETIC BREATH

There are dozens of styles, methods, and ideas about what constitutes "good breathing," and it's easy to be consumed with the idea that there's a particular "right way" to do it. And perhaps, in some settings, it makes sense to practice in a particular way.

But for general health and happiness, the details don't matter much.

In fact, we'd do better to think of the breath in athletic terms. That is, we don't need the diaphragm to do one particular thing; we want it to be strong, agile, and capable of whatever kind of contraction and relaxation the moment calls for. Sometimes we want it to move deep and slow, to help us feel relaxed. Other times, we're lifting a heavy weight, and we want all the muscles of the abdominal core, including the diaphragm, to contract together. This raises the intra-abdominal pressure—a bubble in the center of your body—that helps support your lumbar spine.

All of which argues for a diversity of practice. Do some belly breathing; do some breath holds; do some short, fast breathing. And especially, do some long, sustained, slow inhalations and exhalations. It's all good.

BREATHE YOUR WHOLE BODY

As most of us have heard, the ideal breathing pattern for stimulating the rest-and-digest response is a belly breath. Typically, we're instructed to lie on the floor, put a hand on the belly, and feel the rise and fall with each cycle of breath. It's easy, but the important thing is to synchronize and feel the mind-breath connection. The idea is not to drive or force the breath but to move the mind, attention, and breath together. Stay connected as much as possible. If you get distracted, no worries. Just return to your breath.

When working with the breath, it's easy to assume that the action is all about the diaphragm, the ribs, and the lungs, but the interconnections in the body run deep; it's safe to say that the entire body is involved in the process. To get the feeling, lie down on the floor and try this exercise:

1. Start by simply feeling your belly get big on the inhale.
2. On the next inhalation, feel your chest get into the act.
3. Next, breathe into your back. Now, you're really three-dimensional.
4. Now, recruit even more of your body.
5. Feel deep into your lower abdomen, then higher into your chest and neck . . .
6. Then, all the vast, expansive spaces inside your limbs.
7. Now, you're breathing with every cell in your body.
8. Breathe in the entire power of the biosphere, the vitality of life herself. Imagine clouds and wind, entire atmospheres of circulation. There's gobs of energy out there. Feel it, and welcome it into your body.
9. Next, a whole-body exhale, one big act of letting go. If you're lying down, just sink in and let the floor do all the work of supporting you. With every exhalation, relinquish anything you might be holding on to.

TARGET YOUR BREATH

The abdomen is home base for the breath, but in another sense, we can direct our attention and our breath anywhere we want. This is common practice in the world of massage and body-work, where your therapist might ask you to "breathe into" your shoulder, neck, or hip. Your diaphragm is still doing most of the work, but there seems to be a palpable benefit when we focus our breathing on a particular area, especially a joint or muscle that's in pain.

This focused breathing seems to relax the entire nervous system and provides some relief. Strictly speaking, your painful knee isn't really involved in the process of moving air in and out of your lungs, but when we "breathe into" that area, it's as if we're showing the body and brain that it's OK to feel this place, that it's safe to experience this joint, this muscle, this area of the body. It's no longer necessary to divert our attention or "think away." And if practiced repeatedly, it teaches the body to bring more resources to bear on the area in question.

The process should even work outside the boundary of our skin. Think about something outside your body that's causing you pain—a relationship, an obligation, an upcoming event, or an expectation. Now, breathe into it. Strictly speaking, there's no mechanical causality or relationship there, but by breathing into that painful experience or memory, you're breaking the mental association of fear and tension, teaching the body that it's OK to feel what you're feeling. There's no need to fight or flee; the thing is OK as is. The effect may be subtle and short-lived, and you'll probably still have to address the issue on other levels as well, but at least your body won't be quite so reactive. So, think about what's bugging you and breathe into it.

BE A BREATH OPPORTUNIST

Because breath is so intimately familiar, it's easy to forget the whole thing. Or we find ourselves relying on some particular time and place to pay attention. We work on our breath in yoga class or on the massage table, but otherwise, we mostly ignore it. But there's no reason to exile our breath work into particular settings. Instead, become a "breath opportunist"; look for ways to reweave thoughtful breathing back into the fabric of your everyday life.

The trick is to associate your breath with some event or idea that comes up often: First thing every morning and/or last thing before bed. Before and after every session at your desk. Before every big decision. Before every movement session. Every time you see clouds in the sky, every time you see the trees blowing in the wind. Every time you think about politics. Every time you see someone else take a big breath. Every time your dog relaxes and yawns.

The specifics don't matter. What matters is the doing. When in doubt, when in distress, when you've got a moment, shift your attention to your breath. It's easy, free, and powerful.

HIBERNATION MEDITATION

This meditation is particularly good if you're having trouble falling asleep:

> Imagine this . . .
>
> A distant northern mountain range, deep in winter, late at night. The sky's ablaze with stars and northern lights. Not a sound.
>
> In those mountains, there's a cirque, a U-shaped bowl with high peaks all around. And in that bowl, buried under a deep blanket of snow, lies a sloth of hibernating bears, warm in their dens, curled up, heads on paws.
>
> Their bodies are dormant and relaxed, their metabolism slowed to a crawl. Their breath comes ever so slowly, smoothly, just enough to feed the body. Long slow inhales, long slow exhales.
>
> Feel this breath.
>
> Stretch it out.
>
> The cirque is a refuge and a sanctuary.
>
> You're safe and comfortable in your den.

Time has very nearly stopped.
Breathe with the bears.

MEDITATE

In a moment of stopping, we break the spell
between past result and automatic reaction.
When we pause, we can notice the actual
experience, the pain or pleasure, fear or excite-
ment. In the stillness before our habits arise,
we become free to act wisely.
—Jack Kornfield, *The Wise Heart*

Chaos, confusion, complexity—the lions and tigers and bears of
our modern world are everywhere it seems. Every day another
round of tasks, urgencies, and responsibilities that must be
attended to. We try to keep up with it all by multitasking, but
most of us have gotten the memo from the neuroscience community by now. That is, the brain only attends to one thing at
a time. When we attempt to manage multiple tasks simultaneously, the brain simply increases speed in switching from one
point of attention to another. In moderation, we can manage it,
but this rapid alternation of attention eventually takes a toll on
the whole mind-body. Over the course of months and years, we
become increasingly vulnerable to stress and, in turn, exhaustion and depression.

Overwhelmed by modern life and frustrated with conventional approaches, many of us turn to meditation for relief.
Research suggests that regular practice reduces inflammation,
lowers cortisol, and reduces anxiety, depression, anger, and
fatigue. It also stimulates the vagus nerve, a powerful player in
the autonomic nervous system that helps with healing, tissue
repair, inflammation control, and psychophysical rejuvenation.

The list of benefits is impressive, but once again, it's important to frame our discussion in the right way. In our highly individualistic culture, meditation is often presented as a means to self-improvement, but this may actually be a step in the wrong direction. That is, the very act of trying to improve ourselves strengthens our sense of self, which sets us up for more duality and, in turn, conflict and anxiety. A better approach would be to think of meditation as a practice of nonself. We aren't trying to make ourselves better; we're trying to let go of our ego and merge ourselves with the world. When we succeed, we experience less self, less duality, and, thus, less suffering.

In any case, meditation gives us a chance to step outside the complexity of our normal, daily lives and observe exactly what we're up to. In the process, it gives us an increased understanding of our bodies and our experience. When we allow the chattering, judgmental mind to come to rest, we begin to actually feel what we're feeling. As we let go of the noise of the modern world, we begin to feel the life coursing through our bodies, via the breath.

From a mind-body point of view, the power of meditation lies in the experiential proof that we can coexist with ourselves. We sit quietly for a while, and behold—nothing bad happens. Our minds might get distracted, and we might waste some time ruminating on the dramas in our lives, but these things tend to fade away. In turn, it eventually begins to dawn on us that it's not really necessary to spend every waking moment running away from ourselves or our predicaments. It's not necessary to surround ourselves with distraction and compulsive activity. It's OK to just be.

The beauty of regular meditation practice is that it takes us deeper into the human experience. Some teachers say meditation is all about being in the present moment, but we might also say it's like going back in time, all the way to the preliterate, preverbal days of deep history. Once we let go of our verbal soundtrack and mental ruminations, we return to our primal, ancestral experience. We return to the Great Integrity, the Tao, the time before words. We return to our normal, aboriginal state of mind.

The experience is calming, but it's far more than even that. When we abandon our internal chatter and focus on our bodies and our breath, we might even feel a sense of reunification with the totality of life on Earth and all the power that goes with it. When we relinquish our compulsive narration about our troubles, we're left with a direct experience of a body that's literally millions of years old and continuous with all life. This takes us out of our isolation and back into integration. In this sense, the medical benefits of meditation pale in comparison. Reducing your blood pressure is undoubtedly a good thing, but even better is the chance to unite with the totality of life itself.

LET IT BE

Unfortunately, meditation is often presented as a complex, daunting practice that takes decades to master. There are dozens of styles, hundreds of books, thousands of teachers, and, according to some, layer upon layer of sophistication. This diversity makes for some interesting conversation, but it also distracts us from the essential simplicity we're trying to nurture.

In fact, there's no wrong way to do it. As one meditation teacher puts it, "Just sit down, shut up, and pay attention." Turn off your phone and abandon your concerns about work, your to-do list, and all the things nagging at your mind. Forget about proper posture, breathing technique, attention, mindfulness, compassion, and loving kindness, at least for the moment. Keep it as simple as you can. As you relax, focus your attention on your breath, your most intimate ally, a safe and reliable friend that will show you the way to equanimity and calm.

Of course, if you're anything like a normal human being, your attention will begin to wander almost immediately, and this is the moment of truth. If you try to strong-arm your attention back to your breath, you'll simply produce more noise and wind up even further away from your target. But passivity also fails. If you simply allow yourself to be swept up in whatever thoughts and imagery your mind cooks up, you'll never learn how to stabilize your attention. You'll simply have a nice daydreaming session.

The tricky part is that distraction feeds on itself. We drift off our focal point, and each thought generates another association, memory, or image. Before we know it, we're light-years from our original intent. The solution, as the Buddhists point out, is compassion. There's nothing to be gained by abusing yourself for getting distracted. Every time you drift off target, you get another chance to practice.

So, stick with it. When distraction intrudes on your experience, relax. Don't try to change anything. As Pema Chödrön, author of *When Things Fall Apart*, advises, "soften and stay." Relinquish effort, but maintain focus. Note the pain, the distraction, and the emotion, then return to your breath. Observe the way your mind goes on journeys into the past and future. Observe the chatter, the commentary, and the random images that appear as if from nowhere. Observe all this, and return your attention to your breath.

Whatever you do, keep it simple. In the popular imagination, many of us are inclined to imagine that meditation is a path to some kind of higher, altered state of consciousness, and some of us seek it out precisely for this reason. We want the special thing, the extraordinary state of awareness that will take us to a new level of experience. Just as with almost everything else in the modern world, we want the exceptional, the incredible, and the elite.

But we've got it entirely backward. Meditation is not an altered, exceptional state; it's our normal state. It's our frenzied, anxious modern condition that's the altered state. When we meditate, we simply return to our historically normal, Paleo condition of mind and body. In other words, the meditative state—being still and feeling the breath—is the baseline, the reference point. It's a safe home base. It's who we are.

So, instead of reaching for something rare and astonishing, maybe we'd do better to reach for something modest. Don't worry about sophistication, advanced techniques, or mystical experiences. Stick with simplicity. It's reliable, accessible, and effective.

Of course, most of us claim to be too busy to bother with any of this. The practice takes time and produces no immediate, spectacular payoff, so we simply avoid it in favor of more impulsive activity. But seen from another perspective, this makes no sense whatsoever. After all, we seem to have plenty of time for activities that bring noise, confusion, and complexity into our lives. Why not something that's proven to give us a sense of clarity, depth, and equanimity, if only for a few minutes each day? It's worth a try.

IMAGINE NO TIGERS (EXERCISE)

We've all been there—overcome by events that leave us feeling wrapped up in a stress spiral. Tigers are all around us: false ones, real ones, and we're not sure we can tell the difference. We feel like we're about to explode, implode, or just freeze up. Our mind and spirit are in full rebellion, and it feels like there's nothing to be done except sing the blues.

When you feel like you're at the end of your rope, lie down on the floor and imagine this internal conversation (or read it to a friend in need):

I'm out of options and it feels like there's noth-
ing that I can do. But what if I actually did feel
a sense of calm right now?

What would that feel like?

What if my breath was slow and deep and
regular? What would that feel like?

What if the muscles in my neck and back
were to go slack?

What if my hands and arms suddenly
let go?

What if my hands felt warm?

What if all the bones in my body felt heavy?

What if I simply let the floor do all the work
of supporting my body?

What if the blood vessels in my body were to
relax and expand? What would that feel like?

What would it feel like if I had all the time
in the world?

Now, imagine that your to-do list and your
calendar simply vanished into the digital void,
that your phone melted down, and that all your
work was firmly under control.

Imagine that you're surrounded by people
who care about you.

Imagine that you live in a rest-and-digest
culture that honors the health of the body and
the human animal.

Imagine that all the people in your life are
healthy and taken care of.

Imagine no responsibilities, no urgency,
no demands on your time.

Imagine that your worth isn't measured by
the amount of money you're making or by the

audacity of your achievements. Imagine that you're perfectly OK just the way you are.

Imagine that time is abundant and expansive. There's no urgency to go anywhere or be anywhere. You've got all day, all season, all year. Imagine that your body can take all the time it needs for healing and rejuvenation.

Imagine that all is forgiven. That all the transgressions of your life are seen for what they really are, awkward attempts by a mismatched animal, struggling to navigate a complicated and often alien modern world.

Imagine that all is well in the world and people are relaxed, peaceful, and caring.

Imagine that the future and the past just don't matter in the slightest. Your animal body is smart, strong, and resilient. You can handle any tigers that come your way.

On the face of it, this exercise changes nothing. But imagination is a powerful force that can lead you into more-adaptive behavior, calm, and equanimity. Tigers may well be gathering just outside your door, but if you can imagine another possibility, you can find a better way.

GO TO SLEEP

Even a soul submerged in sleep is hard at work
and helps make something of the world.
—Heraclitus

In conventional conversations about stress, we tend to focus on things we do when we're awake. We read books, do meditations, triage our tasks, focus on our breathing, and all the rest. And sometimes it helps. But what if there was something you could do that would make your body feel great, make you smarter, and replenish your resilience reservoir?

Well, there is such a thing and it's free; all you have to do is go to sleep.

Contrary to popular, modern belief, sleep is not a selfish indulgence. It's absolutely vital for everything we want to do in our lives. Sleep is a heightened anabolic state—a time for the growth and rejuvenation of the immune, nervous, skeletal, and muscular systems. Certain restorative genes are turned on only during sleep, brain function and memory consolidation are enhanced, genes promoting myelin formation are turned on, creativity increases, and synapses are strengthened. Not surprisingly, sleep, learning, and mental well-being are tightly linked. Some researchers have even taken to describing sleep as "overnight therapy." If sleep came in a bottle, it would be—along with physical movement—the most powerful medicine on Earth.

THE WAR ON SLEEP

But tragically, and now stupidly, some segments of modern society continue to insist that sleep is an undesirable obstacle to productivity. It's an adversary, something that we're expected to push back against. We're expected to join the cult of productivity, push the envelope, and get things done. And in this value system, sleep seems like an egregious waste of time.

In an achievement culture, human value is measured by the ability to produce; people are considered worthy if they can get a lot done. We idolize people who claim to get by with less sleep, and in many circles, people who sleep normally are considered to be slackers, a point of view voiced most notably by Thomas Edison, who declared sleep to be "a criminal waste of time."

All of which is consistent with our combative attitude toward life in general. "Shake it off, soldier. Sleep is for sissies." We're all supposed to be entrepreneurs now, building start-up companies, working eighty-hour weeks, killing ourselves for some vague promise of, well, we're not sure exactly what. But everyone's doing it, so we'll do it too.

In short, our adversarial relationship with sleep is a sign of just how far we've drifted from our primal origins. How is it that we could be pushing back against something so fundamental to our bodies and our health? Against something we have in common with every other mammal that has ever lived? Against something that feels so wonderful? This is a cultural pathology of the highest order. Pushing back against sleep is like pushing back against breathing, eating, and sex.

To make matters even worse, our problems with sleep are usually addressed on a person-by-person basis. Like stress, it's treated as an individual matter. We talk about *my* insomnia, *your* sleep disorder, *my* sleep apnea, *your* 2:00 a.m. wake-up pattern, and so on. But this is far bigger than any single individual. This is a systemic, public health problem, a cultural problem, and, ultimately, even an ecological problem and a threat to our collective future.

THE END OF NIGHT

For most of our history on Earth, sleep has been a simple pleasure, a mystery, and a fundamental part of the human experience. Throughout the Paleo, people went to sleep when they felt the need, and no one seemed to fret over the details. It's impossible to say precisely how old sleep is, but we can be sure that the roots go deep. All our mammalian ancestors slept, and it's probable that dinosaurs slept as well. Paleontologists have discovered fossilized skeletons of dinosaurs in what look like sleeping positions, and even jellyfish, some of the oldest creatures on the planet, show sleep-like behavior. As for primates in the wild, sleep is simply not an issue. Go to bed when it gets dark. If something unusual happens, wake up, but that's about it. No one in your group is going to pester you about sleeping; that would be rude.

But with the advent of artificial light, our normal sleep cycles began to fall apart, a trend documented in powerful detail by Paul Bogard in *The End of Night: Searching for Natural Darkness in an Age of Artificial Light*. By the end of the seventeenth century, many European cities had some form of artificial light, and darkness has been under assault ever since. As Bogard tells it, we're now suffering from a very real darkness deficit. Most people are so awash in artificial light that their eyes never make a complete transition to night vision.

Not surprisingly, a considerable body of research concludes that most people in the modern world are substantially sleep deprived. In general, most of us go to bed too late and get up too early. A Gallup poll found that the average number of sleep hours per night dropped from almost 8 in 1942 to 6.8 in 2013. The 2019 Philips global sleep survey, which received more than eleven thousand responses from twelve countries, showed that 62 percent of adults worldwide feel they don't get enough sleep. And as the world warms and nights become hotter, sleep is projected to become even shorter.

The consequences of sleep deprivation are no laughing matter: poor memory, increased impulsiveness, poor judgment, decreased creativity, weight gain, muscle atrophy, suppressed immunity, and increased stress have all been linked to inadequate or poor-quality sleep. In 2005, the National Sleep Foundation found that 75 percent of American adults experienced sleep problems at least a few nights per week. According to Rubin Naiman at the Andrew Weil Center for Integrative Medicine in Tucson, sleep disorders are arguably "the most prevalent health concern in the industrialized world."

But our problem goes even deeper. Research suggests that rapid eye movement (REM) sleep—the period of our most powerful dreaming—is vital to learning and creativity, but as sleep gets shorter, we also suffer an epidemic of REM-sleep loss. "We are at least as dream-deprived as we are sleep-deprived," says Naiman. In essence, we're depriving ourselves of a free, easy form of cognitive and spiritual renewal.

OUR FIRST AND SECOND SLEEP

Sadly, many of us are tortured by the popular belief that sleep must come in a single, unbroken block of roughly eight hours. If we fail to perform in this way, we conclude that we have something called a "sleep disorder," a label that mostly serves to increase our anxiety and, in turn, make it harder to actually sleep well. But in fact, normal human sleep is probably not monolithic and might well depend on culture and environment.

The new thinking holds that humans are naturally inclined toward a segmented form of sleep with two distinct phases. In 2001, historian Roger Ekirch published a seminal paper revealing a wealth of historical evidence that, prior to the modern era, humans slept in two distinct intervals. His book *At Day's Close: Night in Times Past* explores the sleeping behavior of people in the Middle Ages, before electric lighting. He found a common pattern: a "first sleep" from roughly 8:00 p.m. to midnight and a "second sleep" from 2:00 a.m. to sunrise, separated by a period of wakefulness that included socializing, quiet time, conversation, and sex. No one expected to sleep through the night.

This pattern probably held for much of human history but began to disappear with the advent of electric lighting. People began to stay up later in the evening as the night became fashionable, and as the industrial revolution took hold, sleep gradually morphed into the single block we know today.

Of course, few of us are willing to go to bed at 8:00 p.m. or to adopt a segmented sleeping style, but this history tells us that being awake in the middle of the night may not be a disorder at all. More likely, it's a simple expression of our animal nature. As sleep psychologist Gregg Jacobs put it, "Waking up during the night is part of normal human physiology."[71] This new understanding also tells us that sleep is flexible and that there's probably no single "right" way to sleep.

In fact, we're also beginning to suspect that individual variations in sleep patterns probably served an important evolutionary purpose. This is precisely what author Elizabeth Marshall Thomas described in *The Old Way*. In the wild, the bushmen (and -women) of the Kalahari didn't all go to sleep at the same time or sleep for the same duration. At any given time of the night, someone would be up, tending the fire and minding the camp. Some went to sleep early, others late, and people napped whenever they felt the need. Most important, sleep was never stigmatized.

Far from being a problem, this staggered pattern was actually vital to survival. Individual variation meant that someone was always up and vigilant, ready to spot predators and spread the alarm. Today, we no longer worry about being attacked by lions in the middle of the night, but this story of individual variation does put our minds at ease. If your sleeping pattern doesn't happen to fall into line with the modern, conventional standard, maybe that's just your personal variation at work. In another era, your sleeping style would have been a valued asset.

This view of sleep is liberating. We're now free to think of our insomnia not so much as a disease or an affliction but as a normal human variation. Above all, it's not something to be ashamed of. The fact that you're awake in the middle of the night may simply be an expression of an ancient physiological inclination. You're awake because the tribe needs you to check the fire and watch for lions. In all likelihood, there's nothing wrong with you or your brain.

It's also important to remember that most of human history took place in equatorial regions that were often pretty warm, if not outright hot. In this kind of world, people would have risen early for hunting, gathering, and exploring. Then, as temperatures warmed into the afternoon, they would have sought out shade and slept for a few hours. When things cooled off, they'd be active once again. This biphasic, or siesta, pattern is common in many traditional cultures. In other words, napping during the day is probably a pretty normal human behavior too.

SLEEP ACTIVISM AND REFRAMING

By now, we've all heard the common tips and suggestions for better sleep: no caffeine after noon and cut back on screen time before bed. If you're drinking alcohol, do it early and in moderation, and be sure to keep your room cool. These "sleep hygiene" suggestions are sound, but our biggest problem with sleep may well be the way we frame it. If we continue to think of sleep as a selfish act of indulgence that takes us away from our work and family, sleep will continue to be an adversary and we'll feel guilty about getting the sleep we truly need.

In *The Sleep Revolution*, Arianna Huffington calls for a new sleep ethic and declares that "sleep is a basic human right." This is a step in the right direction, but even better, it's essential to recognize that sleep is actually a prosocial act. It's a revolutionary act, a revolution against our chronic, body-hostile culture.

Sleep is a gift to everyone around you and to our world as a whole. When we're rested, we're simply easier to get along with. We're more resilient, and we're probably more sensitive to big-picture views of the world. In this sense, sleep is not just prohealth; it's also profuture. Or to frame it in the inverse, pushing back against sleep isn't just a personal decision; it's socially irresponsible. When you head for the couch or off to bed, you're not being lazy and selfish; you're being smart and altruistic. So, do us all a favor and give sleep the respect it deserves. Sleep is sacred.

REFRAME YOUR INSOMNIA

Likewise, we might do well to reframe our insomnia. In spite of our best efforts and our new understanding of historical sleep patterns, many of us feel cursed to wake up in the middle of the night. We're craving sleep, but our minds race and the anxiety comes in waves.

It might seem like we're stuck, but all is not lost. From a Buddhist perspective, we might say that insomnia is one thing and our resistance to it is another. By itself, insomnia is just wakefulness, but insomnia plus resistance equals suffering. It's one thing to be awake in the middle of the night, but it's another thing to curse the fact that you're awake. You may not have any choice about the fact that you've woken up, but you do have a choice as to whether to resist the experience. You may well prefer to be asleep, but your body has chosen wakefulness, so make something of it. Treat your wakefulness as raw material for something pleasant or creative. And above all, trust your body. Give it the time it needs, and it'll go to sleep when the time is right.

And remember, you're not alone in your effort. When your head hits the pillow, pay attention to your breath, and think about all the people and animals on the planet that are sleeping at this very moment. Billions of creatures, fully absorbed by the sweet comfort of darkness and immersed in the world of dreaming. Taken together, this amounts to a vast, incredibly powerful experience that's sweeping across the planet every

twenty-four hours. Think deeply about this and allow yourself
to participate. Feel their sleep; feel their bodies and their breath.
Sink in and join the sleepers. You're part of something big.

RELATIONAL ARTS

TEND-AND-BEFRIEND

> Human beings are discourse.
> Everything is conversation.
> —Rumi

As we've seen, the body's typical response to stress is to mobilize for action, fighting and fleeing. We imagine ourselves being
attacked by wild animals or doing battle with assailants from
neighboring tribes and escaping by the skin of our teeth. If our
response is powerful and we're lucky, we live to see another day
and maybe even send our genes into the future. But what are
we to do when we get back to camp? How are we to ease our
stress, calm our hyperactive nervous systems, and settle back
down to a more familiar state of mind and body?

One powerful idea has been proposed by Shelley Taylor
and her research team at the University of California, Los
Angeles. As Taylor sees it, humans often ease their stress
by going toward one another for comfort and protection.
This prosocial strategy has been described as the "tend-and-
befriend" response. Some see it as typically female, but men are
just as likely to benefit from social affiliation, friendship, and
mutual protection. Everyone likes to return to camp and share
food, stories, and gossip around the fire. We might even say
that people *are* food (not in the cannibalistic sense!) in the way
that they nourish our lives, our spirits, and even our brains.

For hypersocial primates living in predator-rich environments, this all made perfect sense. The very act of taking care of other people has a distinct salutary effect, not just on our individual psychology but also on the very tissue of our bodies. It's no wonder that we flock to one another. In fact, for the vast majority of human life on this planet, identification with tribe was a fundamental priority. People understood their lives primarily in terms of affiliation. To be was to be a part of the group. I'm part of this tribe, therefore I am.

This prosocial identification shows up in many indigenous and Eastern cultures but is most conspicuous in the African philosophy of *ubuntu* (pronounced uu-boon-too). According to *ubuntu*, there exists a common bond between all human beings, and it is through this bond that we discover our own human qualities; we affirm our humanity when we acknowledge the humanity of others.

For native people, identity is not independent; it is interdependent, intimately connected to the life and welfare of the tribe, the family, the community. People define themselves not as individuals but as participants in a larger social order. As the bushmen of South Africa put it, "We are people through other people" and "I am what I am because of who we are."

Sadly, this sense of human social identity is threatened in our modern world, where society seems held together with duct tape and baling wire. Our deep social instincts remain, but traditional communities are eroding right before our eyes, a process documented most famously by Robert Putnam in his 2001 book *Bowling Alone*. Paradoxically, many people now report feeling lonely, even when surrounded by others.

In 2017, the General Social Survey—the gold standard for social research—found that the number of Americans with no close friends has tripled since 1985. Zero is the most common number of confidants, reported by almost a quarter of those surveyed.[72] Likewise, the average number of people Americans feel they can talk to about "important matters" has fallen from three to two. From a native or indigenous point of view, this is a tragedy in its own right, completely independent of all the other stressors we currently endure.

WE'RE ALL KIN

Most of us desire unity, but how exactly do we tend-and-befriend in a society that encourages us to stand alone? The obvious prescription seems simplistic, but bears repeating:

- Stay in touch
- Reach out
- Listen attentively
- Prepare and share good food

But going deeper, the more important point is to remember our relational common ground. That is, all humans are kin, not just in a metaphorical sense but also in a literal, biological sense. Same species, same genetic foundation, same leaf on the tree of life. The differences may well seem substantial—especially when we're under stress—but this is mostly a distraction from the basic fact of kinship.

When we're relaxed, we understand: they are us, you are me. In turn, we begin to see that tending and befriending others is more than simple altruism. When we tend to others, we're helping them to fill their resilience reservoirs. When they experience the world as a friendly place, their autonomic teeter-totter shifts to feed-and-breed. And quite naturally, this helps us fill our resilience reservoirs too. In other words, tending to others is tending to ourselves.

To put it another way, we can and should start treating people like animals. If this sounds outrageous, you're not thinking biologically. Think like a veterinarian and ask yourself, What do these human animals need? Some things are obvious: everyone wants the basics of food, warmth, and good cheer. Going further, everyone wants to be seen, heard, felt, understood, and respected. Give people these experiences and they're going to be receptive. You don't have to agree with them, and you don't even have to like them; but if you acknowledge their presence and their lives, their stress will moderate, and if all goes well, they'll ease into a state of equanimity.

Tend-and-befriend is all about establishing and maintaining rapport. Start by promoting an atmosphere of safety and calm. Slow down, be consistent, and be at least somewhat predictable. Display competence. Practice genuine conversation with an emphasis on listening. When your people feel safe, they'll relax and do some tending and befriending in your direction as well.

TEND-AND-FORGIVE

Forgiveness is an essential part of this tend-and-befriend practice. In fact, it's bidirectional: When we relax our bodies, we simultaneously become more accepting of one another's transgressions, blunders, and awkwardness. And when we forgive one another, our bodies simultaneously let go of past grievances and outdated threat responses. In the process, we become calmer and more relaxed.

When we forgive, the mind and body come into agreement that it's no longer necessary to hold on to past resentments; it's safe to let go. A popular quip holds that "bitterness and resentment are poisons that we willingly drink, hoping that they will make the other person sick." As we forgive, these poisons flow out of our bodies, and our stress begins to dissipate.

Practicing forgiveness is not just a matter of abstract psychology; it has genuinely beneficial effects on the physical body and health. Studies show that people who forgive are happier and healthier than those who hold resentments. One well-known study showed that, when people merely *think* about forgiving an offender, it leads to improved functioning of their cardiovascular and nervous systems. A study at the University of Wisconsin found that the more forgiving people were, the less they suffered from a wide range of illnesses.[73]

In his work at the Stanford Forgiveness Project, Frederic Luskin found that

> learning to forgive helps people hurt less, experience less anger, feel less stress and suffer less depression. My research also shows that as people learn to forgive they become more hopeful, optimistic and compassionate. As people learn to forgive they become more forgiving in general not just towards one particular person who did them wrong. Our research has also shown that forgiveness has physical health benefits. People who learn to forgive report significantly fewer symptoms of stress such as backache, muscle tension, dizziness, headaches and upset stomachs. In addition people report improvements in appetite, sleep patterns, energy and general well-being.[74]

Not only is forgiveness good for our bodies and spirits, it's also contagious. Every act of forgiveness ripples through tribe and community. People crave this; many of us suffer for years and decades, filled with regret about past behaviors, waiting anxiously for someone to give us a word or gesture of compassion and understanding. Every time we offer this gesture to someone, we heal the lives of people around us. This is why forgiveness and compassion lie at the very heart of so many of the world's religious and spiritual traditions.

Unfortunately, misunderstandings abound. Compassion is not sympathy or pity. It is not an altruistic gift that we give to someone else. It's not as if we're above or outside some suffering soul, offering our condolences. Rather, it's an identification, a sense of being with and suffering with. When we're compassionate, we widen the circle of *ubuntu*. We appreciate, embrace, and feel our shared predicament. We—that is, all living creatures—are fragile, vulnerable, and subject to the ways of a mysterious, sometimes hostile, and chaotic world. The human predicament is universal; every one of us faces the same challenges of ignorance, fear, risk, illness, death, and the unknown.

Naturally, compassion is good for the body and the brain. It is both a cause and effect of parasympathetic activation and tissue repair. It's easy to forget how much psychic and physical energy it takes to maintain our isolation and division from others and the world. We go for years, enforcing boundaries and maintaining distinctions between self and other, us and them. But this vigilance requires enormous attention and distracts us from other, more important creations. As soon as we move toward compassion, we discover immense amounts of energy that we can use for healing, adventure, and learning. In addition, our compassion is contagious. Every time we widen our circle of identity, we inspire others to do likewise, melting conflict and the stress that goes with it.

REHUMANIZE YOUR LIFE

To make all this tending and befriending work on a larger cultural and social scale, we've got to rehumanize our interactions with one another in every domain, including business and the professions. In other words, we've got to reintroduce some humanity into modern life. To put it another way, we've got to stop with the relentless automation of every human activity and replace it with something more organic and natural.

This means getting off the vertical axis of the pyramid and spending more time in horizontal, animal-to-animal interactions—primate to primate, mammal to mammal. The good news is that this human-centered approach is a major inconvenience and forces us to slow down. Horizontal relationships take more time, which reduces productivity and efficiency, but in the long term, the effect might well swing the other way. When human animals have the opportunity to relate horizontally, they form better teams and, ultimately, do better work.

But for control freaks, horizontal relationships are unnerving because they leave us exposed to social uncertainty and ambiguity. When we're accustomed to holding and maintaining a certain rank in a hierarchy, horizontal human encounters can be unsettling, disturbing, or even threatening. We try to keep people in their pigeonholes, but people aren't pigeons.

All of which suggests a simple but challenging trade-off: if you want to rehumanize a school, organization, workplace, or profession, you've got to soften the pyramid and create more space for horizontal, animal-to-animal encounters. De-emphasize rank, give people access to power whenever possible, and, above all, stop being such a chimp. Naturally, this perspective is corrosive to hierarchy as usual, but there really isn't much of a choice. If we continue to buttress our pyramids with an incessant focus on rank, hierarchy, and procedure, the animal is going to be cranky and, in turn, disruptive. Better to stay close to the horizontal axis and treat people like the social animals that they are.

KEEP YOUR FOCUS

> To keep control of passion, one must hold firm
> the reins of attention.
>
> —Baltasar Gracián, *The Art of Worldly Wisdom*

When people talk about the challenges of stress, a common prescription suggests that we can reduce our angst by adjusting our attention and focusing on the right things. The benefit is often expressed in the phrase *What you focus on grows.* In other words, the objects of our attention grow in significance the longer we look. If we choose to focus on the things that make us angry, we become even angrier and more stressed. If we focus on the joys and beauties of the world, we become happier and more content. All of which would suggest that, if we want to experience less stress in life, we should pay less attention to the things that are driving us crazy and more attention to the things that give us comfort and meaning.

This recommendation is supported by many philosophers of the human experience. As William James put it, "The faculty of voluntarily bringing back a wandering attention, over and over again, is the very root of judgment, character and will . . . An education which should improve this faculty would be the education par excellence." Likewise, Mihály Csíkszentmihályi, author of *Flow*, writes: "How much stress we experience depends more on how well we control attention, than on what happens to us."[75]

On the face of it, this all makes sense. After all, modern life feels like one vast conspiracy against focused attention. Every day we're assaulted by a barrage of stimuli that derails our attention and leaves us fragmented, short-tempered, and exhausted. Sales pitches are designed specifically to take advantage of the mind's tendency to fall apart when under pressure. Little by little, our attention is being stolen and chopped into pieces. Compared to our simple, distraction-free lives in the Paleo, the modern world is madness.

It's no wonder we feel so fragmented, no wonder that we hear so many calls for focus. We're reminded to be mindful, to stay in the present moment, and to choose what we pay attention to. If we can manage our attention, we can manage our emotions, our behavior, and the quality of our lives. But these calls can be confusing and even intimidating. Even the word *mindfulness* can be ambiguous and disorienting. Do we really want to spend our entire lives living in the present moment? Isn't learning from the past and planning for the future an inherently human activity? And is it really necessary to spend long hours in meditation to develop these capabilities?

There's no question that our attentional choices have real consequences; the standard prescription is sound advice. What we focus on *does* grow in significance and its power to move us. But there's peril here as well, because selective attention can also put us on the path to avoidance and even denial. Disturbing things make us feel uncomfortable, so we choose to look at beautiful things instead and, yes, we feel better. The destruction of the biosphere really stresses me out, so I choose to pay attention to good food and music. Social injustice and inequality disrupt my equanimity, so I'll focus on planting my garden. Tigers are a real downer, so I'll spend my time looking at kittens instead. And on it goes, our attentional choices building up utopian, insulated, stress-free but ultimately irrelevant lives.

Another popular recommendation tells us that the path to stress relief lies in paying attention to the things that we can control in the world. On the face of it, this, too, makes sense. I can't control what a politician says or writes, so it's a waste of my energy to get upset about it. I can't control the destruction of the Amazon rain forest, so there's no point in grieving about that either. If I focus on my job, my health, and my family, I've got a shot at control, and in turn, my stress will be relieved.

But this, too, is a perilous path because it can take us out of engagement with crucial matters. And who's to say what's truly controllable and what's not? Like selective attention, this approach might well remove us from participation with the world and lead us into evasions of responsibility. If everyone focused exclusively on their domains of personal control, nothing would ever change.

And so our conundrum: selective attention can make us feel better, but it might not do much for the world at large. We've got to stay open and keep our attention broad enough to include the challenging, the ugly, and the difficult. But this is not necessarily the downer we might imagine it to be, because there's always some good to be found. We could focus on the grim, unpleasant facts and suffer the angst and stress that go with them, but there are amazing people doing good work in every domain. There's usually good nested inside the bad, inspiration living inside the "unsolvable" and "insurmountable" challenges of our days. Keep looking and you'll find it.

LOOK TO THE LIVING

Back in the 1960s, psychologist Timothy Leary issued a call for a withdrawal from mainstream culture and a reconnection with the natural forces that sustain our lives. As he saw it, we needed an attentional revolution, a redirection of human consciousness away from the artificial and toward the natural. At the time, the modern world was comparatively simple, and most of our distractions were relatively benign. To be sure, there was plenty of noise in the system, but if you could turn off the TV, you could avoid the worst of it. People still had time for deep engagement with reading, work, and the natural world.

But today, our attention, like so much habitat around the world, is being mined for profit. Human attention is treated like an exploitable resource, a profit center. And like the mining of forests, mountaintops, and seabeds around the world, this has disastrous consequences. The difference is that, this time, the damage is cognitive and psychospiritual. While copper, gold, and lithium mines poison downstream water supplies and habitats, the mining of human attention steals the very fabric of our lives, our intelligence, and our ability to create a viable future.

Leary's attentional revolution is a revolt against the merchants of distraction. As he saw it, the time has come to stop participating in the exploitation of our attention and our consciousness. But unlike more-familiar revolutions, this one requires no political power, no organizing, no legislation, and no fundraising. You won't have to protest in the street, you won't have to paint signs and chant slogans, and you won't have to get arrested. Instead, we make simple choices about where to direct our focus. Stop attending to the shiny lures that chop our attention into shards. Instead, focus on the original, indigenous targets of human attention, especially habitat and continuity with our life-supporting systems. We concentrate on our animal powers, our resilience, and, in particular, our capacity for sapience.

Of course, some observers might describe this attentional revolution as a form of escapism. As we all know, the word *escapist* is widely used to condemn someone's behavior. The person in question is of weak moral character and is avoiding important work. If you're thinking and dreaming about the wonders of the natural world, you aren't being a productive member of society. Shame on you.

But what if we've got it entirely backward? What if the really important work of our time is precisely this—shifting our attention back to living systems? In this sense, the attentional revolution is the precise opposite of escapism; it's the most essential work of our age. You're not daydreaming; you're creating vital attentional links to the world. In fact, returning our attention to nature is the sanest, most fundamental work we can possibly do. It's about preserving and maintaining contact with the very thing that keeps us alive and whole. It's a return to health. It's not a luxury or an escape but a necessity. It's sacred.

The good news is that there's more freedom here than you might think. To be sure, a great many of us are forced to live and work indoors, separated and insulated from the natural world. And yes, a large percentage of our attention must go to the demands of paying the bills and "making a living." But beyond these immediate demands, we are incredibly free. We are free to exercise our biophilia—to think about, read about, and dream about the powers of nature. We're free to notice the plants that burst forth in cracks in the concrete; we're free to notice the way that life leaps back after a long winter and the way that forests regenerate, even after decades of industrial abuse. We're free to think about and even feel the depth of our ancestry and our intimate connection with all of life.

This wild attention doesn't just feel good, it also fills our resilience reservoir, both individually and collectively. In the process, it makes us more powerful. Even better, it's consistent with our ancestral heritage and what we might call "Paleo attention." For the vast, overwhelming majority of our time on Earth, people have paid attention to animals, plants, weather, and water. We're deeply wired for this. All we have to do is remember.

TURN DOWN THE FEAR

As we've seen, one of the biggest drivers of stress in the modern world is our shock-value media. It skews our attention toward danger as it drives us into a state of hypervigilance. It hardens our preexisting beliefs and, no doubt, contributes to the rise in polarization we see around the world. Excessive consumption has been associated with a host of negative mental health consequences, most notoriously depression. And worst of all, modern media often leave us feeling powerless in the face of hypercomplex, systemic problems that no one individual can do much about.

All of this implies a certain responsibility and duty for consumers. If we can't trust "the media" to make good distinctions between real and false tigers, we need to do the job ourselves. In other words, we need to bring educated ears and eyeballs to the process. Listen and watch carefully. Is that rustle on the airwaves a real threat to your life or the biosphere? Is it worth getting worked up about? Where are the real tigers, and why aren't we hearing much about them?

Likewise, the obvious questions: How much media is too much? When does smart consumption turn into obsessive-compulsive, stress-amplifying distraction? How do we know when we've gone too far? When does smart, intentional research become mindless doom scrolling?

Measurement would be folly—who can say what the ideal amount is for any one individual in any given circumstance? It's always going to be a judgment call. And as in all things, there's almost certainly an inverse U-shaped curve of benefit, a sweet spot and a tipping point.

The fundamental questions are simple: Am I exploring and gathering valuable information and ideas by my own volition? Or am I being remotely controlled by forces, agents, and programming in some other corner of the world?

Remember: every time you consume media in any form, your autonomic nervous system is being remotely controlled, for better or for worse, from afar. In other words, you're handing off control of your most intimate and essential physiological functions to people you don't know and can't see—authors, producers, managers, and consultants. Sometimes this remote control serves us well and helps us turn on the appropriate autonomic response. But just as often, it gives us mixed messages and whipsaws us into conflicted and wildly inappropriate reactions.

This is not something to be taken lightly. Handing off control of your body and your spirit to external agents is serious business. Just imagine having a large knob in the center of your chest that other people could turn left or right as they desired. If they turn the knob clockwise, it puts you into feed-and-breed. If they turn it counterclockwise, it puts you into fight-flight. Now, imagine that they're turning the knob not for *your* benefit but for *their* benefit or, more precisely, for the benefit of their shareholders. This is some extremely creepy stuff. You may well believe that you're being entertained, enlightened, or educated, but in fact, your deep body may well be being manipulated for someone else's profit.

Ultimately, the objective is to make our media consumption work for us, not for someone else. To that end, some basic questions are essential:

> *Do I have any conceivable power or control over the events in this report?*
>
> *Does this story enlighten me in any way, or does it simply confirm what I already believe?*
>
> *Does this story offer any real "news"? In other words, does it show me some new way of seeing the world or responding to the world? Or does it simply deepen my perceptual ruts?*
>
> *Does this activity of media consumption displace and distract me away from other, more important concerns?*

Likewise, it makes sense to limit our consumption overall. Modulate your use and be aware of the way it intrudes upon and obscures other life-affirming human activities. If your news consumption overshadows your outdoor time, eating, movement, social time, or lovemaking, it's time to power off. Staying in touch with current events is worthwhile, but staying in touch with our primary circles of life support is far more important.

CIRCLE UP

> We be of one blood, thee and I.
> —Rudyard Kipling, *The Jungle Book*

As we've seen, the ancestral human experience on Earth was fundamentally participatory. For hundreds of thousands of years, we lived in rough harmony with the natural world and saw ourselves as part of the living cosmos. In short, we saw ourselves as part of the circle of life.

And when you're part of the circle, life can be pretty good. To be sure, there were plenty of genuine hardships—real tigers, drought, famine, extremes of heat and cold—but no matter how bad things got, people still had a sense of inclusion. Just knowing that you're part of a group brings a sense of comfort; your body might well be hurting, but you're a part of something bigger. But once you step outside the circle, life begins to feel precarious, no matter what kind of creature comforts you might happen to invent. Suddenly, you're alienated, isolated, and alone. And of course, massively stressed.

This is precisely the story of the modern era. Over the course of just a few thousand years, the circular, indigenous worldview was replaced by a "man against nature" narrative, an adversarial relationship to just about everything. Driven by delusions of human supremacy, we told ourselves that we're better than, separate from, and superior to the rest of creation. And in the process, we've given ourselves a case of crushing, existential dread.

In short, we've created a culture of distance. As mature adults, we're expected to stand apart from whatever it is we're working with. We're encouraged to practice scientific objectivity, medical objectivity, journalistic objectivity, editorial objectivity, professional objectivity, and—even in the world of mental health—"therapeutic distance."

Building on the successes of the early scientific revolution, especially in physics and cosmology, we've come to the conclusion that the best way to know nature is to stand apart from her. Study the world all you like, but whatever you do, don't get involved. Don't get emotionally attached to whatever it is you're working with. Given this kind of mandate, it's no wonder we feel the way we do. When we continually separate ourselves from that which gives us life, we're bound to feel anxious, fragmented, and alienated.

NOURISH THE LONG BODY

All of which calls us back to indigenous philosophy. Almost without exception, native people assume a continuity between their bodies, habitat, tribe, and cosmos. In the Iroquois tradition, people recognize an extended sense of physicality, sometimes referred to as "the long body." Even in the modern era, Alexis de Tocqueville wrote about the larger, highly interdependent "social body." The body, in other words, is far more than an isolated bag of skin or, as some modern people have put it, "a hairy bag of water." In fact, the body is exquisitely sensitive and connected to its surroundings, especially the life-supporting circles of habitat and tribe. Your body, in other words, is functionally bigger than it appears.

A Zen parable put it this way: "To your way of thinking, your skin is a thing which separates and protects you from the outside world. To my way of thinking, my skin is a thing which connects me and opens me to the outside world, which in any case is not the outside world."

In other words, health is a matter not just of individual physical welfare but also of the whole. An early Buddhist teacher stated: "If the people are sick, I, too, am sick; only when everyone is healthy will I, too, be healthy."

Even in ancient Greece, Socrates offered an indigenous view: "This is the reason why the cure of many diseases is unknown to the physicians of Hellas (Greece), because they are ignorant of the whole, which ought to be studied also; for the part can never be well unless the whole is well."[76]

Likewise, a typical indigenous maxim tells us "The hurt of one is the hurt of all. The honor of one is the honor of all." And, by extension, "The health of one is the health of all. The disease of one is the disease of all."

CIRCULAR GOLDEN RULES

The circular, interdependent nature of life is expressed in continual return. Actions do not take place in isolation. Anytime we act, we are acting on the whole, and since we're part of the whole, our actions reflect back upon us. Whatever we do to the world, we do to ourselves. All of our behaviors, you might say, are boomerangs.

We see examples of this karmic worldview throughout the indigenous tradition. Most obviously, we recall the legendary words of Chief Seattle (1786–1866): "What we do to the earth, we do to ourselves." In today's world, we would call this a great sound bite, but this is no mere one-off declaration of interdependence. Across the planet, indigenous people have made similar observations for thousands of years.

STRATEGIES AND ANTIDOTES 225

For normal, native people, habitat and the body are one thing, bound together by an ecological golden rule, a karmic principle of give-and-take. Aboriginal elders in Australia put it this way: "To wound the Earth is to wound yourself, and if others are wounding the Earth, they are wounding you." Likewise, José Ortega y Gasset: "I am I plus my surroundings, and if I do not preserve the latter, I do not preserve myself." The Indian poet and writer Rabindranath Tagore said much the same thing: "The same stream of life that runs through my veins night and day runs through the world and dances in rhythmic measures. It is the same life that shoots in joy through the dust of the earth in numberless blades of grass and breaks into tumultuous waves of leaves and flowers."[77]

Some may suggest that this kind of talk is exclusive to indigenous traditions, but it's not just native people who talk this way. John Muir, Rachel Carson, Aldo Leopold, Henry David Thoreau, Gary Snyder, Alan Watts, E. O. Wilson, and Edward Abbey all advocated for what we today call "deep ecology," biocentrism, and interdependence. What we do to the whole we do to every part of the whole. To abuse the whole is to abuse the self.

In the Eastern tradition, the Sanskrit word *karma* refers to the spiritual principle of cause and effect. It tells us that the intent and actions of an individual influence the future of that individual. Good intent and good deeds contribute to good karma and future happiness, while bad intent and bad deeds contribute to bad karma and future suffering. In popular conversation, we say, "What goes around comes around."

Every religious tradition shares a similar "golden rule." Christianity teaches us "We reap what we sow" and "Do unto others as you would have them do unto you." Of course, we're accustomed to thinking of karma and golden rules strictly in human terms—the "others" are people in our communities, our human neighbors. But the time has come to update our

notion of "others" to include the 99.9 percent of life on Earth—
plants, animals, soils, water, and atmosphere. Now we say, "Do
unto the Earth as you would have the Earth do unto you." Or
as a modernized variation puts it, "Do unto those downstream
as you would have those upstream do unto you."

CONTINUITY IS SACRED

The ultimate remedy to our stress lies in reinvigorating our
participation, intimacy, and compassion for the rest of life. In
this, we seek to reestablish the broken continuities, to put the
fragments back together, to reweave ourselves back into relationship with the world. In joining forces with the circle, we
become calmer and more resilient.

As any biologist will tell us, human life is sustained by circles of life support, most especially habitat and tribe. Habitat
gives us our food, water, and a sense of wonder. Community
gives us a sense of unity, meaning, and safety. There can be no
more-urgent priority, no more-important work on this planet
than remembering and maintaining these links. Everything
else is secondary. Keep this in mind as you triage your tasks and
decisions. Participate in the world of commerce as you must,
but return to the primal essentials whenever possible. If we can
reweave ourselves back into participation with the circle, we've
got a chance. But if we fail at this task, we fail at all of it.

PRACTICAL METHODS

MAKE THE BOULDER SMALLER

Minimalism is an abundance of enough.
—Torley

Sisyphus had a monstrous problem. His boulder was immense, heavy, and unwieldy, intentionally crafted by the gods to give him a case of chronic stress. Over and over, he'd push it up the hill with all his might, only to have the gods wrest it away and send it crashing back down. If only Sisyphus could have made the boulder smaller and more manageable, he might have had a chance.

Like Sisyphus, most of us are cursed to push some kind of boulder up a hill. Giant granite boulders of work, lots of it nonnegotiable. There's work-related work, house work, family work, yard work, work on the car, the taxes, the computer— not to mention all the work that goes into making some kind of functional future for the human animal. And even worse, the boulder only seems to get bigger with each passing day. Obviously, this is not a sustainable situation.

If we're going to succeed, we're going to have to find a way to cut the boulder down to size, but where do we begin? All that work declares itself to be essential and nonnegotiable, but is it really? Can we cut back?

TRIAGE LIKE YOUR LIFE DEPENDS ON IT

One obvious approach is to stop for a moment and consider what exactly it is we're trying to do. When we don't have a point of focus in our lives, all tasks seem equal: everything needs attention, everything must be done. We've got a can-do attitude, and some of us are inclined to be agreeable and say yes to almost any task that's handed to us. And over time, the boulder just keeps growing; we get weaker and exhausted, and after a few years, we're of no use to anyone.

A better approach is to get strategic and start making the hard decisions. What's essential in the service of my core objectives? What can I safely let go? What has to be done right now? What can wait till later? This inquiry is best practiced at regular intervals: each morning at your desk, at the beginning of every week, or at the beginning of each semester, for example. And, in particular, in times of crisis. When you feel the panic coming on, stop and ask about what really matters.

In the extreme version of triage, some business consultants advise people to "say no to almost everything." In other words, don't take on any tasks or new projects unless they're fully aligned with your core vision and purpose. If the task isn't relevant to what you're trying to create, turn it down. This keeps the boulder smaller and manageable. Of course, saying no to almost everything also means saying yes to almost nothing, a strategy with its own set of complications. That is, if we're too militant and disciplined about our work, we might well miss out on the surprises, novelty, and opportunity that can make life wonderful. Obviously, discretion is required; wisdom suggests that we keep some slack in our methods and our philosophies.

In any case, success depends on knowing precisely what it is you're trying to do. What is the One Big Idea that animates your life? What is your mission and purpose? This is no simple inquiry, of course, and it'll demand frequent revision over the course of your life. But the effort is essential. Practice writing it down, and repeat it to yourself often. The more clarity and precision you can get, the better. And once you get that focus, your triage decisions will almost make themselves.

KILL YOUR DARLINGS

A similar strategy for decisiveness shows up in the world of writing, where authors are often advised to "kill your darlings." In other words, be a decisive editor of your work and kill the ideas that don't really fit. Take your most cherished phrases, metaphors, characters, and descriptions and, if they don't fit within the context of your larger vision or creation, delete them.

Of course, there's pain in this process. Writers squeeze their imaginations for every precious word and idea, then come to realize that an entire stream of thought no longer fits their larger story line. Those brilliant insights—possibly, still brilliant—simply don't mesh with the dominant narrative, tone, or theme. If the writer persists in trying to preserve nuggets that don't fit, the process can spiral out of control, consuming weeks or months of effort. This is where the real stress lies: in the endless rounds of confusion and labor, all based on the failure to triage. It may be hard kill your darlings, but it's all for the greater good of the work. So, practice using the Delete key, or save that not-quite-relevant work to a digital archive. It's hard, but it gets easier.

JUST WANT LESS

Sometimes the size of the boulder is nonnegotiable. Work is heaped on our heads and we're just buried. But other times, the boulder is the way it is because of our overactive desires for achievement. We're ambitious and we want everything. Driven by the incessant voice of modern marketing, we want to do everything and be everything. We want to start companies, win gold medals, and climb big mountains. In the process, we become victims of our enthusiasm and desire run amok. In the process, the boulder brings us to our knees and nothing gets done.

The obvious—or not so obvious—solution is to scale back our ambition. In short, want less. Be content now. Enjoy what you've got. Imagine an inverse to-do list. Call it "things I don't have to do":

- Save the world

- Become rich and famous
- Win a championship
- Start a company
- Win a Nobel Prize
- Know everything
- Fix everything
- Rescue everyone around me
- Live forever
- Be perfect

Now it's your turn. Construct your own list of "things I don't have to do." When you're done, review it, and notice what this exercise does for your state of mind and body. This anti-list might well liberate you from that onerous compulsion that you have to do everything and be everything.

GO LIGHT

Another useful way to cut the boulder down to size is to take inspiration from the world of alpine climbing and the practice of minimalism. The history is instructive and even inspiring. In recent decades, the sport has evolved dramatically from its expeditionary roots. Today's equipment is lighter and more functional, and climbers look to climb big mountains in the simplest, most direct way possible. This is often called "alpine style." Famously advocated by Yvon Chouinard, the founder of Patagonia, the goal is to use beautiful, well-crafted tools and clothing to deepen the alpine experience and reduce the impact on the mountain environment. As he famously put it: "He who dies with the least toys wins. Because the more you know, the less you need."

The beauty of alpine style is that it puts climbers in direct physical contact with the ambiguity and joy of the mountain experience. No longer supported by piles of gear, fixed ropes, and numerous camps, climbers are fully exposed to the dangers and beauty of the route, forced to rely on their skills, endurance, and wits. Less work, more sport.

But alpine style is far more than just an elegant way to climb a mountain; it's an incredibly valuable metaphor for our time and a practical answer to the problem of consumerism. It teaches us a fundamental, commonly overlooked life lesson: how to own things. It teaches us to savor experience over possessions, to value what we do own, and to reject the voices constantly shouting at us to buy more.

Moreover, alpine style teaches us to appreciate quality. As it stands, a common rap claims that modern culture is "too materialistic," but perhaps it's precisely the opposite. The reason we buy so much stuff is because we don't really value what we've got, and in this sense, we're not materialistic enough. If we really paid attention to the quality of the things we owned, we wouldn't have to go looking for more. If we took the time to savor good craftsmanship and prime materials, we'd be content. A few simple, beautiful possessions would be enough.

Likewise, it's important to remember that the relationship between possessions and our sense of control follows our familiar inverse U-shaped curve. That is, owning a few key possessions is likely to give us a strong sense of control, which, in turn, buffers our stress and makes us more resilient. More possessions will give us an even greater sense of control, but once we cross the tipping point, the effect goes into reverse. Suddenly, more stuff means *less* control over our circumstances and an increased vulnerability to stress. In this zone, more is really less.

Naturally, the practice is all about proportion. Ask yourself:

Does this thing add meaning to my life?
Is it well crafted?

Does it inspire me?
Is it an appropriate use of technology?
What meanings come along with it?

If the item in question fails to bring meaning and a sense of control into your life, get rid of it. If it fails to inspire you by virtue of its quality, materials, and form, sell it or give it away. If you haven't used it in twenty years, it's safe to assume you're not going to need it.

THE MINIMALIST LIFE

The beauty of minimalism is that it suggests a way, a Tao, for conducting our entire lives. Trimming down our stuff inspires us to reduce complexity everywhere. Clear out the garage and the closets, clear out the mind and spirit. Author Greg McKeown calls this practice "essentialism," the disciplined pursuit of less. We're reminded of the teachings of Thoreau and the Zen masters. Keep it simple. Chop wood, carry water. Stay close to your core experience and don't get distracted by complexity.

In this practice, we lean toward monotasking and single-focus activities. We set up our days to minimize interruptions and distractions. Put one very important thing on your to-do list and do that thing. Don't try to master every skill, sport, or discipline. Survey the options, choose one, and make it your own. Likewise, focus your activism. Don't try to address every crisis or injustice in the world. Instead, concentrate your energies on one issue at a time. Precision activism, like precision living, is a powerful way to make a difference.

In a minimalist, alpine-style culture, we'd frown on excess affluence. A big house filled with stuff would be an embarrassment, not a goal. But to do all this, we'd have to stop listening to the incessant rap that tells us to do more, be more, and, above all, consume more. Close your ears and your vision will become clear. As Chouinard himself put it: "If we could all come to see our consumer products as tools that help us to live our real lives—rather than as substitutes and surrogates for that life—we'd need many fewer products to be happy."

SLOW DOWN

> The greatest discovery of the 21st century will be the discovery that Man was not meant to live at the speed of light.
> —Marshall McLuhan, *The Global Village: Transformations in World Life and Media in the 21st Century*

All of us have heard the story about the slow and plodding tortoise that wins the race against the swift but impulsive hare. It makes for a good parable, but it also leaves us with some nagging questions: Was the hare under stress? Was he experiencing a fight-flight reaction in his autonomic nervous system? Was he fleeing from false tigers or maybe even real ones? Will the chronic stimulation of his stress response make him vulnerable to degenerative diseases later in life? And what of the tortoise? Is he living in a rest-and-digest state of contentment? A feed-and-breed utopia?

Sadly, the parable tells us none of these things, but the metaphor fits. The hare comes across as harried and anxious, a slave to his impulses. Not only does he lose the race, he may well lose his athletic skills, his cognitive smarts, and his sense of perspective. His singular devotion to speed might serve him well in exceptional circumstances, but as a full-time strategy, it'll eventually bring him down. The tortoise, on the other hand, is likely to live a long and fulfilling life.

The thing to keep in mind here is that, historically speaking, the tortoise is the normal one. In other words, a slow pace of life is the status quo for *Homo sapiens*. Just imagine the typical camp setting in prehistory: The hunters and gatherers have returned at the end of the day, and everyone catches up with stories, cooking, and eating. But there's no rushing around, no pushing the envelope, no demands for greater productivity. Why would there be? Except for occasional bursts of activity to get food, avoid predators, or shelter from a storm, there's no urgency whatsoever. In other words, lazy is normal. Lazy is acceptable. Lazy is good. This is our "Paleo pace," sometimes referred to in the modern world as "Africa time." Watch the animals and the weather, gossip with your friends, and enjoy your rest-and-digest time in camp.

In contrast, our modern fast-paced life is wickedly abnormal. Compared to our ancestors, we're living in a state of chronic urgency and stimulation, constantly egging one another on—to do more, achieve more, be more. Whipped up into a frenzy of activity, we hook our identities to continuous production and, above all, speed. Going faster is encouraged, rewarded, and glorified. Fast running, fast driving, fast eating, fast working, fast thinking. If modern culture were a person, it'd be the guy tailgating us on the road, breathing down our necks in line at the grocery store, and cutting us off in conversation. In this modern world, nothing is ever fast enough. In short, we're harebrained.

Today's "speed ethic" is closely related to our work ethic and our productivity ethic. We like to think it's just the pace of modern life, but there are deeper forces at work. We're seduced by speed and its promise that if we just go a little faster, we can have more control over the world. We feel anxious and unsettled, but if we go fast, we can get more done, which gives us the sense of control we seek. If this was a one-off event, that might well be the end of it. But of course, we're never satisfied. If we can gain a little more control by going faster, we could get a lot more control by going faster still. Until something breaks.

There's something paradoxical and unsettling about all this. We've become so accustomed to going fast that slowing down feels odd, alien, boring, and unpleasant. Teachers, coaches, and therapists tell us to slow down and feel our experience; so, we try it, but strangely, we often feel worse. In slowing down, our awareness opens up and we feel our anxiety more acutely. We don't know what to do with ourselves, so we fidget and squirm. The only antidote is to speed back up and close our attention back down.

All of which was vividly illustrated in a widely reported 2014 study revealing that "men would rather give themselves electric shocks than sit quietly."[78] Researchers left participants alone in a room in which they could push a button and shock themselves if they wanted to. The results were startling: 67 percent of men and 25 percent of women chose to shock themselves rather than just sit quietly. Which is precisely why we're going so fast today. Going slow feels uncomfortable, and speed is a distracting balm. It can ease the discomfort and anxiety of stillness, but ultimately, it's no solution at all. And this is the plight of the hare. He can't sit still, so he goes ever faster, running from his own experience, afraid of his own shadow.

SAVE THE SPACE

Throughout history, spiritual leaders and tribal elders have counseled the benefits of patience and reflection in the face of demanding challenges. Give it time, they tell us. Sit with the dilemma, go for a walk, and let the body do its work. Feel what you're feeling, and then, when the process has run its course, act with courage and resolve.

But sadly, the modern world is relentless and merciless in short-circuiting this process and driving stimulus and response ever closer together. Never before in the history of humanity has there been so much pressure to act fast. We're constantly encouraged to work fast, gather information quickly, and generate some kind of profitable product or service in the shortest amount of time. The body wants to metabolize experience, but the marketplace demands action.

Even worse, the marketing industry has evolved into a highly efficient machine for squeezing stimulus and response together into a single reflexive, impulsive act. Advertising has become neurologically sophisticated, and commercial websites are intentionally constructed to ease the path from initial contact to the "Buy Now" click. Everywhere we turn in the modern world, someone is pushing us to swipe our cards, open our wallets, and complete a "call to action." In a historical sense, this is all profoundly abnormal, not to mention hugely destructive to wise action in the face of complexity.

The end result is that we, as a people, are becoming progressively more impulsive and automated with each passing day. As stimulus and response are pushed ever closer together, we become increasingly robotic in our behavior and our relationship with the world. We may well become efficient, but along the way, our humanity and sapience are left in the dust. And this comes precisely at the moment when our planetary predicament demands a new level of reflection. If we could just put some space between stimulus and response, as psychiatrist Viktor Frankl taught, our behavior and our lives would be a lot calmer and a lot more sapient.

HOW TO SLOW DOWN

Many of us understand the pathologies of speed, and we're looking for ways to slow the pace—or, as we might say, to get in touch with our inner tortoise. All of which is really a sign of how confused we've become: that many of us—all of us, more likely—need instruction in what should be a perfectly normal life skill. Our Paleolithic ancestors would be mystified. Is it really true that modern humans need instruction in "how to slow down"? Isn't that just a normal way for people to live?

The thing to remember is that the modern speed ethic is culturally driven. None of us is born wanting to spend our adult lives rushing madly from one task to the next, but somehow, the behavior has become normalized. And so, if we're going to learn the way of the tortoise, we'll have to be countercultural to some degree. We'll have to ignore and reject the constant jabbering, poking, and prodding that seeks to turn us into impulsive and neurotic hares.

Obviously, we need a new—or, rather, an old—approach, something that gives us a chance to breathe into the space between stimulus and response, something to dampen our reactivity. This would be a relaxation ethic, a value system that honors the animal body and, in particular, the autonomic nervous system. Physicians, trainers, coaches, and veterinarians are united in the understanding that all healthy animals need time to simply live. It's time we listened to their advice and stopped rushing to whatever's next. Take more time for everything. Just do less.

Patience will come with age and experience. Just because there's a stimulus doesn't mean you have to act on it. Just because someone or something is poking you doesn't mean you have to respond immediately. You don't have to take the neuromarketing bait that's dangled in front of you. For that matter, you don't have to take *any* bait that tries to manipulate you into fast, impulsive action.

Remember your Paleo pace. Imagine having all the time you need in each day, a sense of temporal affluence, moving and living at the pace of habitat. On the grassland, there are no deadlines. Above all, stop worshiping speed for its own sake. There are times to go fast, but these are occasional events. Instead, stretch out the interval between stimulus and response. Get comfortable in that space. Take a breath. Take a walk. Art comes in its own time. Let the body have its way with the stimulus. Then, only then, act.

KEEP THE BEAT

> The goal of life is to make your heartbeat match the beat of the universe, to match your nature with Nature.
> —Joseph Campbell, *The Joseph Campbell Companion*

As we've seen, one of the most difficult challenges of the modern world is the progressive erosion of our basic life rhythms. The natural world is screaming at us to recognize and participate in the rhythm that exists in all living things, but we persist in our static, relentless approach to almost everything. To say that this is stressful to us as individuals doesn't even begin to describe it. In effect, we are clamping down on the entire biosphere, damping down the oscillations that are essential to all of life. And when the whole is stressed, so are all the parts of that whole.

The impacts on our personal lives are subtle at first, but hugely destructive in the long run. We'd like to maintain the natural rhythm that sustained us in childhood, and we know that it's really important for our health and sanity; but little by little, we give away the contrast and the oscillation that sustains us. We're squeezed for time, and we know full well that we really need to sleep, move, and recharge; but we can't see any other way, so we cope by deal making and brokering:

I'll stay up late.
I'll get up early.
I'll do it on the weekend.
I'll do it on the plane.
I'll make those calls on the road.

It sounds like the right thing to do at the time; but before long, the brokering becomes a habit and, soon, we're running on fumes. We like to think we're working hard and making progress, but it's just not sustainable.

FEED YOUR PALEOLITHIC RHYTHM

Once again, it's essential to remember the profoundly rhythmic nature of our lives in prehistory, long before the first hoe, plows, tractors, fossil fuels, and artificial light. For the vast majority of our time on this planet, humans have lived an oscillating pattern of engagement with the world, hunting and exploring for hours or even days, then resting back in camp.

In their 1988 book *The Paleolithic Prescription*, anthropologists S. Boyd Eaton, Marjorie Shostak, and Melvin Konner described "the Paleolithic rhythm." Without question, this pattern of serious exertion and deep rest is the norm for human beings. Even well into the age of agriculture, natural light ruled human activity, and people lived a rhythmic lifestyle. There can be no question that this kind of oscillation kept us strong and resilient.

Not surprisingly, we also see the power of rhythmic engagement in modern athletic training. If you're a professional athlete or serious amateur, you know the formula for success: When you're training, hit it really hard, but when resting, rest really deep. Go to the gym, the track, or the pool and put in your best possible effort for a couple of hours, then spend the rest of your day listening to music, napping, and lounging. Your body will love it.

Athletic coaches recognize this pattern as an ideal way to build and repair tissue and reorganize the body's nervous system for maximum performance. The body thrives on this kind of oscillation, and the higher the contrast, the better. To put it in technical terms, challenge plus rest promotes "supercompensation," the process by which the body remodels tissue in anticipation of similar future challenges. Typically, we think of muscle tissue, but supercompensation takes place throughout the body: bone, connective tissue, and nervous system circuits all become more robust with oscillations of effort. When we keep this beat, our bodies respond by giving us more of what we need.

This is something that children understand instinctively: play hard for a few hours, rest deep, and then repeat. No instruction or adult guidance is required. This primal rhythm is powerfully anabolic for their bodies and their nervous systems. If they can maintain this pulse throughout childhood, there's a good chance that their bodies will grow strong and capable. But if the rhythm is disrupted by invasive adults and regimented, artificial programs, things are likely to go astray.

Call this the kindergarten model, if you will: play and explore, then take a nap. Students of all ages need this, and it ought to be built into our culture, our programs, and our institutions. If we were truly serious about crafting education that is consistent with what we know about human neurobiology, our schools would look entirely different. Not only would school start later in the day, there would also be more breaks for both students and teachers alike. We'd also pay more attention to seasonal rhythms. Do the academic work indoors in the wintertime, but when the weather gets better, it's time for everyone to go outside.

The Paleolithic-athletic-childhood rhythm is a proven formula for physical training and health, and we'd do well to assume that it works for all human endeavors: relationships, art, music, activism. Dive in with your most concentrated effort, sustain it as long as you can, then back off and rest deep. Naturally, there will be plenty of individual variation here, but the rhythm should still hold. Short bouts with long rests, or long bouts with short rests. Feel what your body wants and go with it.

KEEP THE BEAT

The life lesson is obvious: look for rhythm in everything you do. You might even think of life as one big drum circle. Begin by listening to the beat—the pulsing of the biosphere, your habitat, and the people around you. Feel the movement in your body, listen some more, then join in as best you can. If it feels awkward or you fall off the beat, take a pause, listen again, then pick it back up. Listen, engage, repeat.

Keep this practice in everything you do. Most obviously, try for some kind of normal, circadian oscillation. This is a big ask in the modern world, but the effort is essential. Cut back on the artificial light whenever possible and respect the night. Let the darkness do its work. Likewise, look for a physical-cognitive rhythm, a simple alternation between abstract labor (digital desk work) and physically engaged movement. Don't wait around for a specific workout time. If you've been at your desk and you're starting to squirm, get up and move. While you're at it, feel the locomotor rhythm of walking, skipping, or running. Or pick up a medicine ball and pump it to a beat. And as always, feel the waxing and waning of your breath.

The beauty of rhythm is that it soothes our minds and bodies as it gives us a sense of confidence in the future. Winter will pass, spring will come. Our loneliness, our depression, our injuries, and our illnesses will also pass. We may be stressed, doubtful, and uncertain about how our lives are unfolding, but we can take solace in the fact that, sooner or later, things will come around. Nature is always returning. No storm lasts forever. The wind will die down and the temperature will rise again. It always does.

WATCH YOUR LANGUAGE

> The limits of my language are the limits of my world.
> —Ludwig Wittgenstein

In conversations about stress and trauma, we hear lots of speculation about biomedical evaluation, diagnosis, and, of course, treatment. If we could just measure the cortisol levels in people's bodies, we'd know how much stress they're under and we could, as they say, perform an intervention to help them out. This may sound good on paper, but in practice, these biomedical metrics can never really tell the whole story, because mind and spirit are always getting into the act. A "high" or a "low" level of cortisol may or may not tell us anything meaningful.

In fact, cortisol levels undoubtedly wax and wane with belief, story, culture, and season, and they even change with the words we speak, a process we might call the "language-body connection." Words may look like mere shapes on a page or sounds in the air, but they have real consequences for how our bodies function and how our lives unfold.

In one notable example, legendary psychologist Martin Seligman identified a certain explanatory style he observed in patients with depression. As he listened, he recognized a distinctive pattern in their statements:

Personal: It's all my fault.

Pervasive: I always screw things up.

Permanent: I'll never be any good at any of this.

As Seligman saw it, there was a clear connection between a person's state of mind-body and the language they used. A depressed human tends to speak in a certain way, and in speaking in this way, the depressive state is reinforced. You've no doubt heard people around you use this kind of explanatory style, and maybe you even talk this way yourself on occasion.

As an alternative, Seligman suggested that we shift to a language of optimism:

Transient: This predicament is temporary. I'll feel better about this in a day or so.

Controllable: I can do something about this.

Specific: It was the wrong thing to do at the time.

The language-body connection is bidirectional—which is to say, the body influences the language we choose, and the language we choose influences the body. Each is a reflection of the other. When we choose to speak or write certain words, it inclines our metabolism, our physiology, and our neurotransmitter activity in one direction or another. Likewise, our state of body helps guide our word selection. Words are far more than the chirping of birds, as the Taoist Chuang Tzu suggested. The language-body connection is a powerful driver of what we think, how we behave, and what we might become.

STRESS TALK

It's safe to assume that a similar process takes place in both stressed and unstressed people. Listen carefully to the people around you. Perhaps you've noticed that highly stressed people tend to talk in a particular way. And doesn't their language change when their stress subsides? Most of us would agree that "stress speech" tends to be

- adversarial, an "us versus them" orientation;
- judgmental and blaming, combative and polarizing;
- vigilant, oriented toward defense and security;
- urgent, focused on the need for action;
- categorical, frequent use of statements such as "always" and "never"; and, of course,
- laced with profanity.

To generalize, this is the kind of contracted language we're likely to hear in any high-stress environment: combat, law enforcement, and, of course, action-adventure movies. It's also likely to be common with people who've been traumatized, people who've learned to see the world as a scary, dangerous place.

In contrast, feed-and-breed or rest-and-digest speech is likely to be

- inclusive and integrating;
- focused on unity and a "big tribe" orientation (we're all kin);
- holistic and relational;
- curious, compassionate, and forgiving;
- oriented toward relaxation (let it be);
- nonjudgmental and accepting;
- peppered with *both-and* statements, nuance, and gradients; and
- playful, accepting, and kind.

This is the kind of expansive language we're likely to hear in yoga studios, massage clinics, early childhood education, art schools, healthy workplaces, and romantic relationships. This is the kind of talk we hear around the campfire on summer backpacking trips with our friends. Life is sweet and our language shows it.

All of which makes perfect sense. When we're confronted by tigers, our cognitive capacity is running low, and it feels like time is running out. In this kind of predicament, it's just a lot easier to make simplistic, categorical statements about the world. In a sense, our broad-brush generalizations and adversarial statements are laborsaving devices. Black-and-white views of the world are easier to hold—even if they're not true, even if they wreak havoc in practice.

But when we're relaxed, it all goes the other way. We've got a sense of temporal and cognitive affluence, so it's easier to work with nuance, complexity, and gradients. We've got the capacity and resources to see the richness and diversity of the world, so why contract when you can expand?

Just as posture reflects internal states, so too does speech. When the people around us are talking in adversarial tones, with combative language and broad-brush statements, it's pretty safe to assume that these people are confronting tigers, have a history of stress and trauma, or are modeling the stress talk of their peers. There's no need to measure the stress hormones that are circulating in their bodies; we can tell just by listening.

Likewise, we can diagnose our own condition. What kind of language did you choose today? Did you spew a rant of fight-flight venom? Did you make a series of rash generalizations, punctuated by impulsive, judgmental accusations, laced with profanity? If so, you're probably marinating in cortisol. Maybe some rest-and-digest statements about the world would help: stories of reconciliation, compassion, forgiveness, and appreciation are a good place to begin. Widen your view, take a breath, and talk about things that work, things that are beautiful, and things that heal.

This language-body connection also tells us a great deal about the state of modern culture. Just by listening to the shift in political discourse over the last several decades, we hear a distinct trend away from the feed-and-breed language of an earlier era to fight-flight speak. Talk radio—aka "outrage radio"—reflects this trend in a very distinctive way. Both hosts and callers are quick to make black-and-white generalizations about others, cast blame, and obsess over worst-case possibilities. Listening to the quality of this "discourse," we might just as well call it "stress radio."

It's easy to see how the habitual use of such language can lead to completely different worldviews over time. Consistent use of one form or the other will eventually sculpt and solidify our autonomic nervous system, our relationships, and our futures. We can literally talk ourselves into chronic fight-flight or a state of harmonious feed-and-breed. Words matter.

It really does make a difference whether we use *either-or* statements, ultimatums, or inclusive *both-and* statements. It does make a difference whether we talk in black and white or in color, with lots of gradients. This also suggests that, with some discipline, we might even be able to talk ourselves out of anxiety, out of stress, and out of adversarial worldviews. Try some feed-and-breed speak and see how it goes. Try talking like it's Sunday morning and you've just had a big sleep. Talk like it's the first day of summer vacation, all your work is taken care of, and you've just had a massage. What would that sound like and how would it feel?

SPEAK THE HORIZONTAL

Learning to speak the language of feed-and-breed is a good place to begin our practice, but there's another dimension that calls for our attention. Call it the horizontal-vertical axis. In short, it breaks down like this:

On the vertical, we speak the modern language of the pyramid—the language of status, rank, and hierarchy. Who's higher? Who's lower? Who's winning? Who's losing? We wonder about how the pyramid works and, especially, how to move higher in the ranks. What are the rules for navigating the pyramid, and how can I play them to my advantage? This is where we're likely to hear about dominance and defeat, transactions and legalisms, profit and loss, salaries, self-interest, and win-lose relationships. We hear about advancement, standards, and certifications.

But on the horizontal axis, the conversation sounds completely different. This kind of talk is ancient and universal: primate to primate, mammal to mammal, person to person, human to human. This is the language of childhood—one animal body talking to another animal body. This is our "campfire talk," a place where rank and hierarchy fade away. Status is irrelevant in such a setting; even worse, it's a distraction from what really matters.

In a horizontal conversation, we hear almost nothing about rank or dominance. Instead, we hear questions like:

Where have you traveled?
Who are your people?
What do you like to do for fun?
Do you have a story?
What makes you laugh?

These inquiries are targeted at a person's humanity and their animal nature: their families, their travels, their struggles, their curiosity, and their passions. We're also likely to hear "bioregional talk," people making observations about people and their relationships to habitat: weather, plants, animals, and water. These are universal and timeless interests for all of us.

Looking at conversation from this perspective, it soon becomes obvious why we have so much trouble communicating in the modern world. Some people (let's call them "horizontalists") crave the ancient, primal connection of animal-to-animal talk. They don't care much about rank, hierarchy, or how to navigate the pyramid. They want to know how our human lives are unfolding and how we can connect. "Verticalists," on the other hand, are obsessed with the pyramid. Life is all about moving up, navigating the complexities of hierarchy, and climbing the ladder. For verticalists, our deep humanity is not particularly interesting or relevant.

When these two people meet, there's likely to be some strained conversation and a gulf of mutual incomprehension. If you're looking for a horizontal conversation and your partner is stuck on the vertical, you just aren't going to connect. Which is precisely how a time-travel conversation would play out: Paleolithic people, transported into the modern age, would be mystified and then repelled by the amount of vertical conversation in our world. "Why are you people so obsessed with rank and hierarchy?" they'd ask. "What about the plants, the animals, and the state of the tribe? Have you forgotten what keeps you alive?"

So, what's to be done about our conversational mismatch? Obviously, all of us need to be fluent on the vertical axis if we're going to make our way in the modern world. We need to understand and occasionally speak the language of the pyramid. We need to appreciate the fundamentals of rank and hierarchy and the ways that people and power move up and down.

But if that's the only language we speak, we're in real trouble. Every time we speak on the vertical, we displace our attention away from our historical origins and our primal relationships with body, habitat, and tribe. Call it an opportunity cost, if you will: more vertical means less horizontal. And if this goes on long enough, our amnesia will deepen, and we'll become incapable of having authentic conversations of any kind.

The solution is to spend more time on the horizontal. Forget hierarchy and rank, forget work. In particular, avoid the notorious opening question, What's your job? To be sure, this query sometimes opens up a world of curiosity, but just as often, it serves to remind people of their struggles with duty, tasks, responsibility, hierarchy, and, in particular, stress. Instead, ask people for their stories. Where have you traveled? Where have you lived? Tell me about your people. What's your passion? What are you curious about?

Remember, the vertical axis is historically abnormal. So, don't get distracted by pyramid talk. Keep your attention on the things that really matter to the human animal: body, habitat, people, food, curiosity, and the cosmos. Keep your attention where it belongs.

CREATIVE PRACTICES

CREATE FORWARD

> Develop interest in life as you see it; in people, things, literature, music—the world is so rich, simply throbbing with rich treasures, beautiful souls and interesting people. Forget yourself.
> —Henry Miller

As we've seen, one of the characteristic ways we respond to stress is by engaging in drama. That is, we fall back into the drama triangle, that notorious, dysfunctional set of relationships that begins with our perceived victimhood. When we choose to see ourselves as hapless victims, we spend our days blaming perpetrators and running to rescuers for help. But once we get locked into the drama, our powers wane and our stress gets even worse.

But today, drama is everywhere. Just listen to modern conversation, either your own internal dialogue or eavesdrop on the people around you. How many of these so-called conversations are nothing more than "drama exchanges"? Let's trade grievances: "I'll tell you about the outrageous behavior of my perpetrators, and then you can tell me yours." Or, "My victimhood is bigger and more traumatic than your victimhood." Back and forth it goes, and nothing really comes of it.

To be sure, sometimes we really just need to vent about the frustrations we feel. But if we think about how much of our conversational "airtime" is devoted to drama, we start to wonder just what we're doing. If all we're doing is trading complaints and whining, then what's the point in even having a conversation in the first place?

The same goes for the conversations that take place in our own heads. How much of our internal airtime goes toward complaining about perceived perpetrators and hoping for rescue? The transcripts would be shocking. At the end of the day, the internal dramalogue just amounts to a lot of worthless noise—noise that interferes with our creativity and our sense of peace.

To be sure, some perpetrators must be taken seriously. Real tigers can and do abuse us, and they deserve our condemnation and appropriate pushback. But it's also the case that some of our "perpetrators" are nothing more than false tigers. They aren't really chasing us through the jungle, trying to hunt us down and eat us. They're just fantasy predators, manufactured by our imagination. They only exist to help us maintain our personal sense of victimhood. I may be a lumbering fool, but if I can point the finger of blame at a "tiger," at least I'll have a reason for my predicament. In other words, an excuse.

To make matters a thousand times worse, our personal and cultural habits of victimhood and drama feed one another in a cycle of contagion. When we see the people around us claiming victimhood and blaming perpetrators, we're quick to join the action, and before long, entire societies can get wrapped up in the process, powered by cultural narratives of blame and complaint. Our xenophobia becomes institutionalized, and we may even forget that there's any history involved. This is the logic of the feud; the people across the river are the perpetrators because we say so. This fuels an intergenerational drama triangle that's almost impossible to extinguish.

CREATE YOUR WAY OUT

The way out of the triangle, as many teachers, therapists, and coaches have suggested, is the creative orientation. This is where we exercise responsibility and start building a vision of what we want to become. As we move beyond habits of blaming, complaining, excuses, and wishful thinking, life begins to open up into a world of opportunity and freedom.

In this practice, we actually change our identity. Instead of blaming circumstance or hoping for a rescue, we ask a new set of questions:

What can I do today, right this moment, to advance my creation?
Where can I exercise control?
Where does my power lie?

This is where personal growth and social activism share common ground. At its core, activism is about transcending the drama triangle and taking responsibility for our lives. But the activist (think *artivist*) doesn't just take responsibility for her own life; she takes responsibility for the state of the entire world. This stands in marked contrast to the victim's orientation; when confronted by systemic challenges that afflict our world and communities, the victim's anthem is "It's not my job." In contrast, the creative personality takes responsibility for all of it: the climate crisis, habitat destruction, social injustice, racism, sexism, and every other abuse that people inflict on the Earth and one another. In short, she owns it all. For the activist, "It *is* my job."

To be clear, the activist didn't cause these things, and she's unlikely to solve these problems in her lifetime, but this is very much beside the point. The activist isn't preoccupied by the specific causal chain of events that led to a particular problem, and she's not inclined to spend her time working out the fine-grained details of who's to blame for every human calamity. Instead, she concentrates on what's possible and, in the process, finds a wellspring of meaning and energy.

THINK OUTSIDE THE TRIANGLE

On the face of it, this creative path might seem to be an anti-solution to our stress. After all, doing genuinely creative work means exposure and vulnerability. The artist is sticking her neck out, offering her hard work to a world that may not appreciate it. Truly creative people are often ignored, rejected, misunderstood, arrested, or incarcerated. This may well sound like a recipe for *increasing* our stress.

To be sure, there are plenty of tigers that lie in wait along the creative path. But when we leave the drama triangle behind, we also gain access to some genuine power and capability that was unavailable to us when we were mired in blaming, complaining, and looking for rescue. We've got a different identity now, powered by a sense of meaning and purpose. Perpetrators and rescuers no longer interest us. We've got work to do, and no matter how it's received, there is power and resilience in the doing. Goethe was right: "Boldness has genius, power, and magic in it."

This willingness to accept responsibility is also a defining quality of our most inspiring leaders and superheroes, both real and imagined. These people are not complainers, nor are they seduced by rescue agents, substances, or ideas. They may well be fighting epic battles against powerful forces of destruction and injustice, but they keep their energy focused. It's hard to imagine Rachel Carson, Jackie Robinson, Martin Luther King Jr., Nelson Mandela, Mahatma Gandhi, Colin Kaepernick, or the men and women of Standing Rock blaming, complaining, or looking for a rescue. They're too busy creating the future.

Ultimately, it's all about our orientation. Yes, some predicaments are overwhelming and exhausting, but no matter the depth of the adversity, we are free to choose our interpretations. We're free to choose our stories. We're free to move beyond complaining, blame, excuses, and rescue.

The creative path is not an easy one, but this is where the meaning lies. You may not think of yourself as an artist, and you might be quick to assume you lack the skills, the talents, or the aptitude. But this is all beside the point. Creativity isn't an optional luxury for special or gifted people; it's a foundational practice for human function. All of us are capable, and all of us benefit from the effort. So, think like an artist:

• When the tigers come to visit, double down on your creative work, whatever it might be.

- Start digging into the messy, ambiguous, and perplexing act of making the things that give you meaning.
- Don't wait for inspiration to come to you. Start working.
- Don't waste time bemoaning your lack of talent or aptitude. Start working.

Success lies not in the outcome but in the effort. And in the long run, it's better to fail as a creator than to succeed as a victim.

PLAY IS THE WAY

> The creation of something new is not accomplished by the intellect but by the play instinct acting from inner necessity. The creative mind plays with the objects it loves.
> —Carl Jung, *Psychological Types*

When we're mired in stress, we feel blocked, cornered, and out of options. Everywhere we look we see limitations, restrictions, boundaries, and borders. Our vagility is compromised, and it feels like there's nowhere to turn—we're boxed in. The situation may well feel hopeless, but there's good news hiding in plain sight, a legacy from our childhood, a deeply wired inclination that can move us into fresh understandings, insights, and orientations.

Maybe you think that you've outgrown this childhood delight, but in fact, the play drive is deeply wired into our bodies and our collective unconscious. In fact, it's a human universal, identified as such by anthropologist Donald Brown in his 1991 book *Human Universals.* But not only is it a *human* universal, it's also a *mammalian* universal. In other words, we're in good company: all mammals play, all primates play, and it may even be the case that birds, reptiles, and dinosaurs have felt it too. And this has been going on for tens or maybe even hundreds of millions of years.

We remember play as good fun, but this is actually some really serious business, not only for us as individuals but for society and culture as a whole. Play creates an atmosphere of safety, lowers stress hormones, and raises levels of neurotrophic factors in the brain. Researchers have found that merely *anticipating* laughter boosts the production of mood-elevating hormones called β-endorphins.

Stress contracts, but play and comedy expand. Play moves our minds and spirits as it enlarges our sense of possibility. It dissolves inert, calcified knowledge, helps us generate new behavioral options, and reframes conventional perceptions and ideas. It also helps us transcend "false end points," ideas and methods believed to be complete. Perhaps you remember the legendary high jumper Dick Fosbury and his "Fosbury flop." At the time, coaches assumed that the standard technique was the only possibility—this was a false end point. But Fosbury ignored his coaches, played around, went over the bar backward, and went on to become a world champion. Now, everyone goes over the bar backward.

SEEK THE PLAY STATE

When we feel playful, we're in an ideal state for human function. Playfulness is the optimal physiological state, the optimal athletic state, the optimal learning state, and the optimal relational state. When we're immersed in play, we're lightly stressed; we're on the left side of the inverse U-shaped curve of stress-hormone concentration and benefit. This is the state of engagement and immersion described by psychologist Mihály

Csíkszentmihályi as "flow." And in this sense, it's perfectly appropriate to claim that "play is medicine."

But it's not just an individual benefit. When we engage in play, even playful language and attitudes, we signal safety to those around us. It's safe to assume that people who witness playful behavior experience reduced cortisol and stress levels. Likewise, play gives others a sense of permission: It's OK to move. It's OK to try new combinations of ideas and methods. It's OK to experiment and fail. All of which is essential in crafting, surviving, and thriving in our personal and professional relationships.

Comedians know all this full well. Their playful language bends reality, reframes convention, and offers surprise. Good comedy jumps us out of cognitive ruts and intellectual habit. A good comedic workout is an exercise in flexibility, fluidity, and transformation, which of course is something we all need at this moment in history. It's not a stretch to say that comedians are some of the most important people in modern culture. Like play, comedy is psychosocial medicine.

PLAY DEPRIVATION

As stressed-out adults, we tend to forget about the transformative power of play, or if we do think about it, we trivialize it. Play is just for kids, you know, and we're just too sophisticated for all that. We're busy keeping our lives boxed up, lined up, and organized, so we pigeonhole play into "a fond memory from childhood" and forget about it.

But play is deadly serious business for all social animals, something that we begin to understand when we study its absence. Behavioral scientists who work with rodents have identified a window of play behavior in the development of young rats; if young animals are separated from their peers during this time, they miss out on play opportunities. This turns out to be catastrophic for their development into socially competent adults. Rats that are experimentally isolated and play deprived go on to develop "persistent social deficits"—which is to say, they don't play well with others.[79]

All of which is a rather terrifying message for modern society and culture. Human play behavior is hard to measure because we play in so many ways, but you don't have to be a behavioral scientist to suspect that modern humans are chronically play deprived and that play opportunities are not equally distributed across society. And obviously, many of us are suffering "persistent social deficits" and struggle with adaptation.

In fact, as our work and productivity ethic grows ever more tyrannical, play is becoming an endangered psychospiritual experience. The modern workplace is bad enough, but in the world of sports, particularly youth sports, overzealous adults are systematically turning play into work. More-sophisticated training, more reps, more hours of specialization, and the ever-present emphasis on victory—this professionalization of youth sports is sucking the joy out of childhood and the value out of play. And it's a perfectly avoidable catastrophe; there's no reason whatsoever to impose professional training programs on children who really just want to play. Elite performance is for adults, if that. Give the kids the toys and opportunities and let them do what they do best. The play is the point. Play *is* victory.

PLAY YOUR WAY IN

Of course, serious adults are inclined to be skeptical about all of this. Discipline is there for a reason, and we're taking responsibility to do things right. If we just start playing around like children, we're going to wreak havoc on sensitive methods and established protocols. Without some kind of structure, things will spiral out of control.

All true, but play need not be completely random or impulsive. In fact, creative people understand that the best play takes place within certain guardrails. Artists and athletes call this the principle of "limited sloppiness" or "disciplined anarchy." Set a range, then go wild within those limits. The legendary Hollywood screenwriter Robert McKee calls this "the principle of creative limitation." In his landmark book *Story: Substance, Structure, Style, and the Principles of Screenwriting*, he writes:

> The principle of Creative Limitation calls for freedom within a circle of obstacles. Talent is like a muscle: without something to push against, it atrophies. So we deliberately put rocks in our path, barriers that inspire. We discipline ourselves as to what to do, while we're boundless as to how to do it.[80]

Even in the world of comedy, we see a similar theme. Jon Stewart, former host of *The Daily Show*, put it this way: "Creativity comes from limits, not freedom." In other words, the purpose of rules isn't to inhibit the creative process but to channel and liberate our energies.

This suggests that there's a complementary relationship between play and discipline. We regulate our training, not just because we like being serious adults but also because it helps us play with even greater exuberance and creativity.

BE A PLAY OPPORTUNIST

In any case, it's not easy being a player in our modern world. Our vagility is constantly under threat, and it often feels like no amount of work is enough. So, how do we, as overburdened adults, remember? Can we play our way out of stress? If we've fallen out of the play state, how can we get back in? How do we refresh that feeling of possibility that once moved us to outrageous acts of creativity? Can we play our way back into play? Try this:

1. **Start by reframing the whole thing.** Play is not a distraction from our work; it's a vital element. Being overly serious is not an asset; it's actually a liability. Play is not just for children; it's fundamental to all human creativity. Play is not a sideshow; it lies at the core of whatever it is we're trying to do.

2. **Exaggerate.** Make big things bigger and small things smaller. Exaggerate your exaggerations. Stretch reality as far as it can go. Build unlikely connections, no matter how absurd. Draw from as many disciplines, professions, and experiences as possible. And above all, stop judging your creations—and those of others. There will be plenty of time for that later.

3. **Work from a place of affluence**, even if that affluence is completely imaginary. Remember your best childhood moments and the vista that stretched to the horizon. In this affluence, you've got all the time in the world. There are no constraints, no social limitations, no need to be realistic about anything. It's just you and possibility, with zero judgment. No prejudging, no remorse. No error, no failure. Take the risk and run with it.

4. **Be a play opportunist.** Stay on the alert for play in whatever conditions you might be facing. Be a hunter-gatherer of play. And remember these words from James Carse in *Finite and Infinite Games: A Vision of Life as Play and Possibility*: "A finite game is played for the purpose of winning,

an infinite game for the purpose of continuing the play."

In other words, don't be constrained by the prospect of victory or defeat. The real point is to continue the play. Just ask any kid.

CHANGE THE NARRATIVE

> People think that stories are shaped by people.
> In fact, it's the other way around.
> —Terry Pratchett, *Witches Abroad*

When we're stressed, it's tempting to assume that all tigers are pretty much alike. They prowl around our camps, derail our concentration, and make a mess of things. We wish they'd just go away and leave us in peace, but there's a fundamental distinction that can make our experience a whole lot easier to understand and tolerate. If we can distinguish between objective and subjective tigers, we can think more clearly about what we're up against.

Objective tigers are real, imminent threats to our lives. They're simple, direct, and unambiguous dangers that would impact any animal, any mammal, any primate. Subjective tigers, on the other hand, are products of our imagination. They bother us not because they're inherently dangerous or harmful but because of the meanings we attach to them. And these are the tigers that really drive us crazy.

In one sense, objective tigers are easy. To be sure, they're genuinely dangerous and must be taken seriously, but they're mostly predictable and generally follow physical laws. If we're observant and vigilant, we can learn to protect ourselves from the worst of them. If you learn the ways of gravity, predator

STRATEGIES AND ANTIDOTES   261

behavior, fire, and physical trauma, you can keep most of them at bay.

As for the subjective tigers, these critters require an entirely different approach. Because they're creatures of our imagination, they can't be easily contained, predicted, or manipulated by conventional methods. This is where we turn to narrative and story. If you're plagued by subjective tigers, there might be a way to make them go away or moderate their impact, simply by changing the meaning that you attach to the experience.

On the face of it, this approach may seem soft, but it's actually extremely powerful. In fact, even our objective stressors are fungible and malleable to some degree. Imagine that you're caught out in the mountains overnight without a sleeping bag. Objectively, the stress will be palpable, real, and even life threatening. But if that experience is part of a grand alpine climbing adventure that brings you joy and meaning, it might seem trivial, even welcome and exciting. Story gives meaning, meaning sculpts experience, experience sculpts body. When we change our stories, we change our identity, our relationships, and the trajectory of our lives.

All of which suggests a path forward and a role for the human animal—that of the narrative activist. This may sound like a fancy term for *storyteller*, but it's really much more than that. The narrative activist challenges dysfunctional stories directly, points to their flaws, and generates new narratives to take their place. As the narrative activist sees it, the cure for bad stories is better stories.[81]

ABANDON THE DINOSAUR NARRATIVES

The art begins by going upstream to the origin myths and narratives that shape our personal lives and culture. Instead of simply living the conventional narratives that are handed to us in our youth, we start by identifying defunct, outdated stories that no longer serve us. These are the dinosaur narratives, personal or cultural stories still in circulation but doomed to failure and extinction. These narratives may have served a purpose at some point, but their relevance is coming to an end. We can choose to tell these stories as we wish, but they are no longer useful, as doomed as *T. rex* and all the rest.

In the domain of personal experience, most of us live with dinosaur narratives to some degree, leftover stories from childhood, irrational explanations, or outright fabrications for how people and the world work. We tell ourselves that we're worthless, that we're responsible for our parents' divorce, that we'll never measure up to the expectations laid out for us, and on it goes. These stories were never really true in the first place, and they become even less so over time. We can try to keep them alive, but they're doomed to irrelevance.

Naturally, there's plasticity at work here. Stories are kept alive by repeated circulation through our neural and social networks. It's just like any sensory or motor skill; tell a story enough times and the circuit becomes stronger and eventually solidifies. Keep telling it and eventually the narrative becomes so familiar that we classify it as true and factual, no matter its original veracity. And given what we now know about the unreliability of memory, we might even be solidifying stories that were never really true in the first place. At this point, the narrative becomes wickedly dysfunctional.

NARRATIVE QUAGMIRES

Story has a curious effect on our ability to tolerate and endure stress. Sometimes, it helps. We spin a narrative about how the world works, and we gain a certain comfort in the telling; the world may well be trying and difficult, but at least we've got an explanation that makes sense to us. But over time, we rely more heavily on our interpretation, and slowly, imperceptibly, we fall victim to confirmation bias. That is, we gather facts that fit our narrative and ignore most everything else. In the process, the story solidifies and becomes stronger, even taking over the life of the storyteller himself. As one quipster put it, "First you tell the story, and after a while, the story begins to tell you." Little by little, our understanding of the world becomes distorted, and now we're more vulnerable to stress than we were before.

In the process, we fall into a narrative quagmire. We've invested heavily in a single story or set of stories, and we're unable or unwilling to climb out. This is the tragedy of fundamentalism and the origin of the Latin proverb *"Cave ab homine unius libri"*—that is, "Beware of the man of one book."

THE ART OF REFRAMING

The way out of this quagmire is to develop a sense of narrative flexibility and reframing. When we change the borders around an issue, event, or perspective, we open up new possibilities for awareness, stress relief, and even sapience.

Of course, reframing is as old as storytelling itself and can be used by anyone, for any purpose. Marketing, public persuasion, courtroom presentations, and political campaigning are all about framing and reframing. Most of our difficult conversations and arguments in daily life, romance, and family are about where to put the frame. All of us are reframers to some degree, although some are better at it than others.

The beauty of reframing is that, used wisely, it can move us toward a more functional future. For example, when we reframe lifestyle behaviors such as sleep and regular physical movement as prosocial and profuture, we promote personal and public welfare simultaneously. Likewise, when we reframe a crisis as an opportunity, we change our experience in a fundamental way. Suddenly, our stress and fear feel less overwhelming, and our minds are free to pursue the possibility for creativity. Instead of thinking *adversity is a stressor*, we can reframe the situation as *adversity is a stimulus for adaptation*. We can even reframe our injuries as opportunities to live and move our bodies in new ways. Pain is unpleasant, but it's valuable information that can lead us in new directions.

In the world of activism, reframing can be particularly effective. When people say that "conservation is health care," it shifts our attention to the human-habitat connection and illuminates our continuity with nature. Suddenly, we see the link between our bodies and the world. In 2016, anti-pipeline activists at Standing Rock famously declared, "We are water protectors, not protesters." This kind of shift moved the focus away from militancy and toward the preservation of something universally valuable.

Bioregionalism is another powerful reframe because it inspires us to ask hard questions about the way we've been structuring our politics, our economy, our commerce, and even our relations with one another. It gets us out of the human-centric world and forces us to look at the habitat and creatures that sustain us. Equally powerful is the Rights of Nature movement. A small but growing number of governments are now granting rights to various ecosystems, rivers, and watersheds. The beauty of this reframing is that it forces us to confront the contradiction that lies at the heart of our culture and our failure to give voice to the world that gives us life.

Another powerful reframing comes from the world of neurobiology. For most of human history, we've been quick to condemn people with bad behavior as "evil," "stupid," or of "poor character." We put them in jail, exile them from our communities, medicate them, or kill them outright. But today, we're beginning to understand and appreciate the biological effects of adverse childhood experiences, trauma, concussions, combat, and disease. In this light, people who behave badly aren't bad people—they're people with neurological injuries, and they can be helped. This understanding moves us away from retribution and toward compassionate treatment.

Even the entire field of biology can be described as a reframing. Darwin's *Origin of Species* threw our human identity into a new light, and suddenly, humans went from being the greatest creation the world had ever known to just another animal. For a culture built on the assumption of human supremacy, biology is turning out to be one of the greatest—and most inconvenient—reframings ever.

All of which begs the obvious question: How do we improve our proficiency at reframing? The answer, as we know by way of the SAID principle, is that we get good at reframing stories by practicing that very thing. It's always specific. That is, we get good at narrative flexibility by changing our stories. Start with any story you like, maybe even one that you're really attached to. Change the point of view, the tone, the protagonist, the trajectory. Put it in a different context and give it a different meaning. Don't let it stagnate.

This may all sound like an exercise from an English class, and maybe so. But this is really foundational practice for anyone who wants to survive and prosper in an ambiguous modern world. Far from being grim taskmasters and nitpickers, our English teachers and editors are some of our most valuable allies. Practice reframing and you won't get bogged down in a narrative quagmire again.

STORIES OF A FEATHER

Stand-alone stories are all well and good. We love to watch movies, and we love to hear one another tell a good yarn around the coffee table or the campfire. But in the grand scope of human experience, no story is an island. They're always connected to other stories, other ideas, and other meanings. To put it another way, stories are social animals. They affiliate with one another in groups, packs, schools, flocks, and swarms. And of course, stories of a feather tend to flock together.

A single story may well be meaningful, inspiring, or instructive in its own way, but what really matters is how it connects to other story clusters that circulate across history and through culture. As always, it's about relationship. Does your story reinforce other stories? Does it support or contradict a cultural story cluster that people hold dear? Does it illuminate a path forward, or does it cling to an established set of assumptions about how the world works?

This is where the narrative activist can do some good work. It's not enough to tell an entertaining or even a meaningful story. It's got to connect. Does it build continuity between isolated modern humans and the life-supporting circles that sustain them? Does it build a web of integration?

TELL A BIGGER STORY

It's easy to get wrapped up in the small stories of our personal lives and the local experience of the people around us. But it's equally essential to listen to and tell the big narratives about our species, our big history, our biology, and our affiliation with the natural world. As a people, we're in desperate need of stories about the resilience that lives in our bodies. We need stories of interdependence and affiliation, stories about the circle, the web, of life. When we tell and hear these stories, we become stronger.

Ideally, we'd hear such narratives from our physicians and health care providers, and we'd get reminders of our innate power at every turn. In a truly ecological and health-centric culture, such stories would be an essential part of every doctor-patient encounter. But sadly, these are vanishingly rare events in modern medicine, and most of us are forced to make do on our own.

So, we've got a choice: accept our prevailing cultural story of isolation or start reframing it. Accept the story of humans as independent, stand-alone organisms, or tell a story of strength and interdependence. Look for ways to integrate native and indigenous wisdom with the findings of modern biology and ecological science. Tell a new-old story, one that speaks to our ancestry, our power, our resilience, and our aptitude for adaptation. Ground your story in the actual, biological history of the living world. This will be, or should be, our task for the next thousand years.

DISCOVER WHAT YOU'RE MADE OF

> Character consists of what you do on the third
> and fourth tries.
> —James A. Michener

In the standard narrative, we often talk about stress as a purely negative force that makes our lives miserable. It's all downside and bad news. If we could just make the tigers go away, we could get back to enjoying our lives. But there's actually a powerful reframing we can use to find our way. That is, stress is actually an essential experience that helps reveal our character and gives us an understanding of who we really are.

This perspective comes from what might seem an unlikely source—the world of Hollywood movies and screenwriting. Just imagine a typical movie. As curious viewers, we want to know about the characters involved and what makes them tick. We can get some clues straightaway from the appearance of their faces, their bodies, their clothing, and their mannerisms, but this just doesn't take us very far. What we really want to know is their essence, their true selves. As the story unfolds, we're alert for more clues, but if their lives are easy, we just aren't going to learn much about who they really are.

This is where the screenwriter goes to work, constructing an escalating series of stressful events, all with an eye toward testing and revealing the true character of his characters. This principle holds true no matter the genre, from romantic comedies all the way to the most explosive action adventure or sci-fi movie. The more stress a character endures—the more tigers he encounters—the more completely his character is revealed. The type of stress doesn't much matter; it could be physical, social, romantic, or ethical. As long as the protagonist is under pressure, character will be exposed.

This is precisely the process described by screenwriter Robert McKee in *Story: Substance, Structure, Style, and the Principles of Screenwriting*. For McKee, stress is the means by which character is illuminated on the page and on the screen. Tone and plot are important, but if you really want your audience to know and understand your people, you've got to put them under increasing levels of adversity and show how they respond.

In turn, this tells us a great deal about our own relationship with stress. Tigers, as onerous as they may feel in the moment, are actually doing us a valuable service by illuminating our character. Suppose you're face to face with a big stressor. How will you react? Are you going to buckle in despair, or are you going to respond with courage, persistence, and wisdom? In this sense, stress is not something to be exterminated but something to be respected, honored, and even savored.

Just imagine that the great screenwriter in the sky is revising her script for your life. She's looking at your character and wondering what makes you tick. Who is this person really? Is she strong and resilient? Soft and corruptible? Driven by a sense of purpose? Let's find out. Release the tigers! Build up the stress, step by escalating step. Before long, the audience will know the strength of your character, your resolve, your determination, and maybe even your wisdom.

All of which gives powerful meaning to our stress. It won't make the tigers go away, but at least you can gain some insight: What does this experience reveal about my character? What does it tell me about who I am? And it's not just the movies, by the way; philosophers have long understood that stress is a powerful frenemy, an educational experience that teaches us who we really are. As the Russian revolutionary Leon Trotsky put it: "The depth and strength of a human character are defined by its moral reserves. People reveal themselves completely only when they are thrown out of the customary conditions of their life, for only then do they have to fall back on their reserves."[82]

This changes everything. When our lives are tied up in knots, one of the worst things about it is that the stress seems so inexplicable, so random and without purpose. But with this new understanding, stress begins to make a kind of sense. Even better, it gives us options. It may well feel like there's nothing we can do about the impossible dilemmas we face, but we can always act with dignity, resolve, and honor.

When stress hits the fan, we sometimes daydream about winning the lottery or finding some formula that would make our lives stress free. We'd get our lives all buttoned up, organized, and nailed down. But with this new understanding, we begin to realize that such a utopian life would in fact be a horrible fate, an existence without meaning, passion, or purpose. In the end, it's better to suffer and find out who we are.

And it's not just the character of individuals that's at stake; the same principle is at work at the level of society and culture. What does it say about the character of a nation or a people when they are stricken by chaos, turmoil, or ecological collapse? As tigers circle the perimeter of camp, do the people stand on higher principles of honor, dignity, and wisdom, or do they fragment into petty squabbles, bickering, conspiracy theorizing, victim posturing, and mud throwing? The great screenwriter in the sky is posing these very questions at this very moment, waiting to see what will be revealed about who we really are.

PHILOSOPHICAL PERSPECTIVES

SEE THE GOOD

> The universe is full of magical things, patiently waiting for our senses to grow sharper.
> —Eden Phillpotts, *A Shadow Passes*

As legend has it, Albert Einstein met with reporters late in life and was asked to reflect on the really big questions of human existence. One asked him, "At this point in history, is there one essential question that humanity must ask?" Einstein paused for a moment and answered, "Yes, 'Is the Universe friendly?'"

It's a perfect quip, not just for what it implies on a cosmic, existential scale and for the future of humanity but also for the fact that this is essentially the same question the autonomic nervous system asks throughout life. In every moment of every day, it's always wondering about the nature of its world and what it means for survival. *Is this habitat friendly? Are the people around me friendly?* If the answer is yes, the body activates its anabolic systems and prepares for exploration, affiliation, curiosity, growth, and learning. If the answer is no, it becomes vigilant and prepares for action and defense, fighting or fleeing.

This is where things get interesting. Not only do we have the ability to sense genuine physical threats directly, we also have the ability to imagine them in ways that are completely independent of reality. Mind, story, and culture are always getting into the act, interpreting the meaning of events at every turn.

Acts of imagination have very real physiological consequences; every thought, every mental image, every muse has a downstream physical effect. This is why stress researchers are careful to say that the trigger for the stress response is not a threat to the organism but, rather, a *perceived* threat to the organism. Interpretation is everything. If we perceive our capability to be adequate for the challenge at hand, it's going to be an easy day. But if we judge our skills to be deficient, it's going to be a struggle, no matter the actual nature of our circumstances. In fact, work by June Gruber at Yale University has shown remarkable physiological differences between various kinds of stress events.[83] When a stressor was perceived as a challenge, subjects showed increased cardiac output, increased diameter of circulatory blood vessels, increased blood flow to the brain, and increased cognitive and physical performance. All good things.

In contrast, when a stressor was perceived as a threat, subjects showed decreased cardiac output, decreased diameter of circulatory vessels, decreased blood flow to the brain, and decreased cognitive and physical performance. All bad.

This suggests a narrative strategy for dealing with potential stressors and big events on the horizon. Perhaps you're called upon to step up to speak in public, manage some chaos at work, or navigate the turmoil of a difficult personal drama. Instead of simply reacting to the pressure, try this story:

This situation is simply a challenge and a test of my adaptability. Fortunately, I come from a long line of highly adaptable animals that have been adjusting to difficult and even life-threatening circumstances for millions of years. My body has a rich history of adaptation. My ancestors have found ways to live in

*outrageously challenging circumstances. If they can do
it, so can I.*

Interpretation is such a powerful driver of human experience and physiology that it even affects our long-term health outcomes. Stanford professor Kelly McGonigal describes a study conducted at the University of Wisconsin School of Medicine and Public Health in which researchers asked two very simple questions: How much stress are you under? and Do you believe stress is harmful to your health?

Years later, they compared death records and found a marked difference in mortality. Those who believed "stress is bad for you" were significantly more likely to have died than those who held a friendlier view. The authors concluded: "High amounts of stress and the perception that stress impacts health are each associated with poor health and mental health. Individuals who perceived that stress affects their health and reported a large amount of stress had an increased risk of premature death."[84]

In other words, the belief that stress is bad for your health is actually bad for your health.

PARANOID PRIMATES

The problem is that we don't see reality clearly. Our history as vulnerable bipeds in the predator-rich habitats of prehistory has skewed our attention toward vigilance, even hypervigilance. That rustling in the bushes could be anything, but if you interpret it as a dangerous predator on the prowl, you're more likely to live to see another day and pass your psychophysical disposition down to your descendants. Treat that rustle as something friendly, and you're more likely to wind up in the gut of a hungry carnivore. And so, even in a modern predator-free environment that's generally safe, we tend to see events and conditions as more dangerous and unfriendly than they actually are. In this sense, we're wired for paranoia. The consequences are far-reaching. What was an asset in the Paleo becomes a liability in a modern world that's swarming with stimuli. When you're living in the bush, there's not much of a price to be paid for "false positives." If that rustle in the bushes turns out not to be a leopard, you can simply take a deep breath, laugh it off, and return to your walkabout.

But in the modern world, the false positives add up. Fears that are triggered by a news headline, social media post, or ambiguous social encounter may turn out to be unfounded, but when it happens often enough, the repeated activation of the stress response begins to feed on itself, corroding both our bodies and our cognition. Our vigilance intensifies, and the world begins to look deadlier than it really is.

FRIENDLIER THAN YOU THINK

The good news is, once we understand this primal inclination toward vigilance, we're in a better position to think clearly about the world. Yes, there are genuine threats, but we almost always exaggerate. Our negativity bias tries to keep our bodies safe and alive, but in today's world, it actually makes our problems more intractable. Knowing this, we can remind ourselves that things are probably not as bad as they seem. It's just the human mind doing what it does so well—turning insignificant molehills into gigantic mountains. We can calm down, take a deep breath, and rest assured that things are probably going to work out.

This frees us up to see more of the friendliness around us. In recent years, researchers and therapists have pointed to the beneficial effects of gratitude, kindness, and the intentional practice of focusing on the nurturing qualities of the world.

This advice bears repeating, because for many of us, it just doesn't come naturally.

Our ancient, slightly paranoid brains need to be reminded that, yes, there are plenty of things to celebrate, to savor, and to be grateful for. Predators are real, but so too are the spectacular qualities of the natural world, the friendship and love of the people around us, and the richness of human culture. In this sense, we're actually swimming in a sea of friendship. Friendliness is the norm; unfriendliness is the exception.

Likewise, we're reminded of our creative responsibility. Everyone we meet is wondering about the friendliness of the world, scanning the environment for clues about danger and potential. We are part of that creation. We can sculpt one another's attention toward danger, duality, and hostility, or we can show people the friendliness that exists in almost every moment. This is not just a good thing to do; it's a smart thing to do. When the people around us see friendliness, they relax. They become more receptive and maybe even a little more sapient. Being friendly is far more than just being nice; it's a vital element of health activism.

KEEP YOUR EYE ON WHAT IS

> Life is a series of natural and spontaneous changes. Don't resist them; that only creates sorrow. Let reality be reality. Let things flow naturally forward in whatever way they like.
> —Lao Tzu, Tao Te Ching

Ultimately, stress is about perspective. Sometimes we experience direct threats to our physical survival, but more often our stress is a consequence of the way we explain reality to ourselves. In turn, this suggests a strategy: if we could just give up some of our expectation and judgment, we might feel and perform a whole lot better.

Consider the expectation so many young people grow up with, the standard fantasy model for the modern human life: Go to high school, make lots of friends, excel at sports, get good grades, and have a good time. Get into college, focus on your studies, fall in love, graduate, and get a great job. Build a family and a long, lucrative career in which you'll be respected by your colleagues and peers. Your professional life will be exciting and filled with creative work. People will be fair, honest, and sincere. Later, you'll ease into your senior years in good health and watch as your children and grandchildren go on to success of their own.

It all sounds great, but for most of us, it just doesn't work out that way. To put it bluntly, our standard model is a fantasy that sets us up for frustration. Once our story-driven expectation comes in contact with reality, the stress hits the fan. Reality fails to live up to the narrative, so we blame ourselves. *There must be something wrong with me; I am a failure.*

But the problem is not you; it's the expectation. If there was no expectation, there would be no stress. If there was no expectation, we wouldn't be so completely shattered when it all fails to come true. This is the problem with all of our utopian ideas about how life is supposed to work. On some rare occasions, we fit the model, but for most of us, most of the time, things take a very different turn.

The solution would be to either have a more accurate expectation or, even better perhaps, no expectation at all. Simply live life as it presents itself and adapt on the fly. This may well sound crazy or impossible, but this is precisely the recommendation we hear in the world of martial art, where teachers sometimes advise their students to shift their perspective and remember that "the enemy is never wrong."

This counsel may well sound preposterous to the beginner, but the lesson is sound. The idea is to remain fluid and adaptable; don't get wrapped up in some expectation about what your opponent should or shouldn't be. The enemy—the adversary, the situation—just is. Abandon your psychic resistance and your anger; all it's really doing is gumming up the works and interfering with your creativity. So let it go. Observe reality and adapt accordingly. Fight for what you believe in, but don't get caught up in unnecessary judgment and evaluation. Don't be trapped by your own mind.

This is not to say we should simply accept everything about the enemy or the world as it is. Of course, the destruction of our biosphere is wrong. Of course, the exploitation and domination of other people is wrong. Of course, the manipulation of truth through lies and conspiracy theorizing is wrong. Rather, this is an argument for freedom and adaptation. It's an argument for letting go of expectation and working with the world as it presents itself. The fight remains essential, but the indignation and stress are optional. In the long run, "reality is never wrong" might well be the ultimate koan for stress relief and resilience, the ultimate expression of adaptive psychology.

Outrage and emotion have their place in conflicted encounters, but there comes a time when the best course is to play the situation as it stands. Think of your favorite opponents, grievances, and adversaries. Now, imagine abandoning your expectation and judgment; these things and people simply are what they are. It's a powerful thought experiment that might just free you up, dissolve your stress, and put you in a position for more-skillful action. Remember, life is capable of anything. People are capable of anything. Humans are complex, multifaceted animals, struggling to live in an alien environment. We're driven by ancient impulses that sometimes bubble to the surface, leading us to behave in some strange and incomprehensible ways. Everyone is irrational.

We'd like to have things a certain way, but our expectations are beside the point. Our job is to create and recreate adaptations on the fly. When we get too wrapped up in the wrongness of people, organizations, or events, we become rigid and lose our sapience. We lose our ability to move and, in turn, become even more vulnerable. If we can let go of our indignation, we can start fresh and return to the encounter with a clear vision.

As a stress-relieving practice, this reframing is almost magical. As soon as we say, "Reality is never wrong," our minds turn around and a lot of our angst simply disappears, at least for a while. The conflict and the danger may persist, but the anger and indignation lose their ability to tyrannize us. In turn, this frees us up to bring more of our resources to bear on doing what needs to be done. So, whatever you do, keep your eye on what is.

FIND YOUR WHY

> Life is not an easy matter . . . You cannot live through it without falling into frustration and cynicism unless you have before you a great idea which raises you above personal misery, above weakness, above all kinds of perfidy and baseness.
>
> —Leon Trotsky, *Trotsky's Diary in Exile: 1935*

Tigers prowl the perimeters of our camps, sometimes attacking us outright, sometimes menacing us from afar. We try to learn their ways and fight them as best we can, but there's only so much we can do. Over time, these conditions take a toll on our spirits and our bodies. Some of us buckle under the strain, but some of us manage to summon a resilience, as if from out of nowhere—a power and energy that sustains—even in the face of desperate, trying, and stressful circumstances.

This is what Viktor Frankl observed as he looked around his POW camp and saw suffering all around him. Men were starving and freezing, and some were literally worked to death. There was pain and misery in every moment. Some of the men succumbed to the strain and perished early, but others managed to live and even find fleeting moments of satisfaction in companionship. Frankl wondered, Why do some survive while others weaken and die?

His conclusion, as most of us now know, was that the survivors possessed a sense of meaning and purpose that animated their lives and helped them transcend their conditions. Frankl was fond of quoting Nietzsche: "He who has a why to live can transcend almost any how." Or we might say today, "He who has a why to live can tolerate almost any stressor."

For Frankl, success comes when we get out of ourselves and train our attention on some larger purpose:

> [T]he true meaning in life is to be discovered in the world rather that within man or his own psyche . . . being human always points and is directed, to something, or someone, other than himself—be it a meaning to fulfill or another human being to encounter. The more one forgets himself—by giving himself to a cause to serve or another person to love—the more human he is and the more he actualizes himself.[85]

Quite naturally, this insight has a powerful appeal to those of us living in a hyperstressed environment, and it even suggests that having a "why" might well be the single more important factor in our health and our ability to manage the complexity of the modern world. Suddenly, all our obsessive focus on diet, exercise, and the minutiae of health begins to seem rather trivial and even irrelevant. After all, none of the prisoners in Nazi concentration camps had anything resembling an optimal diet or exercise program. And yet, some of them managed to live and later thrive. Frankl himself lived to the age of ninety-two, animated, we can be sure, by his own powerful sense of why.

BUILD A BIGGER WHY

For many of us, the fundamental problem of our modern lives is that we spend too much of our time chasing after insignificant whys. Frantic and overwhelmed by information overload, stress, and distraction, we don't take time to reflect and, instead, go about chasing superficial meanings—meanings that may not even be our own. Driven by impulse, we chase the whys that are given to us by commercial interests and, in the process, become little more than good consumers. And sadly, these little whys do little or nothing to sustain us in the face of adversity.

Steven Cole at the University of California, Los Angeles, has spent years studying how negative experiences such as loneliness and stress can increase the expression of genes promoting inflammation and, in turn, disease. In 2013, Cole and colleagues examined the influence of well-being and focused on two types: *hedonic*, which comes from pleasure and rewards (think sex, drugs, and rock and roll), and *eudaemonic*, which comes from having a purpose beyond self-gratification.[86]

These two forms were measured by having participants note their well-being over the previous week, how often they felt happy (hedonic) or that their life had a sense of direction (eudaemonic). Although scoring highly in one often meant scoring highly in the other and both correlated with lower levels of depression, they had opposite effects on gene expression. People with higher measures of hedonic well-being had a higher expression of inflammatory genes and a lower expression of genes for disease-fighting antibodies, a pattern also seen in loneliness and stress. For people scoring highest on eudaemonia, it was the opposite. "There were surprises all around," Cole said. "The biggest surprise being that you can feel similarly happy but the biology looks so notably different."

Cole suspected that eudaemonia—with its focus on purpose—decreases the nervous system's reaction to sudden danger, which increases heart rate, breathing, and surges of adrenaline. Overactivation of this stress-response system, as we see with chronic stress, causes harmful inflammation. "There may be something saying 'be less frightened, or less worried, anxious or uncertain.'"

There's a neurological explanation for how this might work. Focusing on something positive and bigger than yourself may activate the ventral striatum, which can inhibit areas like the amygdala, which contributes to the stress response. Similar research shows that higher scores on a scale of purpose correlated with less amygdala activation. Other studies indicate that people with higher eudaemonic well-being have both increased activity in the ventral striatum and lower levels of the stress hormone cortisol. "Things that you value can override things that you fear," said Cole.[87]

Sadly, it's beginning to look like sex, drugs, and rock and roll might not be the true path to health, stress resistance, and sustainability after all. What we need is a big why. And the good news is that most of us already know how to do this. That is, it's a human universal to be moved by the big whys of family, community, country, justice, and the quest for a better future. Intuitively, we seem to understand that life just works better when we focus on something bigger.

Likewise, we begin to see that the self-focused whys of modern culture are abnormal and historically deviant. "I'm working for me" doesn't sustain us in hard times. A narcissistic why can drive us for a while, but it ultimately turns ugly, dysfunctional, and irrelevant. Frankl would surely recognize the poverty of this kind of thinking and would have predicted the demise of any self-focused prisoners in his camp.

Instead, we need to keep our attention extended outside the self, to the bigger circles of life. In particular, connect your sense of meaning to the domain of ecosystems, the biosphere, and the seventh generation. These whys are important, not just for the obvious benefits they bring to the systems and people in question but because of the way they help us prevail in the face of chronic stress and uncertainty. As the Jamaican singer Bob Marley put it: "Live for yourself and you will live in vain. Live for others, and you will live again."

ACTIVISM IS MEDICINE

Our search for a bigger why inevitably leads us into the world of activism and, in turn, brings us to a surprising realization. We're accustomed to thinking that activism is something we do when we want to change the world. We're angry about the way that society is working and resolve to act. We protest, we strategize, we write and talk.

But along the way, we might well come to realize that activism has a powerful set of benefits for the activist herself, completely independent of any success she might have in changing society. And this presents us with a paradox. That is, while activism is often frustrating, stressful, and even maddening, it can also be clarifying and integrating—which is to say, it can help us reduce our stress. In other words, activism might really be a form of medicine.

In the popular imagination, medical practice and political activism are typically described as two completely different animals. Medicine is all about disease, infection, antibiotics, physical exams, diagnostics, and outrageous, inexplicable bills. Activism is all about politics, legislation, organizing, raising money, and messaging. They're completely different domains with miles of empty space between them.

But what if we're wrong about all of this? What if activism isn't just distantly related to medicine but is actually an integral part of health itself? In recent years, lots of people have labeled various activities as medicine. We've heard that "exercise is medicine," "art is medicine," and "music is medicine." But if these activities have medicinal and health benefits for the human organism, why not activism? It hardly seems like a stretch: acting on something you're passionate about almost certainly has an integrating effect on the human mind-body.

As it stands, there isn't much research on the activism-health connection, but if we come at it from the opposite direction, some key insights are revealed. For example, we can say with absolute confidence that *in*activism is bad for our spirit and, in turn, our health. Across history and across the spectrum, writers and activists have taken note of the perils of apathy and nonparticipation:

> Edward Abbey: "Sentiment without action is the ruin of the soul."
> Eleanor Roosevelt: "When you cease to make a contribution, you begin to die."
> Martin Luther King Jr.: "The way of acquiescence leads to moral and spiritual suicide."

These elders are absolutely right: the failure to engage and participate is bad for our lives, and since everything in our lives and bodies is radically connected, it makes sense to suppose

that inactivism will have some very real downstream consequences for our bodies. By the same token, acting and engaging with the world in the service of our meaning and purpose
is likely to have some substantial health benefits.

In fact, a growing body of evidence confirms the power
of purpose and meaning. In 2017, *New Scientist* summarized
the findings: "People with a greater sense of purpose live longer, sleep better and have better sex. Purpose cuts the risk of
stroke and depression. It helps people recover from addiction
or manage their glucose levels if they are diabetic. If a phar-
maceutical company could bottle such a treatment, it would
make billions."

Likewise, Victor Strecher, a public health researcher at the
University of Michigan and author of *Life on Purpose* writes:

> Over the past 10 years, the findings about the
> health benefits of purpose have been remark-
> ably consistent—revealing that, among other
> advantages, alcoholics whose sense of purpose
> increased during treatment were less likely to
> resume heavy drinking six months later, that
> people with higher purpose were less likely to
> develop sleep disturbances with age, and that
> women with more purpose rated their sex lives
> as more enjoyable. These findings persist "even
> after statistically controlling for age, race,
> gender, education, income, health status and
> health behaviours."[88]

The power of meaning is so vital to health that it ought
to be included as a routine part of every medical exam. In the
long run of a person's life, it's probably at least as important as
body weight, blood pressure, and lab results. In fact, most of us
can easily weather minor biomedical abnormalities, but when

a sense of meaning is weak or absent, our resilience, stress resistance, and vitality are all compromised. In other words, an absence of meaning and purpose is a genuine risk factor for disease. So, why is it that we pay so little attention?

If modern medicine is to catch up with the times, it needs to make meaning a regular feature of practice. We might even look forward to the day when "sense of meaning" is given its rightful place as a diagnostic sign, recorded on medical records, and updated regularly. Hippocrates would surely consider this a step in the right direction.

On the surface, it might seem that political activism doesn't have any of the familiar qualities that we've come to associate with promoting good health. Holding up a sign on a street corner doesn't burn many calories; filing a petition or writing a letter expends even fewer. Go to a conference or testify in front of a committee—on the face of it, these things sound stressful, annoying, and even health negative. Who ever heard of someone going into activism specifically as a health practice?

But the value in activism lies in its integrating effect on the human organism. In this respect, it's very much akin to vigorous physical movement, otherwise known as exercise. When we act, particularly in the face of ambiguity and uncertainty, we call on the body to gather its resources into a single, cohesive effort. This integrating effect is powerfully health promoting.

The message is obvious: Get clear about your meaning and purpose. Engage with the world, bang the drum, speak truth to power, and do the important work as you see it. But above all, focus on the why. Write down your purpose, in a single sentence if possible. Post it in a prominent place and revisit it often. Imagine yourself explaining it to your family, friends, and colleagues. Revise and refresh often. This will bring focus and integration to the systems in your body, stimulating them to work in harmony. This is essential work, for you and for us.

> Security is mostly a superstition. It does not
> exist in nature, nor do the children of men as
> a whole experience it. Avoiding danger is no
> safer in the long run than outright exposure.
> Life is either a daring adventure, or nothing.
> —Helen Keller, *The Open Door*

In the popular narrative, we're often counseled to manage the stress in our lives by breathing, relaxing, and letting go. Just relinquish your attachment to whatever it is you're clinging to. This is the Buddhist prescription for equanimity—whatever's bugging you, just let it be. All life is suffering; all life is temporary. It's our attachment and our desire for permanence that's making us unhappy. If we could just let go, we'd feel a whole lot better.

It's solid advice, but as a people, we aren't much inclined to listen, and as a culture, we've gone in the opposite direction altogether. That is, we've gone all-in on the quest for permanence and security. In fact, when we look at it from a psychological perspective, the entire scientific-industrial-technological enterprise begins to look like a relentless effort to lock everything down; the goal is to map all the causalities, identify the leverage points, and, most fundamentally, eliminate all uncertainty, doubt, inefficiency, ambiguity, and suffering from the human experience. In this sense, modern industrial culture is the polar opposite of Buddhist teaching.

THE WAR ON AMBIGUITY

All of which stands in spectacular contrast to human life in pre-history; in other words, it's historically abnormal. In the Paleo, ambiguity was a regular, daily feature of human life. No one thought that uncertainty was a solvable problem, something that could or should be eradicated. It wasn't until the scientific revolution that the flickering promise of certainty and control first emerged. Crude technologies gave us substantial leverage, and for the first time in history, humans imagined that maybe they could nail down the cosmos, solve the riddle of life, and live in a world of security and predictability. Ambiguity might even be something we could eradicate from the human experience altogether.

Thus began a frenzy of activity, research, and investigation, all of it seemingly designed to take control of life once and for all. Science, technology, and capitalism joined forces in the quest to solve the "problem" of ambiguity, to seize the cosmos and give us the certainty we seek. And now, paradoxically enough, this effort even extends to "save the world" efforts with environmental science. Around the planet, well-meaning researchers are now tracking every animal, plant, and substance they can. We might well imagine a day in which every organism in the biosphere has its own radio-tracking collar so we can monitor its whereabouts, trajectory, and state in real time.

This war on ambiguity is also reflected in modern medicine, especially the trend toward "medicalization," famously described by social critic Ivan Illich in his landmark 1976 book, *Medical Nemesis*. For the vast majority of human history, the body was literally and figuratively naked to the world. Like all wild animals, we were exposed to the elements and vulnerable to heat, cold, trauma, and predation. Serious injury or illness was an ever-present danger, and medical care as we know it today was unimaginable.

But beginning with the big-bang discoveries of antiseptics, anesthesia, and antibiotics, medicine became increasingly effective, and a new mindset began to emerge. Physicians became increasingly confident in their powers and began to apply the medical model more broadly, and before long, almost every human experience became a candidate for medical interpretation and intervention: childbirth, athletic training, minor afflictions, mood swings, aging, wrinkled skin, and, of course, death.

Today, medical and health professions lay claim to every cell in the body and almost every aspect of the human experience. We attempt to medicalize exercise, nutrition, sleep, meditation, stress, family and social time, work-life balance, music, travel, and even education. If it touches the body or human life in any way, we attempt to track it, diagnose it, treat it, and, of course, profit from it.

But to what end? Medicalization has become so dominant that many people—physicians and patients alike—now believe that a life without physical and mental suffering is not only possible and desirable but that it's even a birthright. If we can just get all our diagnoses, treatments, substances, and robots pointed in the right direction, our suffering and uncertainty will finally be conquered.

THE WISDOM OF INSECURITY

But what makes us think we can or should be exempt from ambiguity or suffering? Why should the human experience be different from that of any other animal? Every creature suffers at some point in life. In fact, the entire history of life on Earth is one of ambiguity, uncertainty, and suffering. To be sure, nature is often comforting and nurturing to her creatures, but she's also blunt and often brutal. Almost without exception, every creature that has ever lived has either been eaten, died from disease, or struggled with the degenerative changes of old age.

So why should we be exempt? Why is our suffering so intolerable? And even more to the point, what gives us the right to shift the burden of suffering away from ourselves and onto other creatures and their habitat? And where will it end? What would it mean for the human experience if we did in fact succeed in conquering every last uncertainty, every last challenge, every last doubt?

Our war on ambiguity is fundamentally misguided. As the Zen philosopher Alan Watts famously put it:

> There is a contradiction in our desire to be secure in a universe whose very nature is fluidity and movement . . . If I want to be secure, that is, protected from the flux of life, I am wanting to be separate from life. Yet, it is this very sense of separateness that makes me feel insecure. In other words, the more security I can get, the more I shall want.[89]

All of which puts us into a wicked feedback loop, both personally and culturally. We feel stress, so we go in search of control. If we could just get a grip on things, we'd feel better. So, we recruit whatever tools, technologies, and ideas we can in order to control our bodies, our relationships, and our habitat. And sometimes it works, for a while. But our efforts always seem to have side effects and unforeseen consequences. Inevitably, the stress creeps back in; once again, we go searching for control, and this time, we redouble our efforts.

As individuals and a people, we crave security, but we're never going to get it. And if we do get it, it's only going to be temporary at best. And at worst, it will kill the life that we claim to cherish. Our lives and the biosphere are always in flux, living and dying in rhythm. We try to lock things down with tools and technologies, but the most we can do is hold the insecurity at bay for a while. But then the ambiguity comes roaring back, often with catastrophic consequences. The harder we try, the harder we will fall.

The uncertainty and ambiguity of life persist at every level. According to paleontologists, the average lifespan of mammalian species is one million to two million years.[90] In other words, even species are temporary, always in transition to some new form. Nothing in biology is eternal, not our bodies, not ecosystems, not the creatures around us. The Buddha was right: impermanence is the law of life.

THE PATH OF HUMILITY

As it stands, most of us have been conditioned to live with the expectation that ambiguity can and should be cured, conquered, or contained. This belief is baked into the modern narrative, but it's completely at odds with reality and, consequently, generates a vast amount of existential stress. As modern consumers, we're promised security, safety, predictability, and reliability at every turn. And when these things fail to materialize, we feel duped and, in turn, distressed.

The implicit lesson in all of this is simple, if sometimes hard to accept. Human knowledge, as impressive as it may be, is only a glimpse of a magnificent and fundamentally incomprehensible whole. Ambiguity is and will always be the sea we swim in. It's the normal, default condition, and it's not going to go away—not with faster computers, not with better technologies, not with superior policies and practices.

Embrace this ignorance as the human condition. Stop trying to solve ambiguity. Stop trying to nail down the cosmos. Stop trying to make everything fit into human-generated boxes. We are one temporary, semi-sapient species with a very limited view of the universe. We cannot and should not attempt to play biological king of the hill. Mastery isn't just an illusion, it's a counterproductive trap.

There's no shame in admitting any of this. We are fundamentally ignorant about the nature of the cosmos, of human life, of human behavior, and even of the workings of our own minds and spirits. Further acts of discovery may be exciting but will not and cannot "solve" the paradox, the ambiguity, and the dynamism that is fundamental to life. Embrace the mystery and suffer well.

DEATH IS A FALSE TIGER

> There need be no lasting sorrow for the death
> of any of Nature's creations, because for every
> death there is always born a corresponding life.
> —John Muir

Our grand tour of stress inevitably brings us around to what appears to be the alpha stressor of our lives. Death—the biggest tiger of all, or so it would seem.

The fear goes deep, hardwired into every cell of our bodies. Natural selection would make it so. After all, any animal that didn't fear death would be eliminated from the gene pool in short order. Creatures that are utterly fearless don't tend to leave much in the way of viable offspring.

But it's not all about genes. Culture matters too, and in our modern Western technocentric culture, the fear of death is baked into our system. In fact, we build entire industries to keep it at bay. We avoid it, deny it, and pretend that we can somehow beat the game. We exercise like demons, eat perfect diets, buy the latest gadgets, and consult the greatest experts, all under the delusion that, if we just get all the details right, we'll never have to suffer the ultimate fate.

Likewise, we treat aging as a real, monstrous tiger, something to be feared and battled into submission by any means possible. Everyone knows the prevailing narrative by now: aging is one long, depressing decline into degeneration, illness, and loneliness. Certain events are said to be inevitable:

decreased physical and cognitive function, massive medical bills, neurological meltdown, and, perhaps worst of all, social and cultural irrelevance. In short, getting older is a slow-motion train wreck to be avoided by any means necessary.

The outlook is grim, so we medicalize the process and conjure all manner of treatments to slow, stop, or reverse it. Experts claim that we can stop the clock, reverse the damage, delay the onset, and dampen the symptoms. In the process, time becomes our enemy.

But the personal, social, and cultural consequences of this narrative are catastrophic. Not only does it make us increasingly miserable and fearful as time goes by, it also drives the widespread practice of ageism. We begin to see our seniors as nothing more than a drag on society and the economy; old people are a burden and an inconvenience. Human value, in other words, decreases over time.

Not only does this narrative devalue great swaths of human life, it also puts us under an insane level of stress. If you believe your best years are your thirties and forties, followed by a progressive decline into illness and irrelevance, the clock is going to be ticking loud and hard. You've got to hurry up and make something happen, because once your body starts slowing down, it's game over. Even worse, you've got to make yourself a big pile of money right now, because once you hit your golden years, the medical-industrial complex is going to step in and take most of it away.

Sadly, the modern health-and-wellness industry is a powerful enabler of this narrative. For every age-related insult to the human body, someone claims to have a solution. Diets and substances galore, exercise programs for every ailment, exotic treatments of every description—the list is endless. Magazine covers and websites glorify youth and sell us the promise of eternal life. According to the marketing pitch, aging is not inevitable—it's simply the failure to buy the right products and services.

But in the context of human history, today's narrative is, once again, profoundly abnormal. In the Paleo, tribal survival was highly dependent on the experience, knowledge, and wisdom of the elders. The old ones had participated in many hunts and observed the waxing and waning of animal life over the course of decades; they'd seen the tribe suffer and flourish through good times and bad. For Paleolithic people, experience was extremely valuable and tribal elders were held in high esteem. Young people actually *wanted* to be and, yes, look older. In other words, aging wasn't much of a tiger at all.

To make matters worse, much of our modern fear is exacerbated by what we might call the "dead particles" view that, according to some interpretations, is driven by modern science. The entire universe is nothing more than a bunch of matter, driven by energy. Just a bunch of Newtonian billiard balls, organized by natural law. No purpose, no meaning, just a bunch of mindless stuff. And in this kind of universe, death is an even bigger tiger, because once you're dead, there's nothing left to say. We take one last breath and vanish into the void.

But in fact, this is not what modern science reveals. The great discovery of modern science, especially in the twentieth century, is that of complexity and interdependence. From quantum physics to ecology to cosmology, everything connects. Everything touches everything else. Nothing is truly alone or apart. Particles don't really exist. There is no such thing as a thing.

This appreciation of interdependence is the same kind of thinking that moved our ancestors and today's indigenous people. For people who believe in the ultimate continuity of life, the prospect of death just doesn't carry the same dread, the same sense of finality, that we feel in the West. Death is not an end, it's simply a *journey* into another form. And of course it would be this way. When your culture embraces the geometry of the circle and believes in the reality of interdependence, death is more of a transition than anything else. And in this kind of world, our worries are unfounded. No matter what happens, you're still going to be part of the whole.

CHAPTER 6

TEACHING, LEADERSHIP, AND ACTIVISM

Be firm in all you do. Be gentle in how you
do it.
　　　—Animal trainer's motto

As we've seen, the standard narrative holds that stress is an individual problem with individual solutions. It's all about personal health, wellness, athletic performance, and career success. But what about our practices and our work with people? Can an understanding of stress make us better teachers, coaches, trainers, therapists, health professionals, or parents?

This must surely be the case. After all, we're working with human animals, and these animals are extremely sensitive to the emotional tone that we bring to the classroom, the clinic, the home, and the workplace. In fact, our understanding of stress tells us a great deal about how we can do a better job with our people, our clients, our students, and our patients.

Unfortunately, modern professions focus mostly on specialized content delivery and pay less attention to the experience of the humans in question. Stress only enters into the picture from a side door, as enrichment, an occasional consideration to be taken up when students, patients, or athletes are showing signs of burnout. But this is a major oversight. As it turns out, stress has some very important things to tell us about improving our teaching, coaching, health care, and parenting.

TREAT PEOPLE LIKE ANIMALS

To make this process work, we've got to respect people's bodies and their history. In other words, we've got to start treating them like the animals they are. Which of course sounds like crazy talk. In conventional, modern culture, we're quick to distance ourselves from our animal heritage and ancestry. We feel uncomfortable about our flesh and our appetites, and we do everything possible to deny their reality. We don't like referring to ourselves as animals and even statements like "we were treated like animals" imply that nonhuman animals are inferior; we *expect* them to be treated badly.

But in fact, "treating people like animals" is precisely what we need if we want our programs, schools, and organizations to be effective and humane. We've tried treating people like "something other than animals" for a long time now, and it hasn't been working. We've left their bodies in the dust, and now we're suffering a host of physical, mental, and social health consequences.

All across the modern world, our various people-related professions have become fragmented into isolated islands of expertise. Each has its own content, its own specialists, its own techniques, and its own "best practices." A teacher is different from a doctor, a doctor is different from an organizational leader, an organizational leader is different from a parent, a parent is different from a therapist.

But how different are these professions really? They all work with people—which is to say, they all work with the human animal. We might well call this the "veterinarian approach" to the human experience, education, medicine, and commerce. If this sounds preposterous, think again. What's *really* preposterous is to pretend that humans are *not* animals, that we're subject to different laws and different requirements and have different needs.

Of course, all of this is a big ask and a hard sell, especially in organizations and institutions that are historically invested in human exceptionalism. But there's nothing to stop us from thinking like veterinarians when we meet with our athletes, our students, our clients, or our patients. Likewise, it's important to remember that there's nothing demeaning about this perspective whatsoever. To treat people like animals is to show them care and respect. Engage the animal, take care of the animal. Then, when the animal is content, well adjusted, and cared for, proceed to the next step.

All of which suggests that, no matter our position or profession, we must become experiential designers. If you're a teacher, medical professional, manager, or parent, ask yourself: What is the lived experience of the human animals in my care? What exactly are they doing with their bodies, their senses, and their imaginations? Imagine their stress levels. Are they already fighting and fleeing before they begin? What kind of stress experience do they need, to learn their lessons or benefit from their treatment? Do I have any idea where their sweet spot of autonomic function lies? How will I know when they've gone past the tipping point into the realm of toxic stress?

If you can't answer these questions, you've got some work to do.

BE PRECISE

As we've seen, our experience of stress follows the classic inverse U-shaped curve. A little stress makes our brains and bodies work better, but a lot of it inhibits our health, our performance, and our ability to learn new things. This suggests that we ought to be precise in the ways we apply stress to our students, clients, and patients. If we pressure them just the right amount, they're going to do better.

But sadly, we're mostly oblivious to all this. Untrained in the application of optimal challenge, we bring stress into the classroom, clinic, or workplace at random, by habit, or by tradition. Students get stressed when we assign homework or give an exam, and workers get stressed when we do a performance review; but most of this takes place on our schedule or at our convenience, not in relationship to their bodies or their experience. Rarely do we think intentionally about students', patients', or workers' bodies and what effect our methods are having on their autonomic nervous systems.

What we really need is a precise, deliberate, and intentional application of stress. This must not be an afterthought; it should be planned. No matter whether you're a teacher, trainer, coach, health professional, or parent, the same principles apply. What will be the waxing and waning of my people's stress in their experience? Where are the peaks and valleys of their autonomic function? Are my people already prestressed before they engage, or do they actually need more stress to perform at their best? What kind of practices can I create to adjust their experience?

If we can't answer these questions, then we're not really speaking to the body. We're simply delivering content, boilerplate or standardized experiences. We won't know when people are in the sweet spot of stress, when to push harder, and when to back off. And in turn, we can't expect to get good results.

As for finding the sweet spot, we might suppose that technology might give us the information we seek; perhaps some
cortisol measuring device will tell us to ramp up the pressure
or tone it down. But as we've seen, people are highly complex animals, and cortisol levels can never be the whole story.
Instead, we've got to become adept at making the judgment
call on the whole person, the whole animal. What does their
posture say? What about their tone of voice, their facial expressions, and the stories that they tell? This will never be an exact
science, and you might well get it wrong on occasion, but the
effort remains essential.

Likewise, it's essential to put it all in context. Knowing
what we know about the state of modern society and the world
at large, it's safe to assume that most, if not all, of your students, clients, patients, and customers are already prestressed
before they walk in your door. In other words, they're probably
at or beyond the tipping point of the inverse U-shaped curve.
All of which suggests that we tread lightly. Applying powerful
stressors to people who are already struggling is almost certain to backfire.

TALK TO THE AUTONOMIC

No matter our profession or objective, it's essential that we
keep our attention focused on the entire organism, and that
includes the deep, ancient wiring of the autonomic nervous
system. Living as we do in a hyperliterate, left-brained culture,
we're often tempted to focus exclusively on methodology and
technique. As we see it, our objective is to transmit spoken or
written messages to another person, one mind to another. If
we say or type the right words, we've done our job.

But when dealing with the autonomic nervous system, language is wildly overrated. To be sure, some particular words
can put the body at ease or rev it into action, but for the most

part, it's not the words that are doing the talking; it's the experience and the setting. The body has its own language, a preverbal or nonverbal form of dialogue, what we might call an "autonomic vocabulary."

All of which makes perfect sense in a historical context. The autonomic nervous system evolved millions of years before the first human language. In other words, the autonomic nervous system is attentive to ancient ways of habitat, posture, gesture, touch, tone of voice, and pacing, all of it influenced and colored by personal history. Words matter, but experience matters more. In short, experience is the primary, original language of the animal body, including for humans.

This is something that animal trainers know full well. It's not what you say, it's how you say it. It's how you stand, the tone of your voice, and the nuance of your behavior. It's something that lovers, teachers, and parents eventually come to understand, sometimes through harsh experience. That is, you can say precisely the right words, but if you get the autonomic message wrong, nothing else matters. And, by the inverse, you can get the words wildly wrong, but if you get the gestures, touch, tone, and pacing right, you'll probably be OK.

Whatever your job title or professional role, give your animals what they need. Speak to their bodies by creating a context and an atmosphere of safety. Give people time. Listen attentively with curiosity, sincerity, and a nonjudgmental attitude. Be predictable with a rhythmic pattern of behavior and engagement. And above all, fulfill their primal need to be felt, heard, seen, understood, and respected. Whatever you do, keep your focus on the whole human person. Someday, when people say "they treated us like animals," it'll mean "they treated us with kindness, compassion, and attention to our bodies."

U-SHAPED ACTIVISM

It's easy to see how our understanding of stress can inform our practices of teaching, coaching, health care, and parenting, but there are also some valuable lessons that apply in the world of activism. For most of us, this is unexplored territory. Rarely do we think or talk about what stress might mean when we take on really big objectives such as changing the world, and as a consequence, most of us are awkward and ineffective activists. Our strategies and tactics are all over the map. We chant, we write letters, and we click on links. We complain and strategize, hire lawyers, build websites, and raise money. And when we do take action against entrenched power, we apply stress indiscriminately, by accident or impulse. Rarely does it occur to us to use it strategically and intentionally.

Most of us would like to change something about the world but, sadly, few of us receive any instruction or education on how to go about it. The average school curriculum is mostly designed to perpetuate the status quo, not revise it. And even when we agree that change is necessary, we don't know where to begin. Activism, if we think about it at all, mostly seems like a bunch of protesting, pleading, and making our case. Most of us have no idea how to persuade, how to effect change, or how to create a functional future. It's no wonder we're so awkward. We lack a concrete method, based in neurobiology and the animal physiology of our opponents.

The good news is that a useful, practical orientation does exist, and it comes to us in the form of the familiar inverse U-shaped curve. As we've seen, the human animal works best when lightly or moderately stressed. In this zone, memory and performance are strong, while minds and spirits remain open and expansive. People may well hold strong opinions, but those opinions are not rigid or absolute. They're willing to listen and may even be persuadable. But increased stress leads to a tipping point and a shift in cognition and attitude. The animal's mind and spirit become increasingly entrenched and reactionary. He can no longer be persuaded. Indeed, he no longer even listens. For the activist, this suggests a strategy and a method. If you want to change someone's behavior or position, there's almost certainly a sweet spot for adversarial energy and opposition. Naturally, there will be plenty of circumstantial and individual variation, but knowing what we know about the ubiquity of the inverse U-shaped curve, it's safe to assume that the pattern will hold. That is, small amounts of pressure and adversarial energy may produce results, but once we cross the tipping point, the payoff will reverse itself as the process descends into polarization, enmity, and a trench warfare of ideas. This suggests that a moderate touch may be the best strategy for moving the needle in politics, policy, and behavior. If we can stress our decision-makers to the right degree, we can persuade them to adopt our position without sending them over the top into violent opposition.

It sounds good, but can this really work? According to some observers, power politics is a blood sport, and the only way to move people is with maximum stress and ultimatums. Being polite is all well and good, but it just doesn't work. The only way to get anyone's attention is to confront them directly and overpower them with force—cultural force, legal force, political force, or, if all else fails, military force. In other words, don't bother with sweet spots, tipping points, judgment, or sapience, just bring the maximum possible power to bear on every opponent in every interaction. It's the only way to move the needle on the world.

TREAT ADVERSARIES LIKE ANIMALS

To be sure, the modern power pyramid is incredibly high and steep, and largely impervious to pressure from below. Highly entrenched systems and power structures have hardened defenses that are intentionally designed to repel opposition. Some of these systems have been hundreds of years in the making, and they're not going to be overturned by minor challenges or polite requests.

It is a tough challenge, but ultimately, humans are animals and will remain so. Even the most hardened, power-maximizing individuals at the top of corporate and governmental pyramids are still made of flesh, blood, and neurotransmitters, operating on an inverse U-shaped curve of stress response. When we apply maximum stress to these people, we simply reinforce their beliefs and their intransigence. And in so doing, we defeat ourselves.

And no one is talking here about persuasion by simply "being nice." We're talking about the precise application of stress to individuals and institutions: political stress, legal stress, cultural stress, or moral stress. Politeness and civility *are* important, but the real game is stress. Can we engage people and institutions on the left side of the inverse U? Can we disturb their sense of comfort just enough to make them uneasy? Can we make them uncomfortable in their inertia?

In the end, all our political targets are animals. And if you want an animal to change its behavior for the better, that animal needs to feel safe, or maybe slightly challenged. If you can create that kind of atmosphere, you've got a chance for change. But if you push it too far, the animal will freeze up, revert to the familiar, and double down on what it knows. And if that's a philosophy of power maximization, domination, and self-interest, all you will have done is make matters even more intractable.

CHALLENGE, DON'T THREATEN

Think of it from the animal's point of view. Does your opponent feel challenged or threatened? Is this proposal a request, a suggestion, or a black-and-white demand? As we saw earlier, there's a substantial physiological difference between challenges and threats: When a stressor is perceived as a challenge, people show positive physiological changes, but when a stressor is perceived as a threat, people show decreased cardiac output, decreased diameter of circulatory vessels, decreased blood flow to the brain, and decreased cognitive and physical performance—all bad—both for the person in question *and* for the person who is attempting to influence or persuade. Threats may work in action-adventure movies, but in the real world of human animals, they tend to backfire.

Even worse, threat-based approaches are contagious and mostly serve to amp up the stress of everyone in the system. In other words, they normalize hardball tactics. If all we ever hear are threats and demands, we're likely to conclude that's just how the world works. And quite naturally, the whole thing spirals in short order, giving us the kind of society we're living in today.

We'd do better to take a deep breath and speak the language of challenge. "Challenge phrases" are particularly useful because they appeal to a person's better nature. In practice, there's a world of difference between "if you don't stop your slothful behavior, I'm leaving you" and "I challenge you to do better." The animal knows the difference. One statement is a black-and-white, stress-maximizing ultimatum; the other allows for the possibility of growth, adaptation, learning, and transformation.

Our challenge, you might say, is to speak the language of challenge: "I challenge you to protect habitat, reexamine your policies, work for social justice, provide support for disadvantaged communities," and so on. These statements may not produce the kind of dramatic short-term results we'd like, but at the very least, they preserve relationships and keep communication open, something that will surely be valuable when conditions change, as they always do.

Naturally, all of this depends on what you happen to believe about the ultimate nature of human nature. Are we aggressive, power-maximizing chimps that live and die by ultimatums? Or are we social and cooperative bonobos? Are people in power persuadable? Or is the situation so hopeless that threats are the only way forward?

It also depends on the kind of world we're trying to create. If we take the cynical view that people can only be moved by the maximum application of power and stress, we create the heavily armored, militant culture of ego, paranoia, and narcissism that we have today. If we take the view that people can be moved via intelligent stress, civility, challenge, reason, and common purpose, we preserve and nurture what's best about the human animal.

So yes, bring your tiger to your activist encounters, but keep him on a leash. Remind him that challenge is the name of the game and to be a nice kitty. Don't growl at the man behind the desk; he's an animal too.

CHAPTER 7

PRACTICE IS PERFECT

One thousand days to learn, ten thousand days
to refine.

—Miyamato Musashi,
The Book of Five Rings

Lessons, training, and practice are all well and good, but when it comes to our actual encounters with a stressful real world, we always seem to find ways to get it wrong. We forget to breathe, forget to take care of ourselves and the people around us, fall back into automatic behavior, and fall prey to the same old stressors that have bedeviled us for years or even decades. We lose our sense of perspective and get trapped in cycles of angst and bitterness. And on some days, it even feels like we're regressing into bad behaviors that we thought we'd left behind.

So cut yourself some slack and remember that the modern world is a monstrously difficult place to inhabit. Conditions are often wicked, and tough decisions and judgment calls must be made, usually with incomplete information. Of course you're going to falter. You'll be strong when you should have been flexible. You'll be yielding when you should have been assertive. You'll get scared and confused and doubt your capabilities. You'll get suckered by false tigers, and you'll walk blindly into the real ones. You'll overreact to trivial challenges and forget everything you've learned along your way.

All of this is quite inevitable and forgivable but remember this: *you don't have to master the art, only find a better way forward.* Of course you're going to get it wrong from time to time. Of course you're going to endure some sleepless nights, some torturous days, and some deep anxiety about your performance. No amount of training or practice will change this. We are fallible animals, after all.

THE LESSON OF *KAIZEN*

So be modest with your expectations. Forget your utopian ideals of perfect peace and equanimity under pressure. You don't have to be a Zen master. Instead, focus on small steps. This is precisely the lesson of *kaizen*, the Japanese concept of small improvement over time. Beautifully described in *One Small Step Can Change Your Life: The* Kaizen *Way* by Robert Maurer, *kaizen* is a modest but persistent approach to transformation. The power of this approach lies precisely in its humility. As Maurer puts it, "the small steps of *kaizen* disarm the brain's fear response" and allow the body to adapt. *Kaizen* doesn't intimidate us or ask us to make dramatic changes in our lives. It nudges us toward a better way of living.

Legendary basketball coach John Wooden also understood the value of this incremental approach. "When you improve a little each day, eventually big things occur. Don't look for the big, quick improvement. Seek the small improvement one day at a time. That's the only way it happens—and when it happens, it lasts."

Small actions, multiplied by frequent repetition, add up to substantial improvements in our vitality, our physicality, and our relationship with the world. The lifestyle arts of meditation, rhythm, minimalism, and movement are vital and powerful, but they do their work in a surprising and subtle way. You may not notice the benefits at all, at first, but a few years from now you'll wake up and notice that your body and your life are substantially healthier than those of people who failed to make the effort.

FORGIVE YOURSELF

Ultimately, stress is not a game we can win. It's not a skill we can master with finality. There's no destination we can reach, no state of composure we can claim as our own. No matter what happens in the coming decades, the modern world will remain complex, overwhelming, and even incomprehensible. And no matter your discipline, your body will continue to rebel against its mismatched predicament.

So, forgive yourself. Forgive your screwups and your overreactions. Do better next time. Do better tomorrow. Keep waking up. Keep reminding yourself to breathe. Remember your primal physicality and your deep connection with the natural world. Replenish your resilience reservoir at every opportunity: more sleep, more relaxation, more humor, more contact with people and the big outside.

A little more breath, a little more patience, and a little more perspective will sustain you. If you can be just a little bit calmer, a little more balanced, a little more at ease, it will make all the difference in the world.

In the end, the effort is sacred.

GRATITUDES

On the good days, words burst from my keyboard like wild animals, filling my screen with robust energy, leaping, running, and copulating with exuberance. My body rejoices and I breathe deeply. My nervous system relaxes into a state of contentment, resting and digesting, repairing tissues and rejuvenating my entire being. The language flows from my fingertips naturally, smoothly, with scarcely a hint of confusion or doubt. What a wonderful thing, the written word; I'm ready to feed and breed.

But in actual fact, such days are vanishingly rare—exceptional freak moments in my writing life. On a more typical day, the keyboard tortures me with its endless possibilities, and the English language becomes a vicious adversary, mocking my every attempt to make sense of it. I squirm at my desk, my mind and body contract, and the words flee from my screen like rats from a sinking ship. I grind my teeth, and my tissue revolts. Language at war with itself.

Most writers are familiar with this experience and understand the stress that comes with the job. The long hours and the grand effort to build a vast and possibly important creation, only to have it exposed to a distracted, unreliable, sometimes hostile audience, with no guarantee of any kind of success. The lone struggle is filled with tigers, some real, many false.

Fortunately, I've been well supported in this effort by a host of fine human animals:

Michael Campi
Corey Jung
James O'Keefe, MD
Steve Laskevitch
Seby Alary
Jeremy Lent
Dr. Rodney King
Michael Dowd
Steve Myrland
Dana Lyons
Pete Karabetis
Alessandro Pelizzon
Paul Landon
Skye Nacel
Derrick Jensen
Max Wilbert
Susan Fahringer
Sam, Beth, Alex, and Travis Forencich

And big ups to Karen Upson and all the great folks at Girl Friday Productions. In particular, special thanks to Marisa Solis, my editorial shaman and spirit guide to the English language.

NOTES

1   Selye, H. *The Stress of Life.* New York: McGraw Hill, 1956.
Selye, H. (Oct 7, 1955). "Stress and disease." Science. 122
(3171). See also *The End of Stress As We Know It,* by Bruce
McEwen.

2   World Health Organization, https://www.who.int/news-room
/fact-sheets/detail/depression.

3   https://www.sciencedaily.com/releases/2021/02
/210204101640.htm.

4   For some dramatic examples of social and health contagion,
see *Crazy Like Us: The Globalization of the American Psyche,*
by Ethan Watters.

5   See *Kluge: The Haphazard Construction of the Human Mind,*
by Gary Marcus.

6   For a comprehensive look at stress fundamentals, see Robert
Sapolsky's audio series from The Great Courses: *Stress and
Your Body,* https://www.thegreatcourses.com/courses/stress
-and-your-body.

7   For a comprehensive look at our predator-rich history, see
*Monster of God: The Man-Eating Predator in the Jungles of
History and the Mind,* by David Quammen, and *Man the
Hunted: Primates, Predators, and Human Evolution,* by Donna
Hart and Robert W. Sussman.

8   Sapolsky, R. Behave: The Biology of Humans at Our Best and
Worst. New York: Penguin Press, 2017.

9   See the audiobook from Sounds True: *The Neurobiology of
"We": How Relationships, the Mind, and the Brain Interact to
Shape Who We Are,* by Daniel J. Siegel.

10   See *The Plastic Mind: New Science Reveals Our Extraordinary
Potential to Transform Ourselves,* by Sharon Begley. Also see
*The Emotional Life of Your Brain: How Its Unique Patterns
Affect the Way You Think, Feel, and Live—and How You Can
Change Them,* by Richard Davidson.

11   For a great discussion of brain plasticity, see *The Brain That*

Changes Itself: Stories of Personal Triumph from the Frontiers of Brain Science, by Norman Doidge.

12   It's safe to assume an interdependence of body, nervous system, and imagination. The plasticity of imagination is well recognized by generations of artists who've understood the power of practice. See also the work of neuroscientist Antonio Damasio, especially *Descartes' Error: Emotion, Reason and the Human Brain.* For Damasio, the human mind is literally embodied. Mind and body are complementary and reciprocal: "There is no such thing as a disembodied mind. The mind is implanted in the brain, and the brain is implanted in the body."

13   https://en.wikipedia.org/wiki/Eustress.

14   See *Surviving Survival: The Art and Science of Resilience,* by Laurence Gonzales.

15   https://www.researchgate.net/figure/Cortisol-response-in -first-time-and-experienced-skydivers-Predicted-cortisol -is_fig1_274722988.

16   https://quoteinvestigator.com/2017/03/26/learn.

17   See *The Paleolithic Prescription: A Program of Diet and Exercise and a Design for Living,* by S. Boyd Eaton, Marjorie Shostak, and Melvin Konner. Also see *Mismatch: Why Our World No Longer Fits Our Bodies,* by Peter Gluckman and Mark Hanson, and *The Human Zoo: A Zoologist's Classic Study of the Urban Animal,* by Desmond Morris.

18   For the ultimate big-picture, big-history view, see *Origin Story: A Big History of Everything,* by David Christian. Also check out his audio series Big History by The Great Courses.

19   For an in-depth look at the authentic lifeways of ancient, native people, see *The Old Way: A Story of the First People,* by Elizabeth Marshall Thomas. Also, for a fictional but highly dramatic account of Neanderthal-era experience, see *Shaman,* by Kim Stanley Robinson.

20   See also *The World until Yesterday: What Can We Learn from Traditional Societies?* by Jared Diamond.

21   See *The End of Night: Searching for Natural Darkness in an Age of Artificial Light,* by Paul Bogard.

22   https://www.ecowatch.com/animals-captivity-brain-damage -2647869196.html.

23   https://www.ncbi.nlm.nih.gov/pmc/articles/PMC4096361.

24   https://www.discovermagazine.com/planet-earth/the-human -brain-has-been-getting-smaller-since-the-stone-age.

25 https://journals.sagepub.com/doi/abs/10.1177/1745691616662473?journalCode=ppsa&.

26 See *A Green History of the World: The Environment and the Collapse of Great Civilizations*, original and revised editions by Clive Ponting.

27 See *Overshoot: The Ecological Basis of Revolutionary Change*, by William R. Catton Jr.

28 See The Great Work: Our Way into the Future, by Thomas Berry.

29 https://www.frontiersin.org/articles/10.3389/fcosc.2020.615419/full.

30 See *Becoming Attached: First Relationships and How They Shape Our Capacity to Love*, by Robert Karen.

31 Berry, T. The Dream of the Earth. New York: Random House, 1988.

32 http://www.thoreau-online.org/the-maine-woods-page36.html.

33 See The Fall: The Insanity of the Ego in Human History and the Dawning of a New Era, by Steve Taylor, p. 136.

34 https://www.matthieuricard.org/en/blog.

35 Neihardt, J. Black Elk Speaks: The Complete Edition. Lincoln: University of Nebraska Press, 2014.

36 https://www.unl.edu/rhames/courses/current/readings/boehm.pdf.

37 https://quoteinvestigator.com/2016/06/26/shape.

38 See the definitive statement in Damasio, *Descartes' Error*.

39 The Myth Gap: What Happens When Evidence and Arguments Aren't Enough? by Alex Evans.

40 See Naomi Klein, in particular *No Logo*.

41 See Taylor, The Fall, 154.

42 See "E-mail Is Making Us Miserable," https://www.newyorker.com/tech/annals-of-technology/e-mail-is-making-us-miserable.

43 See *Affluence without Abundance: The Disappearing World of the Bushmen*, by James Suzman.

44 https://carlsonschool.umn.edu/sites/carlsonschool.umn.edu/files/2018-12/vohs_2015_money_priming_review_replications_jepg.pdf.
See also: https://carlsonschool.umn.edu/sites/carlsonschool.umn.edu/files/2019-04/savani_mead_stillman_vohs_2016_1.pdf.

45 https://pubmed.ncbi.nlm.nih.gov/26214169.

46   https://www.washingtonpost.com/news/the-fix/wp/2014/05
     /31/watch-americans-trust-in-each-other-erode-over-the
     -last-three-decades/ and https://medium.com/@monarchjogs
     /the-decline-of-trust-in-the-united-states-fb8ab719b82a.
47   See Banksy, Wall and Piece.
48   https://en.wikipedia.org/wiki/Asch_conformity_experiments.
49   https://en.wikipedia.org/wiki/Stanford_marshmallow
     _experiment.
50   See *The Marshmallow Test: Why Self-Control Is the Engine of
     Success*, by Walter Mischel.
51   https://www.nytimes.com/2015/12/06/technology/personaltech
     /cant-put-down-your-device-thats-by-design.html.
52   https://en.wikipedia.org/wiki/Karpman_drama_triangle.
53   https://pubmed.ncbi.nlm.nih.gov/22553896.
54   https://www.statista.com/study/48790/analgesics-report.
55   https://www.who.int/health-topics/noncommunicable
     -diseases#tab=tab_1.
56   See *Learned Optimism: How to Change Your Mind and Your
     Life*, by Martin Seligman.
57   https://www.sciencedirect.com/science/article/pii
     /S0960982213003564.
58   See *The Placebo Effect: An Interdisciplinary Exploration*, by
     Anne Harrington, and *Placebo: Mind over Matter in Modern
     Medicine*, by Dylan Evans. Also see *Meaning, Medicine and the
     "Placebo Effect,"* by Daniel E. Moerman.
59   See *The Biophilia Hypothesis*, by Stephen R. Kellert and E. O.
     Wilson.
60   https://en.wikipedia.org/wiki/Holocaust_survivors
     #Second_Generation_of_survivors.
61   https://www.ncbi.nlm.nih.gov/pmc/articles/PMC5622954.
62   https://greatergood.berkeley.edu/article/item/why_do_we
     _feel_awe.
63   https://pubmed.ncbi.nlm.nih.gov/25603133.
64   https://www.researchgate.net/publication/247497189
     _Approaching_awe_a_moral_spiritual_and_aesthetic_emotion.
65   https://www.apa.org/pubs/journals/releases/psp-pspi0000018
     .pdf.
66   From a forthcoming book by Dacher Keltner (title and pub-
     lisher to be determined).
67   See Deep Ecology: Living as if Nature Mattered by Bill Devall
     and George Sessions.

68 Darwin, C. On the Origin of Species by Means of Natural Selection, or the Preservation of Favoured Races in the Struggle for Life. London: John Murray, 1859.

69 See *Spark: The Revolutionary New Science of Exercise and the Brain,* by John J. Ratey.

70 New York Times interview (1985).

71 https://www.cbtforinsomnia.com/about-us.

72 http://www.gss.norc.org.

73 https://edpsych.education.wisc.edu/staff/enright-robert.

74 https://learningtoforgive.com/2010/04/welcome.

75 https://www.psychologytoday.com/us/articles/199707/finding-flow.

76 http://philosophy.redzambala.com/plato/charmides-plato.html.

77 https://www.goodreads.com/author/quotes/36913.Rabindranath_Tagore.

78 https://www.psychologytoday.com/us/blog/the-introverts-corner/201407/would-you-rather-sit-and-think-or-give-yourself-shock.

79 See *Animal Play: Evolutionary, Comparative and Ecological Perspectives,* edited by Marc Bekoff and John A. Byers. Also see *Animal Play Behavior,* by Robert Fagen.

80 McKee, R. Story: Substance, Structure, Style, and the Principles of Screenwriting. New York: HarperCollins, 2010.

81 See *Winning the Story Wars: Why Those Who Tell—and Live—the Best Stories Will Rule the Future,* by Jonah Sachs. Also see *Houston, We Have a Narrative,* by Randy Olson; *Don't Think of an Elephant: Know Your Values and Frame the Debate,* by George Lakoff; and *Narrative Medicine: The Use of History and Story in the Healing Process,* by Lewis Mehl-Madrona.

82 Trotsky, L. Trotsky's Diary in Exile: 1935. Cambridge: Harvard University Press, 1958.

83 Human Emotion 16.2 Physical Health II (Stress), https://www.youtube.com/watch?v=MWe4B1kTum0.

84 See *The Upside of Stress: Why Stress Is Good for You, and How to Get Good at It,* by Kelly McGonigal.

85 *Man's Search for Meaning,* by Viktor Frankl.

86 "A Functional Genomic Perspective on Human Well-being," https://www.pnas.org/content/110/33/13684.

87 https://www.sciencedirect.com/science/article/abs/pii/S0262407917301793.

88   https://www.newscientist.com/article/mg23331100-500
      -a-meaning-to-life-how-a-sense-of-purpose-can-keep-you
      -healthy.
89   https://alanwatts.org.
90   https://www.livescience.com/how-long-do-species-last.html.

ABOUT THE AUTHOR

Frank Forencich is an internationally recognized leader in health and performance education. He earned his BA at Stanford University in human biology and neuroscience and has over thirty years of teaching experience in martial art and health education.

Frank holds black belt rankings in karate and aikido and has traveled to Africa on several occasions to study human origins and the ancestral environment. He's presented at numerous venues, including the Ancestral Health Symposium, Google, the Dr. Robert D. Conn Heart Conference, and the Institute of Design at Stanford University. A former columnist for *Paleo Magazine*, Frank is the author of numerous books about health and the human predicament and is a member of the Council of Elders at the MindBodyEcology Collective.